W. Wechler

The Concept of Fuzziness in Automata and Language Theory

STUDIEN ZUR ALGEBRA UND IHRE ANWENDUNGEN

Im Auftrage des
Zentralinstituts für Mathematik und Mechanik
der Akademie der Wissenschaften der DDR
herausgegeben von L. Budach und H.-J. Hoehnke

BAND 5

W. WECHLER
THE CONCEPT OF FUZZINESS
IN AUTOMATA AND LANGUAGE THEORY

WOLFGANG WECHLER

THE CONCEPT OF FUZZINESS IN AUTOMATA AND LANGUAGE THEORY

AKADEMIE-VERLAG · BERLIN
1978

Zentralinstitut für Mathematik und Mechanik, 108 Berlin, Mohrenstr. 39
Erschienen im Akademie-Verlag, 108 Berlin, Leipziger Str. 3–4

Lizenz-Nummer: 202 · 100/412/78
Gesamtherstellung: VEB Druckerei „Thomas Müntzer“, 582 Bad Langensalza
Bestellnummer: 762 517 1 (2174/5) · LSV 1025
Printed in GDR
DDR 27,– M

PREFACE

During the past decade, it has been shown that fuzzy sets are useful in various fields of application like pattern recognition, artificial intelligence, automata and language theory, switching theory etc. The concept of a fuzzy set is proposed to reflect what one experiences when dealing with situations in everyday life: considering some properties we often cannot decide whether or not a given object has the property in question, and the best we can do is to estimate in some way the degree in which the property is attained. The usual approach is the probabilistic one, fuzziness was meant as an alternative to it.

In this book, we intend to develop a certain 'calculus of possibility' capable of investigating automata, grammars and languages. For this purpose, Chapter 1 provides a necessary background of a fuzzy set theory based on a generalized (many-valued) logic. Different kinds of fuzziness can be determined by choosing an appropriate algebraic structure on the set of truth values. Chapter 2 is devoted to automata and grammars whose dynamic or rewriting systems possess an inherent incertainty. Chapter 3 discusses closure properties of events recognized by fuzzy automata or generated by fuzzy grammars. Since our formalism is general enough to uniquely describe different kinds of fuzzy automata, a comparison of their acceptance power leads to some interesting problems which are solved at the end of Chapter 3. The appendix (written by V. Dimitrov) is regarded as a typical example for applications. We hope to give some stimulation for reducing the gap between theory and practice of fuzzy sets.

The book is self-contained in the sense that no other sources are needed for the proofs of the results stated as theorems.

I am grateful to many of my colleagues, particularly Gennady Agasandyan, Jirzy Adamek, Vladimir Dimitrov, Marek Karpinski, Jan Pavelka, and Ales Pultr.

Special thanks are due to Winfried Schirotzek for useful comments concerning the manuscript, and to Miss I. Tittel for her care in preparing the final version of the manuscript.

Finally, I wish to thank the Akademie-Verlag for friendly co-operation and quick publication.

Dresden, November 1977 — Wolfgang Wechler

TABLE OF CONTENTS

INTRODUCTION

The rapide development of so-called "soft" sciences, whose key notions cannot precisely be determined as in physics for instance, requires a suitable and convenient mathematical representation for inexact concepts. It seems to be a contradiction in itself unless the modifier "inexact" is explained in this context.

In physics any observable is uniquely defined by a related measurement. By a thorough analysis of these measurement processes, the range of validity of the definitions can be found out, within which they are meaningful. Outside, there is not any possibility of defining such observables because either the considered objects are disturbed in such a way during measurment that they lose their identity or systems are so complex that they have an enormous number of observables whose greater part is more or less irrelevant for investigation. In this case an exact description by a large amount of data in a quantitative manner would not be feasible and even not meaningful. Therefore, an optimum has to be found, namely a description which is as exact (in a quantitative manner) as practicable, on the one hand, and as convenient and suitable as possible, on the other.

Let us illustrate the situation in pattern recognition. The first step in solving a problem is the selection of significant characteristics of a considered object. Only, by such a reduction, the problem becomes conceivable in general. After that the object in question will be compared with standard ones in order to decide the appropriate class of representatives. But this comparison (of handwritten letters for instance) often possesses an inherent uncertainty related more to ambiguity and indeterminancy than to random variations. Thus the calculus of probability cannot be applied in any case. Hence, it is necessary to build up a mathematical formalism which enables us to describe fuzziness generally.

Sometimes fuzziness in a description is not to be seen as inability to register every detail. It is simply a new quality of description being more efficient because of less redundancy. As a case in point, when we give directions for taking a route to a desired destination in a city for example, "inexactness of the description is not a liability, on the contrary, it is a blessing, in that sufficient information can be conveyed with less effort" [28]. Motivations for such situations could be found in areas such as artificial intelligence, linguistics, problem solving etc.

The theory of fuzzy sets proposed by L.A. Zadeh [93] is a first attempt at constructing a suitable mathematical formalism applicable in areas just mentioned. A fuzzy set is a class of objects which does not have sharply defined boundaries but can be distinguished from all objects of a given set by its memebership function with values in the unit interval on the real line. Consequently, for a syntactical representation of fuzzy sets a many-valued logic is necessary. Its basic features have been derived by J.A. Goguen [26]. Indeed, there are close connections to the well-known many-valued logics introduced by E.L. Post and J. Łukasiewicz as well as to intuitionistic logic (cf. [63,64]). J. Pavelka [58] has developed Goguen's approach to a fuzzy propositional calculus whose set of truth values forms a complete lattice with an additional multiplication (residuated lattice). The problem of completeness has been investigated for special structures of the set of truth values.

Chapter 1 deals with fuzzy logic and fuzzy sets. As a preparation, in Section 1.1 algebraic structures on the set of truth values are established. Section 1.2 is concerned with fuzzy propositional and predicate calculi based on different algebraic structures of the set of truth values. By means of fuzzy models of the fundamental ε-theory two kinds of fuzzy sets are introduced in Section 1.3.

In Chapter 2, we apply the formalism of so-called R-fuzzy sets to generalize basic notions of the theory of automata and grammars. Therefore, Section 2.1 develops the calculus of R-fuzzy events, by which the problem of analysis and synthesis of R-fuzzy automata is solved in Section 2.2. The last Section 2.3 of this chapter is devoted to context-free R-fuzzy grammars. We discuss the algebraic characterization of generated R-fuzzy events and the construction of related acceptors.

Closure properties of R-fuzzy events and languages are studied in Chapter 3 in analogy to abstract families of languages [24]. The first Section 3.1 deals with families of R-fuzzy events, whereby an R-fuzzy event can be considered as a mapping from the free monoid X^* generated by a finite set X into a partially ordered semiring R regarded as an algebraic structure on the set of truth values. R-fuzzy languages, investigated in Section 3.2, are defined by means of R-fuzzy events with respect to cut-points as cut-point languages in the case of stochastic automata. Section 3.3 presents some results concerning an R-fuzzy language hierarchy and other comparisons of R-fuzzy language families for different partially ordered semirings R.

PRELIMINARIES

The reader is expected to have some background in set-theoretic pure mathematics. We recall here only the basic notations. The set of those elements having a property π is written as $\{x | x \text{ has property } \pi\}$. The set with no element in it, called the empty set, is denoted by $\emptyset$. We write $x \in X$ if x is an element of a set X, and otherwise $x \notin X$. For sets X and Y, X is a subset of Y (alternatively, Y contains X), in symbols $X \subseteq Y$, if each element of X belongs to Y too. Given a set $\{x_i | i \in I\}$, I is called index set. The union of a family $\{X_i | i \in I\}$ of sets, written

$$\cup \{X_i | i \in I\} \qquad \text{or} \qquad \bigcup_{i \in I} X_i,$$

is the set of elements in at least one of the X_i. The intersection of $\{X_i | i \in I\}$, written

$$\cap \{X_i | i \in I\} \qquad \text{or} \qquad \bigcap_{i \in I} X_i,$$

is the set of elements in all X_i. If I is a finite set, then we write $X_1 \cup X_2 \cup \ldots \cup X_n$ or $X_1 \cap X_2 \cap \ldots \cap X_n$, respectively. The difference of sets X and Y, i.e., the set of all elements in X which do not belong to Y, will be denoted by $X \setminus Y$.

A mapping f from a set X into a set Y is denoted by $f: X \to Y$. The set X is called domain of f and often denoted by dom(f). If X' is a subset of X, then the image f(X') of X' under f consists of all values f(x) at any $x \in X'$, i.e.

$$f(X') = \{y \in Y | \text{there exists some } x \text{ of } X' \text{ such that } y = f(x)\}.$$

Assume Y' is a subset of Y, then the inverse image of Y' under f is defined as follows

$$f^{-1}(Y') = \{x \in X | f(x) \in Y'\}.$$

The product of two sets X and Y, denoted by $X \times Y$, is made up of all pairs (x,y) with $x \in X$ and $y \in Y$. A (binary) relation ϱ on a set X is a subset of $X \times X$. Usually, we write $x \varrho y$ or "$x \varrho y$ holds" to indicate that (x,y) is in the relation ϱ. A relation $\sim$ defined on a set X is said to be an equivalence relation on A provided $\sim$ is reflexive, symmetric and transitive, i.e., for arbitrary elements $x,y,z \in X$, the following conditions are fulfilled

(1) $x \sim x$,

(2) $x \sim y$ implies $y \sim x$

(3) $x \sim y$ and $y \sim z$ imply $x \sim z$.

For every $x \in X$, let $\bar{x}$ denote the set of all $y \in X$ such that $x \sim y$. The sets $\bar{x}$, where $x \in X$, are called the equivalence classes of $\sim$. A partial order on a set X is a relation $\leqq$ on X such that $\leqq$ is reflexive, antisymmetric and transitive, i.e., for arbitrary elements $x,y,z \in X$, the following conditions are fulfilled

(1) $x \leqq x$

(2) $x \leqq y$ and $y \leqq x$ imply $x = y$

(3) $x \leqq y$ and $y \leqq z$ imply $x \leqq z$.

A pair $(X,\leqq)$ is called a partially ordered set. An element t of X is said to be top or greatest element if $x \leqq t$ for every $x \in X$. We call $b \in X$ the bottom or least element if $b \leqq x$ for all $x \in X$. Let S be a non-empty subset of a partially ordered set $(X,\leqq)$. An element x_0 is said to be an upper or a lower bound of S provided $x \leqq x_0$ or $x_0 \leqq x$ holds for all $x \in X$, respectively. If the set of all upper bounds of S contains a least element, then it is called least upper bound of S and denoted by sup(S). The greatest element of all lower bounds of S, if it exists, is called greatest lower bound of S and is denoted by inf(S).

A partially ordered set $(L,\leqq)$ is said to be a lattice if there exist $\sup\{x,y\}$ and $\inf\{x,y\}$ for all $x,y \in L$. The least upper bound of x and y will be denoted by $x \cup y$ and called the join of elements x and y, and the greatest lower bound of x and y will be denoted by $x \cap y$ and called the meet of x and y. It is folklore in lattice theory that every lattice $(L,\leqq)$ can be considered as an abstract algebra $(L,\cup,\cap)$ satisfying the following axioms

(1) $x \cap y = y \cap x$	(1') $x \cup y = y \cup x$
(2) $x \cap (y \cap z) = (x \cap y) \cap z$	(2') $x \cup (y \cup z) = (x \cup y) \cup z$
(3) $x \cap (x \cup y) = x$	(3') $(x \cap y) \cup y = y$

for all $x,y,z \in L$. Thereby $x \leqq y$ if and only if $x \cup y = y$ or equivalent to it $x \cap y = x$. A lattice $(L,\leqq)$ is said to complete if sup(S) and inf(S) exist for any non-empty subset $S \subseteq L$. Assume that a lattice $(L,\leqq)$ has a bottom element 0 and a top element 1. We say an element y is the complement of $x \in L$ if

$$x \cap y = 0 \quad \text{and} \quad x \cup y = 1$$

hold. A lattice is called complemented provided every element of it has a complement. A distributive lattice fulfils the following condition

$$x \cap (y \cup z) = (x \cap y) \cup (x \cap z)$$

for all $x,y,z \in L$. It can easily be seen that the dual equation

$$x \cup (y \cap z) = (x \cup y) \cap (x \cup z)$$

follows from the first one. A Boolean lattice (algebra) is a distributive and complemented lattice.

A monoid consists of a set M and a mapping (operation) $M \times M \to M$. The mapping is not given a name and the image of the pair (m_1,m_2) under this mapping is usually denoted by m_1m_2, but in some cases we write $m_1 \cdot m_2$. This operation is associative, i.e., for any $m_1,m_2,m_3 \in M$

$$(m_1m_2)m_3 = m_1(m_2m_3)$$

is valid. Moreover, there exists a unit element $1 \in M$ such that

$$1m = m = m1$$

for all $m \in M$. M is called commutative if $m_1m_2 = m_2m_1$ holds for all $m_1,m_2 \in M$. A semigroup differs from a monoid only by the omission of the last requirement, that means a semigroup is a set equipped with an associative operation. Let M and M' be monoids, a (monoid) homomorphism $f: M \to M'$ is a mapping satisfying the following two conditions

$$f(m_1m_2) = f(m_1)f(m_2) \qquad \text{for all } m_1,m_2 \in M$$
$$f(1) = 1.$$

Given two subsets X,Y of a monoid M, the product XY is defined as follows

$$XY = \{xy \in M \mid x \in X \text{ and } y \in Y\}.$$

Let M be a monoid. A subset $S \subseteq M$ containing 1 is called submonoid if it is closed under the opertion, i.e. $1 \in S$ and $S^2 \subseteq S$, where $S^2 = SS$. For a subset X of a monoid M, the set

$$X^* = 1 \cup X \cup X^2 \cup \ldots \cup X^n \cup \ldots$$

where $X^{n+1} = X^nX$, is a submonoid of M and is the smallest one containing X. Let X be an arbitrary set. A word (of length $k \geqq 0$) over X is a finite sequence $x_1x_2...x_k$ of elements in X. The word of length zero, called the empty word, is denoted by e. The length of a word w is denoted by $|w|$. If we define the product ww' of words $w = x_1x_2...x_k$ and $w' = x_1'x_2'...x_l'$ as follows

$$ww' = x_1x_2...x_kx_1'x_2'...x_l'$$

then the set X^* of all words over X forms a monoid, where the empty word is the unit element. X^* is called the free monoid generated by X. The basic property of X^* is that any mapping from X into a monoid M admits a unique extension to a homomorphism from X^* into M.

For each finite set (alphabet) X, any subset $L \subseteq X^*$ is called a language (or an event occasionally). We assume that the reader is familiar with the fundamental notions of an automaton and a grammar for defining languages. Nevertheless, these classical concepts will appear as special cases in Chapter 2.

1. FUZZY LOGIC AND FUZZY SETS

The study of systems in the real world requires a new methodological framework to obtain relevant and significant statements.
If we tried to use conventional mathematical concepts and methods in order to derive precise results, then their relevance and significance would diminish as the inherent complexity of real systems increases. Therefore, imprecision or indeterminancy must be taken into consideration. It is well-known that there are two typical sources of such incertainty, namely randomness and fuzziness, whereby the latter is related more to ambiguities than to random variations.

In order to come to terms with such systems it is necessary to apply a mathematical approach whose key notions enable us to describe fuzziness generally. Such an approach has been developed by L.A. Zadeh [93] with his theory of fuzzy sets. A fuzzy set is a class of objects which does not have sharply defined boundaries but can be distinguished from all objects of a given set X by its membership function with values in the unit interval on the real line. J.A. Goguen [25] recognized that the ordering on the unit interval is an essential point of Zadeh's concept.

Consequently, a fuzzy set should be considered as a mapping A from X into a partially ordered set W of so-called truth values. Since the operations between fuzzy sets are defined by means of the related operations on W, the problem arises of constructing as general an algebraic structur as possible on W.

Section 1.1 is concerned with such algebraic structures on the set W of truth values as are suitable for investigating automata and grammars as well as for building up a theory of fuzzy sets in a way syntactically analogous to the usual set theory. This leads to the so-called R-fuzzy and L-fuzzy algebras. Roughly speaking, R-fuzzy algebras are partially ordered semirings and L-fuzzy algebras are complete lattices with an additional multiplication.

In order to see how to construct such universes of fuzzy sets some notions of logic and model theory will be stated in a generalized form in Section 1.2.

Considering fuzzy models of a theory for the relation of membership we are in a position to introduce fuzzy sets in Section 1.3.

Models based on interpretations in R-fuzzy or L-fuzzy algebras lead to so-called R-fuzzy or L-fuzzy sets. Using the Boolean semiring as a underlying fuzzy algebra, we obtain a fragement of set theory.

1.1. Algebraic structures on truth sets

The aim of this section has already been mentioned, namely, to define an algebraic strcture on truth sets as general as possible. If we intend to study automata, grammars and languages in a framework of fuzzy sets over a truth set W, then the basic structure on W must be a partially ordered semiring, that means the partially ordered set W has to be additionally equipped with two binary operations satisfying certain axioms defined precisely later on.

This assertion is supported by the following argumentation. The behaviour of an automaton, for instance, can be regarded as being determined by the set of all possible paths in the associated transition graph whose edges are evaluated by elements of W. In this context the element of W belonging to any particular edge may be interpreted as a measure (truth value) of the related state transition. On this basis, the description of the behaviour depends on the evaluation of all possible paths, which means we need two operations in W defined in such a way that one of them corresponds to alternative branching and the other one to concatenation of paths in the transition graph.

From this intuitive point of view, it seems natural that the two operations in the partially ordered set W are associative and monotonous as well as being connected by distributive laws. Therefore, the algebraic structure on W should be thought of as a partially ordered semiring at least.

At first we recall some necessary basic concepts. A semiring R (cf. [17]) is a set with two binary operations: addition + and multiplication $\cdot$ such that (R,+) is a commutative monoid with 0 as a unit element. Thus

(1) $r + r' = r' + r$

(2) $r + (r' + r'') = (r + r') + r''$

(3) $r + 0 = r.$

With respect to multiplication, R is a monoid with 1 as a unit and 0 as a zero element. Thus

(4) $r\cdot(r'\cdot r'') = (r\cdot r')\cdot r''$

(5) $r\cdot 1 = r = 1\cdot r$

(6) $r\cdot 0 = 0 = 0\cdot r.$

Both operations are connected by the following distributive laws

(7) $r\cdot(r' + r'') = r\cdot r' + r\cdot r''$

(8) $(r + r')\cdot r'' = r\cdot r'' + r'\cdot r''$.

R is called commutative if additionally

(9) $r\cdot r' = r'\cdot r$

holds.

Given two semirings R and R' a homomorphism $f: R \to R'$ is a mapping satisfying

(1) $f(r + r') = f(r) + f(r')$, $f(0) = 0$

(2) $f(r \cdot r') = f(r) \cdot f(r')$, $f(1) = 1$.

A non-trivial semiring R (with $0 \neq 1$) is called positive [17] if $r + r' = 0$ implies $r = r' = 0$ and if $r\cdot r' = 0$ implies $r = 0$ or $r' = 0$.

Definition 1.1. A semiring R is said to be a partially ordered semiring (hereafter abbreviated po-semiring) if R is a partially ordered set under a relation $\leq$ with 0 as bottom element such that both operations are monotonous, i.e.

(1) $r \leq r'$ implies $r + r'' \leq r' + r''$

(2) $r \leq r'$ implies $r \cdot r'' \leq r' \cdot r''$ and $r'' \cdot r \leq r'' \cdot r'$

for all $r, r', r'' \in R$.

Examples. 1) The simplest po-semiring is the so-called Boolean semiring $\underline{2} = \{0,1\}$ with the order $0 < 1$ and $1 + 1 = 1$. Note that the remaining rules of addition $0 + 0 = 0$ and $1 + 0 = 0 + 1 = 1$ are forced by the requirement that 0 is the additive identity. The multiplication is entirely forced by the axioms and is given by $1\cdot 1 = 1$ and $1\cdot 0 = 0\cdot 1 = 0\cdot 0 = 0$.

2) The semiring $\mathbb{N}$ of natural numbers with 0 under the usual ordering is a po-semiring with respect to usual operations.

3) The sets $\mathbb{Q}_+$ and $\mathbb{R}_+$ of all non-negative rational and real numbers, respectively, are po-semirings in the same way.

4) The set $(R)_n$ of all $n \times n$ matrices with elements in a po-semiring R forms a po-semiring by defining the partial order element-wise.

In many important examples, the sum $r + r'$ of two elements r and r' of a po-semiring R coincides with their suprema $r \cup r'$ (least upper bound with respect to the partial order on R). Such an R belongs to the class of so-called complete lattice ordered monoids (cf. [10,26]).

A monoid M is called semilattice ordered monoid (hereafter abbreviated slo-monoid) if M is a partially ordered set having binary suprema and satisfying the distributive laws between suprema and multiplication. A complete lattice ordered monoid (hereafter abbreviated clo-monoid) is a slo-monoid which has arbitrary suprema and satisfies the complete distributive laws:

$$(1) \quad m\cdot(\bigcup_{i\in I} m_i) = \bigcup_{i\in I} (m\cdot m_i)$$

$$(2) \quad (\bigcup_{i\in I} m_i)\cdot m = \bigcup_{i\in I} (m_i\cdot m)$$

for $m, m_i \in M$ and any index set I.

It is known that a partially ordered set with arbitrary suprema also has arbitrary infima, that means M is a complete lattice. A clo-monoid is said to be integral if the unit of the monoid M is the top element of the partial order. Clearly, every clo-monoid is a po-semiring.

Remark. Since a slo-monoid M with a special element 0, which is a multiplicative zero of the monoid M as well as being the bottom element of the partial order on M, can already be regarded as a po-semiring, this kind of structure will also be used here and M shall be called a slo-monoid with zero.

Examples. 1) Any complete distributive lattice can be considered as a clo-monoid.

2) The subsets of a monoid under complex multiplication and set-inclusion form a clo-monoid.

3) Let X be a set. Then the set Rel(X) of all binary relations on X is a clo-monoid under set-inclusion and usual product of relations.

4) The unit real interval with the usual ordering forms a clo-monoid by defining $a\cdot b = ab$ (usual product of real numbers) or $a\cdot b = \max\{a + b - 1, 0\}$.

5) If the ordering on the unit interval is defined dual to the usual one, then it forms a clo-monoid by different multiplications: $a\cdot b = \min\{a + b, 1\}$, $a\cdot b = a + b - ab$ or $a\cdot b = (a + b)/(1 + ab)$.

6) The sets of all natural numbers with 0, all non-negative rational or all non-negative real numbers form slo-monoids with zero under the usual ordering and product.

A more general concept has been introduced by S. Eilenberg [17] with his notion of a complete semiring, for which the sum of a family $(r_i)_{i\in I}$ of elements $r_i \in R$ is a well defined element of R for any index set I. Moreover, the following axioms are satisfied:

(1) $\sum_{i\in I} r_i = \sum_{j\in I} (\sum_{i\in I_j} r_i)$ provided $I = \bigcup_{j\in J} I_j$ is a disjoint partion of I

(2) $r\cdot(\sum_{i\in I} r_i) = \sum_{i\in I} r\cdot r_i$

(3) $(\sum_{i\in I} r_i)\cdot r = \sum_{i\in I} r_i\cdot r$

for all $r, r_i \in R$ and any index set I. A po-semiring is said to be complete if R is a complete semiring.

Examples. 1) Any clo-monoid can be considered as a complete semiring.

2) Let $\mathfrak{N}$ be the semiring $\mathbb{N}$ with 0 completed by the adjunction of an element ∞, where addition and multiplication are extended by the rules

$$n + \infty = \infty + n = \infty + \infty = \infty$$

$$n \cdot \infty = \infty \cdot n = \infty \text{ if } n > 0$$

$$\infty \cdot \infty = \infty, \quad 0 \cdot \infty = \infty \cdot 0 = 0$$

and ∞ be the greatest element of usual ordering. $\mathfrak{N}$ is a complete po-semiring.

3) In the same way, every po-semiring R can be enlarged to a complete po-semiring $\mathfrak{R}$ by adjunction of ∞.

Definition 1.2. An algebraic structure $(A,\cap,+,\cdot,\rightarrow)$ with four binary operations called intersection, sum, product and residuation is said to be a fuzzy algebra provided the following axioms are fulfilled:

(1) $(A,\cap)$ is a semilattice. (The induced partial order will be denoted by $\leqq$)

(2) $(A,+,\cdot)$ is a po-semiring.

(3) $a \rightarrow b = 1$ if and only if $a \leqq b$

(4) $a \leqq a'$ implies $a' \rightarrow b \leqq a \rightarrow b$

(5) $b \leqq b'$ implies $a \rightarrow b \leqq a \rightarrow b'$.

With each po-semiring $(R,+,\cdot)$, a fuzzy algebra $(R,\cap,+,\cdot,\rightarrow)$ may be associted by setting

$$r \cap r' = \begin{cases} \inf\{r,r'\} & \text{if } \inf\{r,r'\} \text{ exists} \\ 0 & \text{otherwise} \end{cases}$$

and

$$r \to r' = \begin{cases} 1 & \text{if } r \leqq r' \\ 0 & \text{otherwise} \end{cases}$$

for $r,r' \in R$.

Definition 1.3. A fuzzy algebra $(R,\cap,+,\cdot,\to)$ is called R-fuzzy algebra if the possible values of $\to$ are only 0 and 1, i.e.

$$\{r \in R \mid r = r' \to r'' \text{ for some } r',r'' \in R\} = \{0,1\}.$$

This severe restriction on residuation prevents us from building up a fuzzy set theory syntactically analogous to the usual case. Therefore, a more general definition of it is needed.

Definition 1.4. A partially ordered set A with a greatest element 1 is said to be an implication algebra*) if A is equipped with a binary operation $\to$ satisfying the following axioms

(1) $a \to b = 1$ if and only if $a \leqq b$

(2) $b \leqq b'$ implies $a \to b \leqq a \to b'$

(3) $a \to (b \to c) = b \to (a \to c)$.

Examples. 1) Any chain A with a greatest element 1 is an implication algebra by defininining

$$a \to b = \begin{cases} 1 & \text{if } a \leqq b \\ b & \text{if } a > b \end{cases}$$

2) Consider the real closed interval $[0,1]$. Then there are e.g. the following possibilities of defining $\to$, so that $([0,1],\to)$ is an implication algebra:

$$a \to b = \begin{cases} 1 & \text{if } a \leqq b \\ b/a & \text{if } a > b \end{cases}$$

or the Łukasiewicz operation

$$a \to b = \min\{1,1-a+b\}.$$

*) J.C. Abbott and H. Rasiowa (cf. [63]) use this notion in a different way.

<u>Theorem 1.1</u>. In any implication algebra $(A,\rightarrow)$, the following conditions hold for a, a', b, b' and c of A.

(1) $a \rightarrow 1 = 1$

(2) $a \rightarrow a = 1$

(3) $a \leqq b \rightarrow c$ if and only if $b \leqq a \rightarrow c$

(4) $a \rightarrow (b \rightarrow a) = 1$

(5) $a \rightarrow ((a \rightarrow b) \rightarrow b) = 1$

(6) $1 \rightarrow a = a$

(7) $a \rightarrow b \leqq (b \rightarrow c) \rightarrow (a \rightarrow c)$

(8) $b \rightarrow c \leqq (a \rightarrow b) \rightarrow (a \rightarrow c)$

(9) $a \leqq a'$ implies $a' \rightarrow b \leqq a \rightarrow b$

(10) $(a \rightarrow b) \rightarrow (a \rightarrow c) \leqq a \rightarrow (b \rightarrow c)$

(11) $a \leqq (a \rightarrow b) \rightarrow a$

Proof. (1) and (2) are trivial consequences of axiom (1).

(3) is an equivalent formulation of axiom (3).

(4) Since $a \rightarrow a = 1$, we have $b \leqq a \rightarrow a$ and, by (3), $a \leqq b \rightarrow a$, i.e., $a \rightarrow (b \rightarrow a) = 1$.

(5) From $a \rightarrow b \leqq a \rightarrow b$ follows $a \leqq (a \rightarrow b) \rightarrow b$ by (3), which proves the assertion $a \rightarrow ((a \rightarrow b) \rightarrow b) = 1$.

(6) $1 \rightarrow a \leqq 1 \rightarrow a$ implies $1 \leqq (1 \rightarrow a) \rightarrow a$. Since 1 is top element $(1 \rightarrow a) \rightarrow a = 1$ and, therefore, $1 \rightarrow a \leqq a$. From $a \rightarrow a = 1$, we conclude $a \leqq 1 \rightarrow a$, i.e., $1 \rightarrow a = a$ holds.

(7) Because of (5), $b \leqq (b \rightarrow c) \rightarrow c$ holds. Thus, by axiom (2), $(a \rightarrow b) \rightarrow b \leqq (a \rightarrow b) \rightarrow ((b \rightarrow c) \rightarrow c)$ follows directly. Since $a \leqq (a \rightarrow b) \rightarrow b$ by (5), we get $a \leqq (a \rightarrow b) \rightarrow ((b \rightarrow c) \rightarrow c)$ and, consequently, $a \rightarrow b \leqq a \rightarrow ((b \rightarrow c) \rightarrow c) = (b \rightarrow c) \rightarrow (a \rightarrow c)$ by axiom (3).

(8) follows from (7) and (3).

(9) If $a \leqq a'$, then $a \rightarrow a' = 1$. Applying (8), we have $a' \rightarrow b \leqq (a \rightarrow a') \rightarrow (a \rightarrow b) = 1 \rightarrow (a \rightarrow b)$. Together with (6), the assertion $a' \rightarrow b \leqq a \rightarrow b$ can be derived.

(10) results from (4) and (9). Because $b \leqq a \rightarrow b$ by (4) and, therefore, $(a \rightarrow b) \rightarrow (a \rightarrow c) \leqq b \rightarrow (a \rightarrow c)$. Now, the assertion can be proved by means of axiom (3).

(11) follows from (4).

Theorem 1.2. Assume $(A,\rightarrow)$ is an implication algebra which is at the same time a lattice, then the following conditions are satisfied for all $a,a',b,b' \in A$

(1) $(a \cup a') \rightarrow b = (a \rightarrow b) \cap (a' \rightarrow b)$

(2) $a \rightarrow (b \cap b') = (a \rightarrow b) \cap (a \rightarrow b')$

(3) $(a \rightarrow b) \cup (a' \rightarrow b) \leqq (a \cap a') \rightarrow b$

(4) $(a \rightarrow b) \cup (a \rightarrow b') \leqq a \rightarrow (b \cup b')$

Proof. Equation (1) is proved in two steps. (i) $a \leqq a \cup a'$ and $a' \leqq a \cup a'$ imply $(a \cup a') \rightarrow b \leqq a \rightarrow b$ and $(a \cup a') \rightarrow b \leqq a' \rightarrow b$, respectively. Hence $(a \cup a') \rightarrow b \leqq (a \rightarrow b) \cap (a' \rightarrow b)$.
(ii) By Theorem 1.1. (5), we have $a \leqq (a \rightarrow b) \rightarrow b$ and $a' \leqq (a' \rightarrow b) \rightarrow b$. Because $(a \rightarrow b) \rightarrow b \leqq ((a \rightarrow b) \cap (a' \rightarrow b)) \rightarrow b$ and $(a' \rightarrow b) \rightarrow b \leqq ((a \rightarrow b) \cap (a' \rightarrow b)) \rightarrow b$, successively, we get $a \cup a' \leqq ((a \rightarrow b) \cap (a' \rightarrow b)) \rightarrow b$, which is equivalent, by axiom (3), to $(a \rightarrow b) \cap (a' \rightarrow b) \leqq (a \cup a') \rightarrow b$.

(2) can be proved in analogy to (1).

(3) Since $a \cap a' \leqq a$ and $a \cap a' \leqq a'$, $a \rightarrow b \leqq (a \cap a') \rightarrow b$ and $a' \rightarrow b \leqq (a \cap a') \rightarrow b$. Hence $(a \rightarrow b) \cup (a' \rightarrow b) \leqq (a \cap a') \rightarrow b$.

(4) can be proved in analogy to (3).

Definition 1.5. A fuzzy algebra $(L,\cap,+,\cdot,\rightarrow)$ is called an L_+-fuzzy algebra provided

(1) $(L,+,\cdot)$ is a complete po-semiring with 1 as top element.

(2) $(L,\rightarrow)$ is an implication algebra.

(3) $a \cdot b \leqq c$ if and only if $a \leqq b \rightarrow c$

An L_+-fuzzy algebra is said to be an L-fuzzy algebra if the following axioms are additionally fulfilled

(4) $(L,\cap)$ is a complete semilattice.

(5) $+$ is an idempotent operation.

Remark. By definition, any L-fuzzy algebra $(L,\cap,+,\cdot,\rightarrow)$ is a complete lattice with respect to $\cap$ and $+$. Moreover, L forms an integral clo-monoid under multiplication. The operation $\rightarrow$ is a residuation in the sense of semigroups (cf. [10,26]). Therefore, L-fuzzy algebras coincide with integral residuated clo-monoids. Fuzzy algebras characterize, from the algebraic point of view, fuzzy logic to be discussed in

Section 1.2. By considering complementation in lattices, the difference from other ncn-classical logics shall be shown. In all these logics the law of excluded middle is not valid. This is a basic assumption for studying fuzziness.

By a complement of an element a in a lattice L with bottom element 0 and top element 1, an element $b \in L$ is meant such that

$$a \cap b = 0 \qquad \text{and} \qquad a \cup b = 1.$$

L is called complemented if all its elements have complements. It is known (cf. [63]) that in any distributive lattice complements are unique. In this case $\bar{a}$ denotes the complement of a. A complemented distributive lattice is said to be a Boolean lattice (algebra).

Let L be a distributive lattice with 0 and 1. Then the set of all elements which have a complementforms a Boolean lattice B. Furthermore, B is not only a sublattice of L but also the largest sublattice of L which is at the same time a Boolean one.

Every complete Boolean lattice L can be considered as an L-fuzzy algebra by setting

$$a + b = a \cup b, \qquad a \cdot b = a \cap b \qquad \text{and} \qquad a \rightarrow b = \bar{a} \cup b.$$

Let a and b be elements of a lattice L. An element $c \in L$ is said to be the pseudo-complement of a relative to b if c is the greatest element of the set $\{x \in L | a \cap x \leqq b\}$. The pseudo-complement of a relative to b is denoted, if it exists, by the symbol b:a. Therefore, for every $x \in L$ we have,

$$x \leqq b{:}a \qquad \text{if and only if} \qquad a \cap x \leqq b.$$

This equivalence can be considered to be another definition of b:a. A lattice L is called relatively pseudo-complemented (or Brouwerian algebra) if b:a exists for all $a,b \in L$. Any relatively pseudo-complemented lattice is distributive and has a top element 1. If such a lattice also has a bottom element 0, then L is said to be a pseudo-Boolean lattice (cf. [63]). In this case the element $\neg a = 0{:}a$ is called the pseudo-complement of a.

If an element a of a distributive lattice L has the complement $\bar{a}$, then for every $b \in L$ the pseudo-complement b:a of a relative to b exists, and $b{:}a = \bar{a} \cup b$. Assuming an element a of a pseudo-Boolean lattice has the complement $\bar{a}$, then the pseudo-complement $\neg a$ is equal to $\bar{a}$. Therefore, any complemented pseudo-Boolean lattice is a Boolean lattice.

Let L be a pseudo-Boolean lattice and $B = \{a \cup L | a \cup \neg a = 1\}$, then B is the largest Boolean sublattice of L.

Every complete pseudo-Boolean lattice can be considered as an L-fuzzy algebra by setting

$$a + b = a \cup b, \quad a \cdot b = a \cap b \quad \text{and} \quad a \to b = b{:}a .$$

Pseudo-Boolean lattices are related to non-complemented logics as positive or intuitionistic ones (cf. [63]). A major difference between pseudo-Boolean or Boolean lattices and L-fuzzy algebras is the fact that multiplication in L-fuzzy algebras is generally non-idempotent.

But this argument is also true for many-valued Łukasiewicz logic. Consider the related algebraic structure on the real closed interval [0,1] defined by

$$a \cap b = \min\{a,b\}$$

$$a + b = \max\{a,b\}$$

$$a \cdot b = \max\{0, a+b-1\}$$

$$a \to b = \min\{1, 1-a+b\}$$

for all $a,b \in [0,1]$. Obviously, this structure, denoted by Ł, is an L-fuzzy algebra with an idempotent multiplication too. Therefore, L-fuzzy logic will be a generalization of classical logic including positive, intuitionistic as well as many-valued logics properly.

Next, restrictions on implication algebras are proposed in order to show connections between L-fuzzy algebras, on the one hand, and pseudo-Boolean or Boolean lattices, on the other hand. It turns out that the properties (10) and (11) of Theorem 1.1 are essential in the following sense. If equality in property (10) is required, then any L-fuzzy algebra is a pseudo-Boolean lattice. Each L-fuzzy algebra, for which in properties (10) and (11), equality holds, is a Boolean lattice. To prove this fact some preparation is necessary.

Definition 1.6. An implication algebra $(A,\to)$ is said to be positive provided

$$a \to (b \to c) \leqq (a \to b) \to (a \to c)$$

holds for all $a,b,c \in A$. $(A,\to)$ is called strong implication algebra if, in addition,

$$(a \to b) \to a \leqq a$$

is valid for all $a,b \in A$.

Theorem 1.3. Let $(L,\cap,+,\cdot,\rightarrow)$ be an L_+-fuzzy algebra such that $(L,\rightarrow)$ is a positive implication algebra. Then multiplication coincides with intersection, i.e. $a\cdot b = a \cap b$ for all $a,b \in L$.

Proof. At first, the idempotence of multiplication will be shown. Let a, b and c be arbitrary elements of L. By assumption $a \rightarrow (b \rightarrow c) \leq (a \rightarrow b) \rightarrow (a \rightarrow c)$, from which it follows that $a \rightarrow b \leq (a \rightarrow (b \rightarrow c)) \rightarrow (a \rightarrow c)$ in accordance with property (3) of Theorem 1.1. Setting $a = b$, we get $a \rightarrow (a \rightarrow c) \leq a \rightarrow c$ and, therefore, $a\cdot a \rightarrow c \leq a \rightarrow c$ by axiom (3) of a L_+-fuzzy algebra. If $c = a\cdot a$ is chosen, then $1 = a \rightarrow a\cdot a$ or $a \leq a\cdot a$. On the other hand, $a\cdot a \leq a\cdot 1 = a$. Consequently, $a\cdot a = a$ for all $a \in A$.

Since 1 is top element, $a\cdot b \leq a \cap b$ holds otherwise, $a \cap b \leq a$ and $a \cap b \leq b$ imply $(a \cap b)\cdot(a \cap b) \leq a\cdot b$. Because of the idempotence of multiplication $a \cap b \leq a\cdot b$ is valid. Both inequalities yield $a\cdot b = a \cap b$ for all $a,b \in A$.

Theorem 1.4. An L-fuzzy algebra $(L,\cap,+,\cdot,\rightarrow)$ is a (complete) pseudo-Boolean lattice if and only if $(L,\rightarrow)$ is a positive implication algebra.

Proof. Let $(L,\cap,+,\cdot,\rightarrow)$ be an L-fuzzy algebra.

(1) Assume that L is a pseudo-Boolean lattice, then $(L,\rightarrow)$ is an implication algebra by setting $a \rightarrow b = b:a$, as already mentioned. In order to prove $(L,\rightarrow)$ is positive let x be an arbitrary element of L satisfying $x \leq a \rightarrow (b \rightarrow c)$ for the given elements $a,b,c \in L$. By definition, we derive $x \cap a \cap b \leq c$. Together with $a \cap (a \rightarrow b) \leq b$ we obtain $x \cap a \cap (a \rightarrow b) \leq c$, which is equivalent to $x \leq (a \rightarrow b) \rightarrow (a \rightarrow c)$. Hence $a \rightarrow (b \rightarrow c) = (a \rightarrow b) \rightarrow (a \rightarrow c)$, i.e. $(L,\rightarrow)$ is a positive implication algebra.

(2) Let $(L,\rightarrow)$ be a positive implication algebra. By Theorem 1.3, it is easily seen that L is a (complete) pseudo-Bollean lattice.

Theorem 1.5. In any strong implication algebra $(A,\rightarrow)$ the following conditions are satisfied

(1) $(a \rightarrow b) \rightarrow b = (b \rightarrow a) \rightarrow a$

(2) $(a \rightarrow c) \leq ((b \rightarrow c) \rightarrow (((a \rightarrow b) \rightarrow b) \rightarrow c))$

for all $a,b,c \in A$.

Proof. (1) can be shown in two steps.(i) Property (5) of Theorem 1.1 yields $a \leq (a \rightarrow b) \rightarrow b$. From this $(b \rightarrow a) \rightarrow a \leq (b \rightarrow a) \rightarrow ((a \rightarrow b) \rightarrow b)$ is derived and, by axiom (3) of an implication algebra,

$(b \to a) \to a \leq (a \to b) \to ((b \to a) \to b)$. Because of the assumption that $(L,\to)$ is a strong implication algebra, $(b \to a) \to b$ equals b, consequently, $(b \to a) \to a \leq (a \to b) \to b$.
(ii) is proved in analogy to (i).

(2) Using property (8) of Theorem 1.1, we have
$(c \to b) \to (a \to b) \leq ((a \to b) \to b) \to ((c \to b) \to b)$. By Theorem 1.1 (7), $a \to c \leq ((a \to b) \to b) \to ((c \to b) \to b)$. Since $(c \to b) \to b = (b \to c) \to c$, by (1), the following inequality $a \to c \leq ((a \to b) \to b) \to ((b \to c) \to c)$ holds, which proves the assertion.

Theorem 1.6. An L-fuzzy algebra $(L,\cap,+,\cdot,\to)$ is a (complete) Boolean lattice if and only if $(L,\to)$ is a strong implication algebra.

Proof. (1) Let $(L,\cap,+,\cdot,\to)$ be an L-fuzzy algebra, which is a Boolean lattice too. Then $(L,\to)$ is a positive implication algebra by Theorem 1.6. It only remanis to show that the equation $(a \to b) \to a = a$ holds for all $a,b \in L$. Since in a Boolean lattice $a \to b = \bar{a} + b$, where $\bar{a}$ is the complement of a and + coincides with suprema, we can conclude $(a \to b) \to a = (\bar{a} + b) + a = (a \cap \bar{b}) + a = a$, i.e. $(L,\to)$ is a strong implication algebra.

(2) Suppose $(L,\cap,+,\cdot,\to)$ is an L-fuzzy algebra such that $(L,\to)$ is a strong implication algebra. By Theorem 1.6, L is a (complete) pseudo-Boolean lattice. Therefore, it is sufficient to verify $\neg a + a = 1$ for all $a \in L$, where $\neg a = a \to 0$ is the pseudo-complement of a. At first, the following equation shall be derived: $a + b = (a \to b) \to b$ for all $a,b \in L$. By Theorem 1.1 (5), $a \leq (a \to b) \to b$ and $b \leq (b \to a) \to a$ hold. Applying $(b \to a) \to a = (a \to b) \to b$ for strong implication algebras we have $a + b \leq (a \to b) \to b$. The opposite inequality results from property (2) of Theorem 1.5, because $a \leq a + b$ and $b \leq a + b$ imply $((a \to b) \to b) \to (a + b) = 1$, which is equivalent to $(a \to b) \to b \leq a + b$. Especially, $\neg a + a = (a \to 0) + a = ((a \to 0) \to a) \to a$ and hence $\neg a + a = 1$, since $(a \to 0) \to a = a$ by assumption.

Theorem 1.7. Let $(L,\cap,+,\cdot,\to)$ be an L_+-fuzzy algebra, then the following conditions are fulfilled for all $a,b,c \in L$

(1) $a \cdot b = b \cdot a$

(2) $a \cdot (a \to b) \leq b$

(3) $a \to (b \to c) = (a \cdot b) \to c$

(4) $a \leq b \to (a \cdot b)$

(5) $a \to b \leq (a \cdot c) \to (b \cdot c)$

(6) $(a \to b) \cdot (b \to c) \leq a \to c$

(7) $a \cdot b \leq a \cdot (a \to b)$

(8) $(a \to b) \cdot b \leq b$.

Proof. (1) follows from axiom (3) of an L_+-fuzzy algebra by means of axiom (3) of an implication algebra.

(2) follows from property (5) of Theorem 1.1.

(3) and (4) are direct consequences of axiom (3).

(5) Let x be an arbitrary element of L satisfying $x \leq a \to b$ for given $a, b \in L$. Then $x \cdot a \leq b$ holds and, therefore, $x \cdot a \cdot c \leq b \cdot c$ for any $c \in L$. Hence $x \leq (a \cdot c) \to (b \cdot c)$, i.e. $a \to b \leq (a \cdot c) \to (b \cdot c)$.

(6) results from property (7) of Theorem 1.1.

(7) Since 1 is top element, $b \cdot a \leq b$ is valid for all $a, b \in L$. Thus $b \leq a \to b$ and, consequently, $a \cdot b \leq a \cdot (a \to b)$ because of the monotony of multiplication.

(8) For any $a, b \in L$, $a \to b \leq 1$ holds and, therefore, $(a \to b) \cdot b \leq b$ follows.

Remark. If the multiplication in an L_+-fuzzy algebra is idempotent, then equality holds in (7) as well as in (8).

In analogy to Theorem 1.2 the following statements can be proved.

Theorem 1.8. In every L-fuzzy algebra $(L, \cap, +, \cdot, \to)$ the following properties are satisfied for all a, a_i, b and b_i of L, $i \in I$, where I is an arbitrary indexing set.

(1) $(\sum_{i \in I} a_i) \to b = \bigcap_{i \in I} (a_i \to b)$

(2) $a \to (\bigcap_{i \in I} b_i) = \bigcap_{i \in I} (a \to b_i)$

(3) $\sum_{i \in I} (a_i \to b) \leq (\bigcap_{i \in I} a_i) \to b$

(4) $\sum_{i \in I} (a \to b_i) \leq a \to (\sum_{i \in I} b_i)$.

Remark. Observe that any L-fuzzy algebra $(L, \cap, +, \cdot, \to)$ is a complete lattice $(L, \cap, +)$ too, i.e. intersection and sum are defined for arbitrary families of elements.

Let $(L, \cap, +, \cdot, \to)$ be an L-fuzzy algebra. By biresiduation we shall understand the derived operation

$$a \leftrightarrow b = (a \to b) \cap (b \to a).$$

<u>Theorem 1.9</u> [58]. Let $(L,\cap,+,\cdot,\to)$ be an L-fuzzy algebra. The biresiduation in L has the following properties.

(1) $a \leftrightarrow 1 = a$

(2) $a = b$ if and only if $a \leftrightarrow b = 1$

(3) $a \leftrightarrow b = b \leftrightarrow a$

(4) $(a \leftrightarrow b)\cdot(b \leftrightarrow c) \leqq a \leftrightarrow c$

(5) $(a \leftrightarrow b) \cap (a' \leftrightarrow b') \leqq (a \cap a') \leftrightarrow (b \cap b')$

(6) $(a \leftrightarrow b) \cap (a' \leftrightarrow b') \leqq (a + a') \leftrightarrow (b + b')$

(7) $(a \leftrightarrow b)\cdot(a' \leftrightarrow b') \leqq (a\cdot a') \leftrightarrow (b\cdot b')$

(8) $(a \leftrightarrow b)\cdot(a' \leftrightarrow b') \leqq (a \to a') \leftrightarrow (b \to b')$.

Proof. (1), (2) and (3) are trivial consequences of the definition.

(4) For any $a,b,c \in L$, we have $(a \leftrightarrow b)\cdot(b \leftrightarrow c) \leqq (a \to b)\cdot(b \to c)$ and $(a \leftrightarrow b)\cdot(b \leftrightarrow c) \leqq (c \to b)\cdot(b \to a)$. By (6) of Theorem 1.7, $(a \leftrightarrow b)\cdot(b \leftrightarrow c) \leqq a \to c$ and $(a \leftrightarrow b)\cdot(b \leftrightarrow c) \leqq c \to a$ hold. Hence $(a \leftrightarrow b)\cdot(b \leftrightarrow c) \leqq a \leftrightarrow c$ by definition.

(5) For any $a,a',b,b' \in L$, we can derive $((a \leftrightarrow b) \cap (a' \leftrightarrow b'))\cdot$ $\cdot(a \cap a') \leqq ((a \to b) \cap (a' \to b'))\cdot(a \cap a') \leqq ((a \to b)\cdot a) \cap$ $\cap ((a' \to b')\cdot a') \leqq b \cap b'$ because of $a\cdot(a \to b) \leqq b$ and $a'\cdot(a' \to b') \leqq b'$ by Theorem 1.7 (2). Therefore $(a \leftrightarrow b) \cap (a' \leftrightarrow b') \leqq$ $(a \cap a') \to (b \cap b')$. By the symmetry of definition we also get $(a \leftrightarrow b) \cap (a' \leftrightarrow b') \leqq (b \cap b') \to (a \cap a')$. The last two inequalities already yield assertion (5).

(6) In accordance with the axioms of a po-semiring we derive $((a \leftrightarrow b) \cap (a' \leftrightarrow b'))\cdot(a + a') = (((a \leftrightarrow b) \cap (a' \leftrightarrow b'))\cdot a) +$ $(((a \leftrightarrow b) \cap (a' \leftrightarrow b'))\cdot a') \leqq ((a \to b)\cdot a) + ((a' \to b')\cdot a') \leqq b + b'$. Therefore $(a \leftrightarrow b) \cap (a' \leftrightarrow b') \leqq (a + a') \to (b + b')$. By symmetry the statement (6) can be verified in analogy to (5).

Because of the same argument used in (5) and (6), it suffices to show only one part of (7) and (8).

(7) By associtivity of multiplication $(a \leftrightarrow b)\cdot(a' \leftrightarrow b')\cdot(a\cdot a') \leqq$ $((a \to b)\cdot a)\cdot((a' \to b')\cdot a') \leqq b\cdot b'$ can be proved. Hence, the first part of (7) results, namely, $(a \leftrightarrow b)\cdot(a' \leftrightarrow b') \leqq (a\cdot a') \to (b\cdot b')$.

(8) From $(a \leftrightarrow b)\cdot(a' \leftrightarrow b')\cdot(a \to a') \leqq (b \to a)\cdot(a' \to b')\cdot(a \to a')$ follows $(a \leftrightarrow b)\cdot(a' \leftrightarrow b')\cdot(a \to a') \leqq b \to b'$ by Theorem 1.7 (6). Consequently, $(a \leftrightarrow b)\cdot(a' \leftrightarrow b') \leqq (a \to a') \to (b \to b')$ holds.

1.2. Fuzzy logic and fuzzy models

As a good deal of well-known applications of fuzzy sets in various fields like pattern recognition (cf. [9]), artificial intelligence (cf. [28,29]), automata (cf. [48,49,53,91]), switching theory (cf. [35,36,46]) etc. has shown fuzzy concepts and methods to be useful, a rigorous treatment of a calculus of fuzzy sets becomes desirable now. Its goal should be a self-contained universe governed by the fundamental membership relation. Such an approach has to be a 'set theory' in a certain sense, that means the universe in question must be determined by a fuzzy interpretation of an associated ε-theory. This requires a generalized logic.

Ordinary logic represents exact concepts syntactically. It can be thought of as a mechanism for manipulation with names of concepts. By means of selected axioms and rules of inference, valid manipulations can be distinguished from invalid ones. On the other hand, exact concepts are represented by usual sets semantically. From this point of view, a logic of inexact concepts [26] is needed to serve as a suitable logic in which a fuzzy set theory can be built up. Such kinds of logics are called fuzzy although 'it is shocking to associate the word fuzzy with the word logic' [38]. But it has been clear since the twentieth of this century that it is, in fact, not a matter of having one unique logic, but having as many logics as one wishes. It all depends on the axiomatization chosen (cf. [63]).

J. A. Goguen [26] illustrates the representation of inexact concepts by fuzzy sets resolving the ancient paradox called sorites or falakores.The original form can be paraphrased as follows: If you add one stone to a small heap, it remains small. A heap containing one stone is small. Therefore, by induction, every heap is small. Besides using fuzzy sets, the most important discovery is the fact that the validity of a chain of nearly valid deductions decreases as the length of the chain increases. This leads to a hint how to evaluate rules of inference as it has been done in [58]. Section 1.2.1 is devoted to this problem.

A different approach for approximate reasoning was proposed by L. A. Zadeh [95]. 'We reason in approximate terms when we decide on how to cross a traffic intersection, which route to take to a destination, how much to bet in poker and what approach to use in proving a theorem.' It is suggested to use truth values as fuzzy sets with linguistic labels like true, false, not true, very true, quite true, not very true, not very true and not very false, etc. The truth value set is assumed to be generated by a context-free grammar with a semantic rule providing a means of computing the meaning of each linguistic truth value as a fuzzy set. The characistic feature of approximate reasoning, namely fuzziness of premises and of inference rules, is similar to the approach mentioned above. In this section we will not deal with that kind of fuzzy logic.

Our aim is a fuzzy logic capable of building up a fuzzy set theory. The crucial point is the notion of a fuzzy model which will be introduced in Section 1.2.2.

Some interesting notes concerning fuzzy logic have been made in [54], where C. G. Morgan and F. J. Pelletier state that presentations of fuzzy logics have been semantic in nature and the syntax has been ignored. But without such a syntax consisting of a set of inference rules and a set of axioms, the semantical intuitions behind a fuzzy logic cannot be formulated in any orderly manner, and their value will correspondingly be diminished. The basic question is whether it is possible to axiomatize fuzzy logic. For this purpose a language is developed which is capable of mirroring the semantic in the syntax. The standard remedy (cf. [65]) is to introduce special one-place operators. They have the form 'I_k', where the subscript k is one of truth values. Intuitively, prefexing such an operator before a formula α has the effect of saying α has exactly the truth value k. Now, the statement is that fuzzy logic is not axiomatizable. But a way out of this dilemma will be shown in Section 1.2.1.

It seems quite natural to ask for application of fuzzy logic in switching theory if one has in mind the relationship between classical propositional logic and combinational switching systems (cf. [36,46]). By means of a fuzzy logic based on Zadeh's truth value set, A. Kandel [35] has studied static hazards in combinational switching systems. A further application of fuzzy logic concerns modelling of retrieval processes (cf. [56,57]). But all such possible kinds of applications will not be dealt with in this section.

In order to generalize the basic notions of logic, universal algebra provides a convenient framework. Therefore, a necessary amount of related concepts will be presented in the sequel. The reader is expected to have some **familiarities** with algebraic notions because examples for motivations are omitted.

An operator domain Ω is a disjoint sequence of sets Ω_n ($n = 0,1,\ldots$) of n-ary operator symbols. An Ω-algebra is a pair (A,d) consisting of a set A and a mapping d which assigns an n-ary operation $d_\omega: A^n \to A$ to each ω of Ω_n.

Given two Ω-algebras (A,d) and (A',d'), an Ω-homomorphism from (A,d) into (A',d') is a mapping $f: A \to A'$ which preserves all the Ω-operations, that is, for all $\omega \in \Omega_n$, $n \geq 0$, and each n-tuple $(a_1,a_2,\ldots,a_n)$ of A^n, we have

$$f(d_\omega(a_1,a_2,\ldots,a_n)) = d'_\omega(f(a_1),f(a_2),\ldots,f(a_n)).$$

An equivalence relation $\sim$ on A is called Ω-congruence relation on (A,d) if

$$a_i \sim a'_i,\ i = 1,2,\ldots,n, \text{ implies } d_\omega(a_1,a_2,\ldots,a_n) \sim d_\omega(a'_1,a'_2,\ldots,a'_n)$$

for each $\omega \in \Omega_n$, $n \geq 1$, and all $a_1,a_2,\ldots,a_n,a'_1,a'_2,\ldots,a'_n$ of A. The set of all equivalence classes of elements of A forms an Ω-algebra called the factor algebra.

Let X be a set, let $(F_\Omega X,\varphi)$ be an Ω-algebra and let $i: X \to F_\Omega X$ be an injective mapping. We say that $(F_\Omega X,\varphi)$ is a free Ω-algebra on the set X (of free generators) if, for every Ω-algebra (A,d) and any mapping f from X into A, there exists a unique Ω-homomorphism $f^{\#}: F_\Omega X \to A$ satisfying $i \cdot f^{\#} = f$. It is well-known (cf. [7,45]) that, for any set X and any operator domain Ω, there exists a free Ω-algebra $(F_\Omega X,\varphi)$ on X. This free Ω-algebra on X is unique up to ismomorphism. $F_\Omega X$ can be constructed as union

$$F_\Omega X = \bigcup_{n\geq 0} F_\Omega X_n$$

of sets $F_\Omega X_n$ defined inductively as follows

(1) $F_\Omega X_o$ is disjoint union of X and Ω_o.

(2) Assume $F_\Omega X_m$ is already defined for $0 \leq m < n$.
Then put
$F_\Omega X_n = \{\omega t_1 t_2 \ldots t_k | \omega \in \Omega_k,\ t_i \in F_\Omega X_{n_i} \text{ with } \sum_{i=1}^{k} n_i = n - 1\}$.

The elements of $F_\Omega X$ are called Ω-terms. They are given in Polish notation. But it is allowed to use another notation. The mapping φ is determined by

$$\varphi_\omega = \omega \qquad \text{for } \omega \in \Omega_o$$

$$\varphi_\omega(t_1,t_2,\ldots,t_n) = \omega t_1 t_2 \ldots t_n \qquad \text{for } \omega \in \Omega_n,\ n \geq 1.$$

Now, the basic notions of logic will be fuzzyfied, that means, the two truth value 0 (false) and 1 (true) of the classical logic have to be replaced by a (possibly infinite) set W of truth values containing 0 and 1. Moreover, the set of usual logical connectives $\wedge$ (conjunction), ∇ (disjunction), and $\Rightarrow$ (implication) must be extended by an additional connective Δ (called context or coimplication) to yield $C = \{\wedge,\nabla,\Delta,\Rightarrow\}$. Accordingly, a new universal quantifier $\forall$, which is related to Δ, must be added to the set Q of usual quantifiers $\bigwedge$ (universal quantifier) and $\exists$ (existential quantifier). On the basis of this formal language, a W-valued logic will be built up. Its semantic interpretation in a fuzzy algebra $(A,\cap,+,\cdot,\rightarrow)$ is essentially determined by the following correspondence

logical connectives	operations in A
$\wedge$ conjunction	$\cap$ intersection
∇ disjunction	$+$ addition
Δ context	$\cdot$ multiplication
$\Rightarrow$ implication	$\rightarrow$ residuation

Convention. For sake of convenience, Ω-algebras whose operator domain is specified by $\Omega_0 = W$ and $\Omega_2 = C$ or $\Omega_0 = W$, $\Omega_1 = \{(qx) \mid q \in Q \text{ and } x \in V\}$ and $\Omega_2 = C$, where all $\Omega_n = \emptyset$ otherwise, are called (W,C)- or (W,Q,C)-algebras, respectively. Thereby, V is an infinite set which will be fixed later on.

1.2.1. Fuzzy proposition calculi

In this section we mainly review results obtained by J. Pavelka [58]. His interesting paper is stimulated by J. A. Goguen's comprehensive article [26].

Definition 1.7. The free (W,C)-algebra on V, denoted by $\mathcal{P}_W(V)$, is said to be the algebra of the fuzzy proposition calculus on the set V of propositional variables. The (W,C)-terms are called W-propositions.

The set of all W-propositions may also be described by the following rules

(1) Any proposition variable v of V is a W-proposition.

(2) Any element of W is a W-proposition called logical constant or internal truth value.

(3) If α and β are W-propositions, so are $\alpha \wedge \beta$, $\alpha \nabla \beta$, $\alpha \Delta \beta$, $\alpha \Rightarrow \beta$.

(4) There are no W-propositions other than those constructed from the atomic ones, described in (1) and (2), or obtained by means of successive applications of the rules given in (3).

In any algebra of W-propositions, some derived operations are introduced by

(1) $\neg\alpha = \alpha \Rightarrow 0$

(2) $\alpha \Leftrightarrow \beta = (\alpha \Rightarrow \beta) \wedge (\beta \Rightarrow \alpha)$

(3) $\alpha^n = \alpha \Delta \alpha \Delta \ldots \Delta \alpha$ (n-times), $n \geq 1$

for W-propositions α and β. The connectives $\neg$ and $\Leftrightarrow$ are called negation and biimplication, respectively. The derived unary connective $\alpha \mapsto \alpha^n$ is called the n-th context power.

In order to describe fuzzy interpretation of W-propositions in a fuzzy algebra $(A,\sqcap,+,\cdot,\to)$ within the formalism of Ω-algebras, fuzzy algebras must be considered as (W,C)-algebras. Therefore, a mapping from W into A assigning a_w to each w of W has to be introduced so that $a_0 = 0$ and $a_1 = 1$ hold. Indeed, $(A,\{a_w | w \in W\},\sqcap,+,\cdot,\to)$ is a (W,C)-algebra now. In all cases to be studied later on, W will be identified with $\underline{A} = \{\underline{a} | a \in A\}$ for simplicity.

<u>Definition 1.8.</u> A fuzzy interpretation of $\mathcal{P}_W(V)$ in a fuzzy algebra $(A,\sqcap,+,\cdot,\to)$ is a (W,C)-homomorphism $f: \mathcal{P}_W(V) \to A$. The set of all fuzzy interpretations is denoted by $\mathrm{Sem}_{(W,C)}(V,A)$.

<u>Remark.</u> Since $\mathcal{P}_W(V)$ is a free (W,C)-algebra on V, for any mapping f from V into A there exactly exists $f^* \in \mathrm{Sem}_{(W,C)}(V,A)$ such that $f(v) = f^*(v)$ for all v of V. Once we define the value of a fuzzy interpretation f of $\mathrm{Sem}_{(W,C)}(V,A)$ on V, then

(1) the values of f on $\{\underline{a} | a \in A\}$ are determined by the condition that f preserves all nullary operations, i.e.

$$f(\underline{a}) = a \qquad \text{for all } a \in A$$

(2) the values of f on non-atomic W-propositions are uniquely determined by the preservation of binary primitive operations, i.e., for all $\alpha,\beta \in \mathcal{P}_W(V)$, we have

$$f(\alpha \wedge \beta) = f(\alpha) \sqcap f(\beta)$$
$$f(\alpha \nabla \beta) = f(\alpha) + f(\beta)$$
$$f(\alpha \Delta \beta) = f(\alpha) \cdot f(\beta)$$
$$f(\alpha \Rightarrow \beta) = f(\alpha) \to f(\beta).$$

Since an Ω-homomorphism of Ω-algebras preserves all derived operations, each f of $\mathrm{Sem}_{(W,C)}(V,A)$ interpretes the biimplication $\Leftrightarrow$ as biresiduation $\leftrightarrow$ in A.

We are now going to generalize the notion of semantic consequence $X \models \alpha$, where X is a set of assumptions and α is a proposition in the classical logic. Instead of a subset X of propositions, we have to take a mapping X from $\mathcal{P}_W(V)$ into A. Every assumption of X is only true with a certain value. Following J. Pavelka [58], the truth value of semantic consequence is defined by

$$X \mid\!\!== \alpha = \bigcap\{f(\alpha) \mid f \in \mathrm{Sem}_{(W,C)}(V,A) \text{ such that } f \geq X\},$$

where $f \geq X$ means that $f(\beta) \geq X(\beta)$ for all $\beta \in \mathcal{P}_W(V)$. We say that X semantically implies α with degree $X \mid\!\!== \alpha$. The inequality $(X \mid\!\!== \alpha) \geq a$ will often be expressed in the alternative form

$$X \mid\!\!==_a \alpha.$$

Let $\emptyset$ be the mapping from $\mathcal{P}_W(V)$ into A defined by $\emptyset(\alpha) = 0$ for all α of $\mathcal{P}_W(V)$. A W-proposition α is called W-tautology provided $\emptyset \mid\!\!==_1 \alpha$ holds. Next, some W-tautologies will be derived. For this purpose, the following schemata of W-propositions are introduced:

(1) For any $a,b \in A$, we put

$$\sigma_1(a,b) = (\underline{a} \wedge \underline{b}) \Rightarrow \underline{a \cap b}$$
$$\sigma_2(a,b) = (\underline{a} \Rightarrow \underline{b}) \Rightarrow \underline{a \rightarrow b}.$$

(2) If $\alpha,\beta,\gamma \in \mathcal{P}_W(V)$, we put

$$\sigma_3(\alpha,\beta,\gamma) = \alpha \Rightarrow \underline{1}$$
$$\sigma_4(\alpha,\beta,\gamma) = \alpha \Rightarrow \alpha$$
$$\sigma_5(\alpha,\beta,\gamma) = (\beta \Rightarrow \gamma) \Rightarrow ((\alpha \Rightarrow \beta) \Rightarrow (\alpha \Rightarrow \gamma))$$
$$\sigma_6(\alpha,\beta,\gamma) = (\alpha \Rightarrow (\beta \Rightarrow \gamma)) \Rightarrow (\beta \Rightarrow (\alpha \Rightarrow \gamma))$$
$$\sigma_7(\alpha,\beta,\gamma) = (\alpha \wedge \beta) \Rightarrow \alpha$$
$$\sigma_8(\alpha,\beta,\gamma) = (\alpha \wedge \beta) \Rightarrow \beta$$
$$\sigma_9(\alpha,\beta,\gamma) = (\beta \Rightarrow \alpha) \Rightarrow ((\gamma \Rightarrow \beta) \Rightarrow (\gamma \Rightarrow (\alpha \wedge \beta)))$$
$$\sigma_{10}(\alpha,\beta,\gamma) = \alpha \Rightarrow (\alpha \nabla \beta)$$
$$\sigma_{11}(\alpha,\beta,\gamma) = \beta \Rightarrow (\alpha \nabla \beta)$$
$$\sigma_{12}(\alpha,\beta,\gamma) = (\alpha \Rightarrow \gamma) \Rightarrow ((\beta \Rightarrow \gamma) \Rightarrow ((\alpha \nabla \beta) \Rightarrow \gamma))$$
$$\sigma_{13}(\alpha,\beta,\gamma) = \alpha \Rightarrow (\beta \Rightarrow (\alpha \Delta \beta))$$
$$\sigma_{14}(\alpha,\beta,\gamma) = (\alpha \Rightarrow (\beta \Rightarrow \gamma)) \Rightarrow ((\alpha \Delta \beta) \Rightarrow \gamma)$$
$$\sigma_{15}(\alpha,\beta,\gamma) = (\alpha \Delta \underline{1}) \Leftrightarrow \alpha.$$

Theorem 1.10 [58]. The semantic consequence has the following properties:

(1) $\emptyset \mid\!\!==_a \underline{a}$, $\emptyset \mid\!\!==_{a \cdot b} \underline{a} \Delta \underline{b}$ and $\emptyset \mid\!\!==_{a \rightarrow b} \underline{a} \Rightarrow \underline{b}$ for all $a,b \in A$.

(2) For all $a,b \in A$, the schemata $\sigma_1(a,b)$ and $\sigma_2(a,b)$ are W-tautologies.

(3) For any $\alpha,\beta,\gamma \in \mathcal{P}_W(V)$, the schemata $\sigma_i(\alpha,\beta,\gamma)$, $i = 3,4,\dots,15$, are W-tautologies provided the underlying fuzzy algebra is an L-fuzzy algebra.

Proof. (1) is trivial by definition. For instance, $\emptyset \mid\!==_{a\cdot b} \underline{a} \mathbin{\Delta} \underline{b}$ if and only if $\bigcap \{f(\underline{a} \mathbin{\Delta} \underline{b}) \mid f \in \mathrm{Sem}_{(W,C)}(V,A)\} \geq a\cdot b$. Because of $f(\underline{a} \mathbin{\Delta} \underline{b}) = a\cdot b$, the required inequality holds.

(2) In order to show that $\sigma_2(a,b)$ is a W-tautology, we have only to prove

$$f(\underline{a} \Rightarrow \underline{b}) \leq f(\underline{a \to b}) \qquad \text{for all } a,b \in A.$$

Since $f(\underline{a} \Rightarrow \underline{b}) = f(\underline{a}) \to f(\underline{b}) = a \to b$ and $f(\underline{a \to b}) = a \to b$, the inequality above is valid.

(3) To prove Statement (3) we have to verify that

$$f(\sigma_i(\alpha,\beta,\gamma)) = 1 \qquad \text{for all } f \in \mathrm{Sem}_{(W,C)}(V,A)$$

and arbitrary W-propositions α,β,γ of $\mathcal{P}_W(V)$ holds. For this purpose, the properties of L-fuzzy algebras listed in Theorems 1.1, 1.2 and 1.7 are used. Let us, for example, show that $\sigma_{14}(\alpha,\beta,\gamma)$ is a W-tautology. It is sufficient to prove

$$f(\alpha \Rightarrow (\beta \Rightarrow \gamma)) \leq f((\alpha \mathbin{\Delta} \beta) \Rightarrow \gamma),$$

that is

$$f(\alpha) \to (f(\beta) \to f(\gamma)) \leq f(\alpha)\cdot f(\beta) \to f(\gamma)$$

for each $f \in \mathrm{Sem}_{(W,C)}(V,A)$ and each $\alpha,\beta,\gamma \in \mathcal{P}_W(V)$. Setting $f(\alpha) = a$, $f(\beta) = b$ and $f(\gamma) = c$, we obtain

$$a \to (b \to c) \leq a\cdot b \to c,$$

which holds true by Theorem 1.7 (3).

Remark. In [58] further W-tautologies are derived for special L-fuzzy algebras such as chains, finite chains with Lukasiewicz's operations or the unit interval of real numbers with the same operations. For instance, if the L-fuzzy algebra $(L,\cap,+,\cdot,\to)$ is a chain with respect to ordering, then

$$\lambda_o(\alpha,\beta) = (\alpha \Rightarrow \beta) \wedge (\alpha \Rightarrow \beta)$$

$$\lambda_n(\alpha,\beta) = (\alpha \mathbin{\nabla} \beta)^n \Rightarrow (\alpha^n \mathbin{\nabla} \beta^n),\ n \geq 1$$

are W-tautologies for all $\alpha,\beta \in \mathcal{P}_W(V)$.

Concerning the questions of soundness and adequacy, we have to generalize, besides the concept of semantic consequence, that of syntactic consequence. By a syntax on $\mathcal{P}_W(V)$, we mean a couple (Ax,Inf) consisting of a fuzzy set Ax of logical axioms and a set Inf of fuzzy inference rules. Ax is a mapping from $\mathcal{P}_W(V)$ into the underlying fuzzy algebra.

Let $(L,\cap,+,\cdot,\rightarrow)$ be an L-fuzzy algebra. Observe that, in particular, L is a complete lattice with respect to intersection and addition. An n-ary fuzzy inference rule on $\mathcal{P}_W(V)$ $(n \geq 1)$ is a couple $\rho = (\rho',\rho'')$, where

(1) ρ' is a partial n-ary operation on $\mathcal{P}_W(V)$ with the domain $\mathrm{dom}(\rho) \subseteq \mathcal{P}_W(V)^n$

(2) ρ'' is an n-ary operation on L satisfying the semicontinuity condition, i.e., if $I \neq \emptyset$, $k = 1,2,\ldots,n$, $a_1,\ldots,a_{k-1},a_{k+1},\ldots,a_n \in L$ and $a_{k_i} \in L$ for all $i \in I$, then

$$\rho\,(a_1,\ldots,a_{k-1},\sum_{i\in I} a_{k_i},a_{k+1},\ldots,a_n) =$$

$$\sum_{i\in I} \rho\,(a_1,\ldots,a_{k-1},a_{k_i},a_{k+1},\ldots,a_n).$$

In other words, in each variable the operation ρ'' preserves all non-empty sums (joins) in L.

Examples. 1) Consider $\rho_1 = (\rho_1',\rho_1'')$ with $\mathrm{dom}(\rho_1') = \{(\alpha,\alpha \Rightarrow \beta)\,|\,\alpha,\beta \in \mathcal{P}_W(V)\}$ and

$$\rho_1'(\alpha,\alpha \Rightarrow \beta) = \alpha, \qquad \rho_1''(a,b) = a\cdot b$$

for all $\alpha,\beta \in \mathcal{P}_W(V)$ and $a,b \in L$. ρ_1 is a binary fuzzy rule of inference. In analogy to current notation, ρ_1 may also be expressed in the form

$$\frac{\alpha,\alpha \Rightarrow \beta}{\beta} \quad \left[\frac{a,b}{a\cdot b}\right].$$

2) Let a be an arbitrary element of L. Then $\rho_{2,a} = (\rho_{2,a}',\rho_{2,a}'')$ with $\mathrm{dom}(\rho_{2,a}') = \mathcal{P}_W(V)$ and

$$\rho_{2,a}'(\alpha) = \underline{a} \Rightarrow \alpha, \qquad \rho_{2,a}''(b) = a \rightarrow b$$

for all $\alpha \in \mathcal{P}_W(V)$ and $b \in L$, is a unary fuzzy rule of inference denoted by

$$\frac{\alpha}{\underline{a} \Rightarrow \alpha} \quad \left[\frac{b}{a \rightarrow b}\right].$$

A mapping $X\colon \mathcal{P}_W(V) \to L$ is said to be closed with respect to an n-ary fuzzy inference rule $\rho = (\rho', \rho'')$ if the inequality

$$X(\rho'(\alpha_1, \alpha_2, \dots, \alpha_n)) \geq \rho''(X(\alpha_1), X(\alpha_2), \dots, X(\alpha_n))$$

holds whenever $(\alpha_1, \alpha_2, \dots, \alpha_n) \in \mathrm{dom}(\rho')$. We shall say that X is closed with respect to a set Inf of fuzzy inference rules provided X is closed with respect to all elements of Inf.

Theorem 1.11 [58]. Let (Ax,Inf) be a syntax. For any $X\colon \mathcal{P}_W(V) \to L$ there exists the smallest mapping $\mathrm{Ded}(X)\colon \mathcal{P}_W(V) \to L$ such that

(1) $Ax \leq \mathrm{Ded}(X)$ and $X \leq \mathrm{Ded}(X)$

(2) Ded(X) is closed with respect to Inf.

Remark. The set of all mappings from $\mathcal{P}_W(V)$ into L is ordered in a canonical way.

For a given syntax (Ax,Inf) on $\mathcal{P}_W(V)$ and a given $X\colon \mathcal{P}_W(V) \to L$, we define for any W-proposition α:

$$X \mid\!\!-\!\!- \alpha = \mathrm{Ded}(X)(\alpha).$$

We call α a syntactic consequence of X with degree $X \mid\!\!-\!\!- \alpha$. As before, the inequality $(X \mid\!\!-\!\!- \alpha) \geq a$ will be expressed by

$$X \mid\!\!-\!\!-_a \alpha.$$

α is said to be a theorem if $\emptyset \mid\!\!-\!\!-_1 \alpha$ holds.

By definition, it follows that, for any n-ary fuzzy inference rule $\rho = (\rho', \rho'')$ of Inf and any $X\colon \mathcal{P}_W(V) \to L$, the assumptions $(\alpha_1, \alpha_2, \dots, \alpha_n)$ of $\mathrm{dom}(\rho')$, $X \mid\!\!-\!\!-_{a_i} \alpha_i$, $i = 1, 2, \dots, n$, imply $X \mid\!\!-\!\!-_{\rho''(a_1, \dots, a_n)} \rho'(\alpha_1, \dots, \alpha_n)$.

Remark. In [58] the deductive system Ded(X) is also described by the concept of a proof.

As usual, the algebra $\mathcal{P}_W(V)$ of the W-propositions with the semantic system $\mathrm{Sem}_{(W,C)}(V,L)$ relative to an L-fuzzy algebra L is said to be axiomatizable if there exists a syntax (Ax,Inf) such that this fuzzy logic is sound, i.e. $X \mid\!\!-\!\!-_a \alpha$ implies $X \mid\!\!=\!\!=_a \alpha$, and adequate, i.e. $X \mid\!\!=\!\!=_a \alpha$ implies $X \mid\!\!-\!\!-_a \alpha$ for all $X\colon \mathcal{P}_W(V) \to L$, $a \in L$ and $\alpha \in \mathcal{P}_W(V)$. J. Pavelka [58] has shown the fuzzy logic is **axiomatizable** if the L-fuzzy algebra is a finite chain with respect to ordering. But the case of L-fuzzy algebras carried by the unit interval of the real numbers is more interesting. Among all the $2^{\aleph_0}$ isomorphism types of L-fuzzy algebras only the

Łukasiewicz L-fuzzy algebra $Ł = ([0,1],\min,\max,\cdot,\to)$, whereby $a\cdot b = \max\{0,a+b-1\}$ and $a \to b = \min\{1,1-a+b\}$ is axiomatizable.

Theorem 1.12 [58]. Let Ł be the Łukasiewicz L-fuzzy algebra. If the fuzzy set Ax: $\mathcal{P}_W(V) \to L$ of logical axioms and the set Inf of fuzzy inference rules are defined as follows, then the syntax (Ax,Inf) provides an axiomatization:

$$(1)\quad Ax(\alpha) = \begin{cases} a & \text{if } \alpha = \underline{a} \\ a\cdot b & \text{if } \alpha = \underline{a} \,\Delta\, \underline{b} \\ a \to b & \text{if } \alpha = \underline{a} \Rightarrow \underline{b} \\ 1 & \text{if } \alpha \in Ax_1 \\ 0 & \text{otherwise} \end{cases}$$

for all $a,b \in L$ and

$$(2)\quad Inf = \{\rho_1\} \cup \{\rho_{2,a} \mid a \in L\}.$$

Thereby, Ax_1 is the following subset of W-propositions

$$Ax_1 = \Sigma \cup \Lambda \cup I \cup J$$

with

$$\Sigma = \{\sigma_i(a,b) \mid i = 1,2 \text{ and } a,b \in L\}$$
$$\{\sigma_i(\alpha,\beta,\gamma) \mid i = 3,4,\ldots,15 \text{ and } \alpha,\beta,\gamma \in \mathcal{P}_W(V)\}$$

$$\Lambda = \{\lambda_n(\alpha,\beta) \mid n \geq 0 \text{ and } \alpha,\beta \in \mathcal{P}_W(V)\}$$

$$I = \{i(\alpha,a,b,a',b',n) \mid \alpha \in \mathcal{P}_W(V) \text{ and } 0 \leq a' < a \leq 1,\ 0 \leq b < b' < 1,\ n > 0,\ n\cdot a + b \leq n\cdot a' + b'\}$$

$$J = \{j(\alpha,a,b,a',b',n) \mid \alpha \in \mathcal{P}_W(V) \text{ and } 0 \leq a < a' \leq 1,\ 0 \leq b < b' < 1,\ n > 0,\ n\cdot a - b \geq n\cdot a' - b'\},$$

where $i(\alpha,a,b,a',b',n) = ((\underline{a} \Rightarrow \alpha)^n \Rightarrow \underline{b}) \Rightarrow ((\underline{a}' \Rightarrow \alpha) \Rightarrow \underline{b}')$ and $j(\alpha,a,b,a',b',n) = ((\alpha \Rightarrow \underline{a})^n \Rightarrow \underline{b}) \Rightarrow ((\alpha \Rightarrow \underline{a}')^n \Rightarrow \underline{b}')$.

Sketch of proof. (1) Soundness. We have to show

(i) $Ax(\alpha) \leq (\emptyset \models\!= \alpha)$ for all $\alpha \in \mathcal{P}_W(V)$

(ii) every $\rho \in$ Inf is sound, that is, any fuzzy interpretation f of $Sem_{(W,C)}(V,L)$ is closed with respect to ρ.

Since $\emptyset \models\!=_a \underline{a}$, $\emptyset \models\!=_{a\cdot b} \underline{a} \,\Delta\, \underline{b}$ and $\emptyset \models\!=_{a\to b} \underline{a} \Rightarrow \underline{b}$ by Theorem 1.10 (1), it follows $Ax(\alpha) \leq (\emptyset \models\!= \alpha)$ for $\alpha = \underline{a}$, $\alpha = \underline{a} \,\Delta\, \underline{b}$ and $\alpha = \underline{a} \Rightarrow \underline{b}$ for all a,b $\in$ L. By Theorem 1.10 (2), all W-propositions of Σ and Λ are W-tautologies (cf. remark to Theorem 1.10). Therefore, it remains to verify that I and J only contain W-tautologies. But this can be done by a simple computation (cf. [58]). Thus condition (i) is fulfilled.

Condition (ii) is proved if the following two inequalities can be derived:

$$f(\rho_1'(\alpha, \alpha \Rightarrow \beta)) \geq \rho_1''(f(\alpha), f(\alpha \Rightarrow \beta))$$

$$f(\rho_{2,a}'(\alpha)) \geq \rho_{2,a}''(f(\alpha)) \qquad \text{for all } a \in L$$

for any fuzzy interpretation f of $Sem_{(W,C)}(V,L)$ and $\alpha, \beta \in \mathcal{P}_W(V)$. Let us consider fuzzy detachment rule ρ_1. Applying property (2) of Theorem 1.7, we get

$$f(\rho_1'(\alpha, \alpha \Rightarrow \beta)) = f(\beta) \geq f(\alpha) \cdot (f(\alpha) \Rightarrow f(\beta)).$$

Since $f(\alpha) \Rightarrow f(\beta) = f(\alpha \Rightarrow \beta)$, it follows

$$f(\rho_1'(\alpha, \alpha \Rightarrow \beta)) \geq f(\alpha) \cdot f(\alpha \Rightarrow \beta) = \rho_1''(f(\alpha), f(\alpha \Rightarrow \beta)).$$

Thus ρ_1 is sound. For the fuzzy lifting rules $\rho_{2,a}$, a $\in$ L, the required inequality holds because of

$$f(\rho_{2,a}'(\alpha)) = f(\underline{a} \Rightarrow \alpha) = a \rightarrow f(\alpha) = \rho_{2,a}''(f(\alpha))$$

for all a $\in$ L.

(2) The adequacy is proved by means of the technique based on Lindenbaum-Tarski algebra and ultrafilter trick.

1.2.2. Fuzzy predicate calculi

The classical predicate calculus (of first order) will be generalized to such an extend that the definition of fuzzy models (of first order theories) becomes possible. Let P be a set of predicate symbols divided in disjoint classes P_n, $n \geq 1$, where P_n contains the predicate symbols of order n.

The free (W,Q,C)-algebra on the set P<V> of atomic formulas will be denoted by $F_{(W,Q,C)}P\langle V\rangle$. Atomic formulas are obtained by filling the empty spaces of a predicate symbol with individual variables of V, i.e.

$$P\langle V\rangle = \{\pi(x_1, x_2, \ldots, x_n) \mid \pi \in P_n,\ x_1, x_2, \ldots, x_n \in V,\ n \geq 1\}.$$

For our purpose, $F_{(W,Q,C)}P\langle V\rangle$ must be factorized by a certain (W,Q,C)-congruence $\sim$ in order to express the fact that variables in quantifiers are dummy. The desired (W,Q,C)-congruence will be defined by means of the depth $|t|_Q$ of quantification of a (W,Q,C)-term t:

(1) $|t|_Q = 0$ for $t \in W$ or $t \in P\langle V\rangle$

(2) $|ct_1t_2|_Q = \max\{|t_1|_Q, |t_2|_Q\}$ for $c \in C$, $t_1, t_2 \in F_{(W,Q,C)}P\langle V\rangle$

(3) $|(qx)t|_Q = 1 + |t|_Q$ for $q \in Q$, $x \in V$, $t \in F_{(W,Q,C)}P\langle V\rangle$.

Let T_n denote the subset of all (W,Q,C)-terms whose depth of quantification equals n. Two (W,Q,C)-terms t and t' are said to be congruent, in symbols $t \sim t'$, if one of the following conditions are fulfilled (cf. [7]):

(1) $t, t' \in T_o$ and $t = t'$

(2) $t, t' \in T_n$, $n \geq 1$, and there exist (W,Q,C)-terms t_1, t_2, t_1' and t_2' satisfying either (2a) or (2b):

(2a) $t = ct_1t_2$, $t' = ct_1't_2'$ with $t_1 \sim t_1'$ and $t_2 \sim t_2'$ for some $c \in C$

(2b) $t = (qx)t_1$, $t' = (qx')t_1'$ with ($x = x'$ and $t_1 \sim t_1'$) or (there is a (W,Q,C)-term $\bar{t} = \bar{t}(x)$ such that $t_1 \sim \bar{t}$ and $t_1' \sim \bar{t}[x/x']$) for some $q \in Q$, $x, x' \in V$.

The notation $t = t(x)$ is to point out that x is a variable in t. By $t[x/x']$ we mean substitution of x by x' in t supposed x' is not yet a variable in t.

<u>Definition 1.9.</u> The factor algebra $\mathfrak{F}_W(V,P) = F_{(W,Q,C)}P\langle V\rangle/\sim$ is said to be the algebra of the fuzzy predicate calculus (of first order) on the set V of individual variables and the set P of predicate symbols. The elements of $\mathfrak{F}_W(V,P)$ are called W-formulas.

Let α be a W-formula. Then $\mathrm{var}(\alpha)$ denotes the set of free variables of α, where $\mathrm{var}(\alpha) = \mathrm{var}(t)$ for a representative t of the congruence class α and $\mathrm{var}(t)$ is defined as follows

(1) $\mathrm{var}(w) = \emptyset$ for $w \in W$

(2) $\mathrm{var}(\pi(x_1, x_2, \ldots, x_n)) = \{x_1, x_2, \ldots, x_n\}$ for $\pi \in P_n$, $n \geq 1$, $x_1, x_2, \ldots, x_n \in V$

(3) $\mathrm{var}(ct_1t_2) = \mathrm{var}(t_1) \cup \mathrm{var}(t_2)$ for $c \in C$ and $t_1, t_2 \in F_{(W,Q,C)}P\langle V\rangle$

(4) $\mathrm{var}((qx)t) = \mathrm{var}(t) \setminus \{x\}$ for $q \in Q$, $x \in V$ $t \in F_{(W,Q,C)}P\langle V\rangle$.

Since $t \sim t'$ implies $var(t) = var(t')$, the set of free variables in α is well defined. For a subset F of W-formulas, we put

$$var(F) = \bigcup_{\alpha \in F} var(\alpha).$$

It can easily be seen that for any W-formula α, there is a representative $\tilde{\alpha}$ of α such that no variable $x \in V$ appears in $\tilde{\alpha}$ more than once in a quantifier (qx) with $q \in Q$ and no $x \in var(\alpha)$ appears at all in a quantifier (i.e., $\tilde{\alpha}$ has no repeated dummy variables, and no free variables also appear as dummies). We assume henceforth that any $\alpha \in \mathcal{F}_W(V,P)$ is represented by an $\tilde{\alpha} \in F_{(W,Q,C)}P\langle V\rangle$ having the form described above. We shall also usually abuse notation and not distinguish between α and $\tilde{\alpha}$.

Next, W-formulas have to be interpreted. We think of the elements of V as names of objects, and the predicate symbols as A-valued relations among those objects, where $(A,\sqcap,+,\cdot,\rightarrow)$ is a fuzzy algebra. Let M be a set (of objects). Then an n-ary A-valued relation on M is a mapping from M^n into A. We call an algebraic structure

$$\mathfrak{M} = (M,\{\pi_{\mathfrak{M}} \mid \pi \in P\})$$

with $\pi_{\mathfrak{M}}: M^n \rightarrow A$ if $\pi \in P_n$, $n \geq 1$, a fuzzy model (of the theory with an empty system of axioms).

<u>Definition 1.10</u>. Let $(A,\sqcap,+,\cdot,\rightarrow)$ be a fuzzy algebra. The pair $(\mathfrak{M},v)$ is said to be a fuzzy interpretation of $\mathcal{F}_W(V,P)$ in M if $\mathfrak{M}$ is a fuzzy model and v is a mapping from $\mathcal{F}_W(V,P) \times M^V$ into A such that for all mappings $f: V \rightarrow M$ the following conditions are satisfied:

(1) $v(\pi(x_1,x_2,\ldots,x_n),f) = \pi_{\mathfrak{M}}(f(x_1),f(x_2),\ldots,f(x_n))$ for $\pi \in P_n$, $x_1,\ldots,x_n \in V$

(2) $v(-,f)$ is a (W,C)-homomorphism

(3) Assume that $(qx)\alpha$ has the depth $n + 1$, where $q \in Q$, $x \in V$ and $\alpha \in \mathcal{F}_W(V,P)$. Let $f: V \rightarrow M$ be an arbitrary mapping. For $m \in M$, we define a mapping f_m as follows: $f_m(x) = m$ and $f_m(x') = f(m)$ for $x' \in V \setminus \{x\}$. Suppose $(\mathfrak{M},v)$ is already a fuzzy interpretation for all W-formulas with a depth less than n, then put

$$\text{(3a)}\quad v((\wedge x)\alpha) = \begin{cases} \bigcap_{m \in M} v(\alpha,f_m) & \text{if it exists} \\ \text{undefined} & \text{otherwise} \end{cases}$$

$$(3b)\quad v((\exists x)\alpha) = \begin{cases} \sum_{m\in M} v(\alpha,f_m) & \text{if it exists} \\ \text{undefined} & \text{otherwise} \end{cases}$$

$$(3c)\quad v((\forall x)\alpha) = \begin{cases} \prod_{m\in M} v(\alpha,f_m) & \text{if it exists} \\ \text{undefined} & \text{otherwise.} \end{cases}$$

For a given fuzzy model $\mathfrak{M}$, a fuzzy interpretation $(\mathfrak{M},v)$ is uniquely determined by the mapping $f\colon V \to M$. Therefore, we can define

$$(X \mid\!\!== \alpha)_{\mathfrak{M}} = \bigcap\{v(\alpha,f) \mid f\colon V \to M \text{ and } v(\beta,f) \geq X(\beta) \text{ for all } \beta \in \mathcal{F}_W(V,P)\}.$$

We shall say that $X\colon \mathcal{F}_W(V,P) \to A$ semantically implies $\alpha \in \mathcal{F}_W(V,P)$ with degree $(X \mid\!\!== \alpha)_{\mathfrak{M}}$. A W-formula α is called valid in $\mathfrak{M}$ if $(\emptyset \mid\!\!== \alpha)_{\mathfrak{M}} = 1$. Let $\alpha \in \mathcal{F}_W(V,P)$ with $\mathrm{var}(\alpha) = \{x_1,x_2,\dots,x_n\}$. Then there exists a mapping $\|\alpha\|$ from M^n into the underlying fuzzy algebra A defined as follows

$$\|\alpha\|(m_1,m_2,\dots,m_n) = v(\alpha,f),$$

where $f\colon V \to M$ is an arbitrary mapping satisfying $f(x_i) = m_i$ for $i = 1, 2,\dots,n$. For sake of convenience, we shall write $\|\alpha(m_1,m_2,\dots,m_n)\|$ instead of $\|\alpha\|(m_1,m_2,\dots,m_n)$. It can easily be seen that

$$(\emptyset \mid\!\!== \alpha)_{\mathfrak{M}} = \bigcap_{m_1,m_2,\dots,m_n\in M} \|\alpha(m_1,m_2,\dots,m_n)\|$$

holds for any $\alpha \in \mathcal{F}_W(V,P)$ with $\mathrm{var}(\alpha) = \{x_1,x_2,\dots,x_n\}$.

Definition 1.11. A (first order) theory is a triple $\mathfrak{T} \doteq (P,Ax,K)$ consisting of a set P of predicate symbols, a subset $Ax \subseteq \mathcal{F}_W(V,P)$ of (mathematical) axioms and a set K of (individual) constants, where $K \subseteq V$ for some V such that $V \setminus K$ is infinite. The constants are free variables of Ax, i.e. $K = \mathrm{var}(Ax)$. While the language of $\mathfrak{T}$ is the subset $\mathcal{L}(\mathfrak{T}) = \{\alpha \in \mathcal{F}_W(V,P) \mid \mathrm{var}(\alpha) \subseteq K\}$ of $\mathcal{F}_W(V,P)$.

Definition 1.12. Let $\mathfrak{T} = (P,Ax,K)$ be a theory. We call $\mathfrak{M} = (M,\{\pi_{\mathfrak{M}} \mid \pi \in P\})$ a fuzzy model of $\mathfrak{T}$ if there exists a fuzzy interpretation such that each axiom α of Ax is valid in $\mathfrak{M}$. Any W-formula of $\mathcal{L}(\mathfrak{T})$ valid in $\mathfrak{M}$ is said to be a theorem of $\mathfrak{T}$.

Example. Consider the theory of non-deterministic automata $\mathfrak{T}_{Aut} = (P,\emptyset,\emptyset)$ where $P_1 = \{\sigma_o,\sigma_f\}$, $P_2 = \{\delta_x \mid x \in X\}$ with a finite set X of inputs and $P_n = \emptyset$ for $n \geq 3$. A fuzzy model of $\mathfrak{T}_{Aut}$ is a system $\mathcal{A} = (S,S_o,S_f,\{d(x) \mid x \in X\})$. Such systems called fuzzy automata will be studied in Section 2.2.

1.3. Fuzzy sets

The aim of this section is to define fuzzy models of a so-called ε-theory whose predicate symbols only are ε (membership) and ρ (equality). Constructing different fuzzy models over certain fuzzy algebras, we shall develop, in Section 1.3.1, an R-fuzzy set theory capable of investigating automata, grammars and languages as well as an L-fuzzy set theory, in Section 1.3.2, which could be thought of as a fuzzy model of classical set theory like Gödel-Bernays theory for instance.

Convention. Let x and y be individual variables. As usual, instead of $\varepsilon(x,y)$ and $\rho(x,y)$ we will write $x \in y$ and $x = y$, respectively. W-formulas are expressed in common form, that means logical connectives are put between the parts of a W-formula. For instance, the following W-formula $(\bigwedge x)(\bigwedge y)(\Rightarrow \rho(x,y)\rho(y,x))$ is expressed by $(\bigwedge x)(\bigwedge y)((x = y) \Rightarrow (y = x))$. Moreover, W-formulas can be simplified by appropriate rules of omitting parentheses. The W-formulas $\neg (x \in y)$ and $\neg (x = y)$ will be abbreviated by $x \notin y$ and $x \neq y$, respectively.

Definition 1.13. A theory $\mathcal{I} = (\{\varepsilon,\rho\},Ax,\emptyset)$ is called ε-theory if Ax contains the following axioms:

(α_1) $\bigwedge x(x = x)$

(α_2) $\bigwedge x \bigwedge y(x = y \Rightarrow y = x)$

(α_3) $\bigwedge x \bigwedge y \bigwedge z(x = y \Rightarrow (y = z \Rightarrow x = z)$

(α_4) $\bigwedge x \bigwedge y \bigwedge z(x = y \Rightarrow (x \in z \Rightarrow y \in z)$

(α_5) $\bigwedge x \bigwedge y \bigwedge z(x = y \Leftrightarrow (z \in x \Leftrightarrow z \in y)$

(α_6) $\bigwedge x(x \notin x)$.

Therefore, a fuzzy model of the ε-theory is an algebraic structure $\mathfrak{M} = (M,\{\varepsilon_{\mathfrak{M}},\rho_{\mathfrak{M}}\})$ equipped with two mappings $\varepsilon_{\mathfrak{M}}$ and $\rho_{\mathfrak{M}}$ from $M \times M$ into a fuzzy algebra. The images $\varepsilon_{\mathfrak{M}}(x,y)$ and $\rho_{\mathfrak{M}}(x,y)$ will be denoted by $x \mathrel{\dot{\in}} y$ and $x \mathrel{\dot{=}} y$, respectively. Occasionally, the point may be omitted if no confusion arises.

1.3.1. R-fuzzy sets

Throughout this section, the underlying fuzzy algebra always is an R-fuzzy algebra $(R,\sqcap,+,\cdot,\rightarrow)$. At first, Zadeh's approach will be generalized by constructing an appropriate R-fuzzy model. Let U be a set, then R^U denotes the set of all mappings from U into R.

Theorem 1.13. Let U be a set. The algebraic system $\mathfrak{M}_1 = (U \cup R^U, \{\varepsilon_{\mathfrak{M}}, \rho_{\mathfrak{M}}\})$, where the mappings $\varepsilon_{\mathfrak{M}}$ and $\rho_{\mathfrak{M}}$ are defined as follows, is an R-fuzzy model of the ε-theory:

$$x \mathrel{\dot{\in}} y = \begin{cases} y(x) & \text{if } y \text{ belongs to } R^U \text{ and } x \text{ belongs to } U \\ 0 & \text{otherwise} \end{cases}$$

$$x \mathrel{\dot{=}} y = \begin{cases} 1 & \text{if } x = y \text{ in } U \text{ or } R^U \\ 0 & \text{otherwise.} \end{cases}$$

Proof. Obviously, the axioms α_1, α_2 and α_3 are valid in $\mathfrak{M}_1$.

(α_4) We have to show

$$\|\bigwedge x \bigwedge y \bigwedge z(x = y \Rightarrow (x \in z \Rightarrow y \in z))\| = 1.$$

But this equation holds if and only if

$$\{(x \mathrel{\dot{=}} y \rightarrow (x \mathrel{\dot{\in}} z \rightarrow y \mathrel{\dot{\in}} z)) \mid x,y,z \in U \cup R^U\} = 1.$$

Therefore, it is sufficient to prove that

$$x \mathrel{\dot{=}} y = 1 \quad \text{implies} \quad (x \mathrel{\dot{\in}} z \rightarrow y \mathrel{\dot{\in}} z) = 1$$

for all $x,y,z \in U \cup R^U$. Let $x = y$ (in U or R^U) and assume that z belongs to U, then $x \mathrel{\dot{\in}} z = 0$ and $y \mathrel{\dot{\in}} z = 0$. Thus $(x \mathrel{\dot{\in}} z \rightarrow y \mathrel{\dot{\in}} z) = 1$. In case z belongs to R^U, we derive

$$x \mathrel{\dot{\in}} z = z(x) = z(y) = y \mathrel{\dot{\in}} z$$

yielding $(x \mathrel{\dot{\in}} z \rightarrow y \mathrel{\dot{\in}} z) = 1$. Hence α_4 is valid in $\mathfrak{M}_1$.

(α_5) The validity of α_5 in $\mathfrak{M}_1$ can be verified analogously.

(α_6) Axiom α_6 is valid in $\mathfrak{M}_1$ if and only if

$$\|\bigwedge x(x \notin x)\| = \{(x \mathrel{\dot{\in}} x \rightarrow 0) \mid x \in U \cup R^U\} = 1.$$

Since $x \mathrel{\dot{\in}} x = 0$ for all x of $U \cup R^U$ by definition, α_6 is valid in $\mathfrak{M}_1$.

Definition 1.14. The elements of $\mathfrak{M}_1$ belonging to R^U are said to be R-fuzzy sets (of first type).

One aim of this approach is to describe R-fuzzy sets syntactically. Let α be a W-formula of $\mathcal{F}_W(V,\{\varepsilon,\rho\})$ with one free variable. Then we want to construct an R-fuzzy set A such that $x \mathrel{\underset{\bullet}{\in}} A = \|\alpha(x)\|$ holds.

Theorem 1.14. Let $\alpha = \alpha(x)$ be a W-formula of $\mathcal{F}_W(V,\{\varepsilon,\rho\})$ with one free variable x of V such that $\|\alpha(x)\|$ is well defined for all x of $U \cup R^U$. If $\|\alpha(x)\| = 0$ for x of R^U, then there exists an R-fuzzy set A with the property

$$x \mathrel{\underset{\bullet}{\in}} A = \|\alpha(x)\| \qquad \text{for all x of } U \cup R^U.$$

Proof. Let α be a W-formula fulfilling the stated assumption. Then there exists a mapping $\|\alpha\|: U \to R$. Define an R-fuzzy set A by

$$A(x) = \|\alpha(x)\| \qquad \text{for all x of U.}$$

Obviously, $x \mathrel{\underset{\bullet}{\in}} A = A(x) = \|\alpha(x)\|$ holds for all x of U and $x \mathrel{\underset{\bullet}{\in}} A = 0 = \|\alpha(x)\|$ for all x of R^U. Hence the R-fuzzy set A has the required property.

Convention. Assume that α is a W-formula satisfying the premises of Theorem 1.14. The corresponding R-fuzzy set will be denoted by

$$A = \{x|\alpha(x)\}.$$

Accordingly, the notation $A = \{x \in B|\alpha(x)\}$ will be used if A is defined by $x \in A = (x \in B) \wedge \alpha(x)$.

Definition 1.15. Let A and A' be R-fuzzy sets and let r be an arbitrary element of R. The scalar product rA, the sum A + A', the intersection $A \cap A'$ and the bold intersection $A \mathbin{\pmb{\cap}} A'$ are defined by setting

$$(1) \qquad rA = \{x|x \in A \mathbin{\Delta} r\}$$

$$(2) \qquad A + A' = \{x|x \in A \mathbin{\nabla} x \in A'\}$$

$$(3) \qquad A \cap A' = \{x|x \in A \wedge x \in A'\}$$

$$(4) \qquad A \mathbin{\pmb{\cap}} A' = \{x|x \in A \mathbin{\Delta} x \in A'\}.$$

Definition 1.16. The inclusion $A \mathrel{\underset{\bullet}{\subseteq}} A'$ of two R-fuzzy sets A and A' is defined as follows

$$A \mathrel{\underset{\bullet}{\subseteq}} A' = \|\bigwedge x(x \in A \Rightarrow x \in A')\|.$$

<u>Theorem 1.15</u>. The set of all R-fuzzy sets of $\mathfrak{M}_1$ forms a po-semiring $(R^U,+,\cap)$ with respect to the inclusion $\subseteq$ as partial order.

Proof. By definition, R-fuzzy sets can be considered as mappings from U into R. Therefore, we have

(1) $(A + A')(x) = A(x) + A'(x)$

(2) $(A \cap A')(x) = A(x) \cdot A'(x)$

for all x of U. Moreover, the inclusion $\subseteq$ is a two-valued predicate satisfying

(3) $A \subseteq A' = 1$ if and only if $A(x) \leq A'(x)$ for all x of U.

Since operations and partial order are defined element-wise, R^U is a po-semiring.

The model established so far is too restrictive to be used for generalizing set theoretic operations. Thus our next construction is based on a set theory in the sense of Zermelo-Fraenkle enriched by an additional axiom (cf. [14,31]):

For every set X there exists a universe containing X as an element.

Thereby, a set $\mathfrak{U}$ is called a universe if the following conditions are fulfilled:

(1) Let $(X_i)_{i\in I}$ be a family of sets X_i of $\mathfrak{U}$ for any $i \in I$ with I in $\mathfrak{U}$, so $\bigcup_{i\in I} X_i$ is an element of $\mathfrak{U}$.

(2) For any element x, the set $\{x\}$ belongs to $\mathfrak{U}$.

(3) Let X be a set of $\mathfrak{U}$, then each x of X is an element of $\mathfrak{U}$.

(4) If X is a set of $\mathfrak{U}$, so is the power set of X.

(5) For all elements x and y of $\mathfrak{U}$, the ordered pair (x,y) is in $\mathfrak{U}$.

Let $\mathfrak{U}$ be a universe containing R. Then we set

$$\mathfrak{F} = \{A \mid A \text{ is mapping from } X \text{ into } R \text{ for some set } X \text{ of } \mathfrak{U}\}..$$

Since the set of all mappings from X into R is a set of $\mathfrak{U}$, every mapping $A: X \to R$ belongs to $\mathfrak{F}$. Thus $\mathfrak{F}$ is a subset of $\mathfrak{U}$.

Theorem 1.16. Let $\mathfrak{U}$ be a universe containing R. Then $\mathfrak{M} = (\mathfrak{U},\{\varepsilon_{\mathfrak{M}},\rho_{\mathfrak{M}}\})$ is an R-fuzzy model of the ε-theory provided $\varepsilon_{\mathfrak{M}}$ and $\rho_{\mathfrak{M}}$ are defined as follows

$$x \underset{\cdot}{\in} y = \begin{cases} 1 & \text{if } x \in y \text{ (in } \mathfrak{U}) \\ y(x) & \text{if } y \text{ in } \mathfrak{F} \text{ and } x \text{ belongs to dom}(y) \\ 0 & \text{otherwise} \end{cases}$$

$$x \underset{\cdot}{=} y = \begin{cases} 1 & \text{if } x = y \text{ (in } \mathfrak{U}) \\ 0 & \text{otherwise.} \end{cases}$$

Proof. Since $\underset{\cdot}{=}$ coincides with the classical two-valued equality relation, α_1, α_2 and α_3 are valid in $\mathfrak{M}$.

(α_4) In analogy to the proof of Theorem 1.13, it sufficies to show that

$$x = y \quad \text{implies} \quad x \underset{\cdot}{\in} z \leq y \underset{\cdot}{\in} z$$

for all x,y,z of $\mathfrak{U}$. But, by definition, this condition is fulfilled.

(α_5) and (α_6) are trivial.

Definition 1.17. The elements of $\mathfrak{F}$ are called R-fuzzy sets (of higher types). An R-fuzzy set A is said to be crisp, or a set shortly, if either $x \underset{\cdot}{\in} A = 0$ or $x \underset{\cdot}{\in} A = 1$ for all x of $\mathfrak{U}$.

Let A be an R-fuzzy set. We call

$$|A| = \{x | x \in A \neq 0\}$$

support of A, which is a crisp set.

The comprehension principle is valid in $\mathfrak{M}$ in the following form.

Theorem 1.17. Let α be a W-formula of $\mathfrak{F}_W(V,\{\varepsilon,\rho\})$ with one free variable. Assume that $\|\alpha(x)\|$ is defined in $\mathfrak{M}$ for all x of $\mathfrak{U}$. If an R-fuzzy set X of $\mathfrak{M}$ exists such that $\|\alpha(x)\| \neq 0$ if and only if $x \in |X|$ holds, then there is an R-fuzzy set A in $\mathfrak{M}$ satisfying

$$x \in A = \|\alpha(x)\| \qquad \text{for all } x \text{ of } \mathfrak{U}.$$

Proof. Suppose that $\alpha = \alpha(x)$ is a W-formula of $\mathfrak{F}_W(V,\{\varepsilon,\rho\})$, then there exists a mapping $\|\alpha\|: \mathfrak{U} \to R$ under the assumption stated above. Now, an R-fuzzy set A can be defined as follows

$$A(x) = \|\alpha(x)\| \qquad \text{for all } x \in |X|.$$

In analogy to the proof of Theorem 1.14, it can easily be seen that A possesses the required property.

The following principle of subset building can be derived as a conclusion.

Theorem 1.18. Let B be an R-fuzzy set and let α be a W-formula. Then there exists an R-fuzzy set A such that

$$x \in A \Leftrightarrow (x \in B \wedge \alpha)$$

is valid in $\mathfrak{M}$.

We can define the power set $\mathfrak{P}_R(A)$ of a given R-fuzzy set in $\mathfrak{M}$ so that

$$X \underset{\cdot}{\subseteq} A = 1 \quad \text{implies} \quad X \underset{\cdot}{\in} \mathfrak{P}_R(A) = 1$$

for any R-fuzzy set X. For application in Chapter 2, however, a modified power set is needed. For this purpose, a new inclusion $\underset{\cdot}{\subseteq}'$ is introduced as follows

$$A \underset{\cdot}{\subseteq}' A' = |A| \underset{\cdot}{\subseteq} |A'|$$

for arbitrary R-fuzzy sets A and A'.

Definition 1.18. Let A be an R-fuzzy set. We say

$$\mathfrak{I}_R A = \{A' | A' \underset{\cdot}{\subseteq}' A\}$$

is the set of all R-fuzzy sets with support A. Furthermore, the notation $\mathfrak{I}_R^f A$ is used for the following set

$$\mathfrak{I}_R^f A = \{A' \in \mathfrak{I}_R A | A' \text{ has a finite support } |A'|\}.$$

Definition 1.19. Let A and B be R-fuzzy sets, then

$$A \underset{\cdot}{\times} B = \{x | \exists a \exists b (x = (a,b) \wedge a \in A \wedge b \in B)\}$$

is called the (Cartesian) product of A and B.

Remark. For all R-fuzzy sets A and B, the product $A \underset{\cdot}{\times} B$ is well defined although two existential quantifiers not always interpretable in $\mathfrak{M}$, occure in the definition. But because of the two-valued equality $x = (a,b)$, $A \underset{\cdot}{\times} B$ always exists and is representable as mapping from $|A| \times |B|$ into R as follows

$$(A \underset{\cdot}{\times} B)(a,b) = A(a) \cap B(b)$$

for all pairs (a,b) of $|A| \times |B|$.

As usual, the direct sum of two R-fuzzy sets A and B is defined by $A \oplus B = (A \times \{1\}) + (B \times \{2\})$. Evidently, the direct sum of two (crisp) sets coincides with their disjoint union.

Definition 1.20. Let A and B be R-fuzzy sets. Then

$$\mathrm{Rel}_R(A,B) = \{\rho \mid \rho \subseteq' A \times B\}$$

is the set of all (binary) R-fuzzy relations between A and B. We write

$$\mathrm{Rel}^f_R(A,B) = \{\rho \in \mathrm{Rel}_R(A,B) \mid \rho \text{ has a finite support } |\rho|\}$$

for the set of all R-fuzzy relations with a finite support. Instead of $\mathrm{Rel}_R(A,A)$ and $\mathrm{Rel}^f_R(A,A)$ we will shortly write $\mathrm{Rel}_R A$ and $\mathrm{Rel}^f_R A$, resp.

Definition 1.21. The product $\rho \cdot \sigma$ of two R-fuzzy relations ρ of $\mathrm{Rel}_R(A,B)$ and σ of $\mathrm{Rel}_R(B,C)$ is the following R-fuzzy relation

$$\rho \cdot \sigma = \{x \mid \exists a \exists b \exists c(x = (a,c) \mathbin{\Delta} (a,b) \in \rho \mathbin{\Delta} (b,c) \in \sigma)\},$$

where A, B and C are R-fuzzy sets.

Remark. Let A,B be R-fuzzy sets and let $\rho \in \mathrm{Rel}_R(A,B)$. For any $A' \in \mathfrak{T}^f_R A$ as well as for any $B' \in \mathfrak{T}^f_R B$, we define

$$A' \cdot \rho = \{b \in B \mid \exists a(a \in A' \mathbin{\Delta} (a,b) \in \rho)\}$$

and

$$\rho \cdot B' = \{a \in A \mid \exists b((a,b) \in \rho \mathbin{\Delta} b \in B')\}.$$

Theorem 1.19. Let A, B and C be R-fuzzy set. Assume that B has a finite support. Then the product $\rho \cdot \sigma$ of two R-fuzzy relations $\rho \in \mathrm{Rel}_R(A,B)$ and $\sigma \in \mathrm{Rel}_R(B,C)$ is well defined.

Proof. By definition, $\rho \cdot \sigma$ is a mapping from $|A| \times |C|$ into R given by

$$(\rho \cdot \sigma)(a,c) = \sum_{b \in |B|} \rho(a,b) \cdot \sigma(b,c)$$

for all $(a,c) \in |A| \times |C|$. Since $|B|$ is assumed to be finite, the summation is well defined in any po-semiring. Hence $\rho \cdot \sigma$ is well defined.

Theorem 1.20. For any R-fuzzy set A, the set $\mathrm{Rel}^f_R A$ forms a semiring with respect to addition and multiplication of R-fuzzy relations.

Proof. Let ρ and σ be R-fuzzy relations of $\mathrm{Rel}^f_R A$. We conclude

(1) $(\rho + \sigma)(a,b) = \rho(a,b) + \sigma(a,b)$

(2) $(\rho \cdot \sigma)(a,b) = \sum_{c \in |A|} \rho(a,c) \cdot \sigma(c,b)$

for all a and b of A. Obviously, $\mathrm{Rel}^f_R A$ is a semiring. The empty relation $\emptyset_A$ is zero and the identical relation id_A is unit element.

1.3.2. L-fuzzy sets

The concept of a fuzzy set was intended to reflect what one experiences when dealing with situations in everyday life: considering some properties we often cannot decide whether or not a given object has the property in question and the best we can do is to estimate in some way the degree in which the property is attained. The usual approach to such situations is the propabilistic one, fuzziness was meant as an alternative to it.

L. A. Zadeh [93] has defined operations on fuzzy sets via algebraic operations on the reals in analogy to the way that Boolean operations on $\underline{2}$ induce the Boolean algebra structure of the power set of a given set. Very soon it was realized that the replacement of $\underline{2}$ by $[0,1]$ is not compulsory and that there are more possibilities in choosing the algebra of truth values as shown in Section 1.1. The calculus of R-fuzzy sets developed in Section 1.3.1 presents one of them. But, nevertheless, a crucial point for further investigations is to find out a kind of fuzzy algebra which offers the most fruitful generalization of the calculus of set theory. Supported by the results obtained so far (cf. [26,27,62]), the structure of an L-fuzzy algebra seems to be one of the likly candidates.

The current efforts of a growing number of papers to introduce fuzzy versions of as many mathematical structures as possibly indicates that the authors would like the fuzzy set theory to become a world for mathematical objects to live in, in the same way as the universe of sets. In this context M. A. Arbib and E. G. Manes [2] say 'the time has come to face up to the fact that we live in a 'fuzzy' world - there is no guarantee that we can be sure of the next state of a system in the real world'.

Whenever the expression 'set theory' is used, most mathematicians visualize a self-contained universe governed by a single binary relation of membership, and we suggest that such a universe should become the goal of fuzzy set theory too. The fuzzy model we exhibit in this section is intended as a step towards this goal. It should be emphasized that the motivation for its construction was not just to have any fuzzy model of the ε-theory but to have a natural one, capable of further development. Constructing the underlying class we, therefore, tried to keep the objects representing sets as near to the image of a mapping into the L-fuzzy algebra as possible. That is also why we wanted regularity - at least in the form of axiom α_6.

Let $(L,\cap,+,\cdot,\rightarrow)$ be an L-fuzzy algebra. By transfinite induction L-fuzzy models $\mathfrak{M}_\xi = (M_\xi,\{\varepsilon_{\mathfrak{M}}^{\xi},\rho_{\mathfrak{M}}^{\xi}\})$ are defined for any ordinal number ξ, whereby $x \in_\xi y$ and $x =_\xi y$ shall be written instead of $\varepsilon_{\mathfrak{M}}^{\xi}(x,y)$ and $\rho_{\mathfrak{M}}^{\xi}(x,y)$ henceforward.

(1) $M_0 = \{\emptyset\}$ with $\emptyset \in_0 \emptyset = 0$ and $\emptyset =_0 \emptyset = 1$.

(2) Let α be an ordinal number. Assume that $\mathfrak{M}_\xi = (M_\xi, \{\varepsilon^\xi_{\mathfrak{M}}, \rho^\xi_{\mathfrak{M}}\})$ is already an L-fuzzy model of the ε-theory for all $\xi < \alpha$. Moreover, τ is a mapping from $\bigcup_{\xi<\alpha} M_\xi$ in α defined by

$\tau(x) = \min\{\xi | x \in M_\xi\}$

(2a) If α is a limit number, so put

$M_\alpha = \bigcup_{\xi<\alpha} M_\xi$ with $x \in_\alpha y = x \in_\eta y$ and $x =_\alpha y = x =_\eta y$,

where $\eta = \max\{\tau(x), \tau(y)\}$

(2b) If α is not a limit number, i.e. $\alpha = \beta + 1$, so put

$M_\alpha = M_\beta \cup \langle M_\beta, L\rangle$ with

$$x \in_\alpha y = \begin{cases} x \in_\beta y & \text{if } x \text{ and } y \text{ belong to } M_\beta \\ y(x) & \text{if } x \text{ of } M_\beta \text{ and } y \text{ of } M_\alpha \setminus M_\beta \\ 0 & \text{otherwise} \end{cases}$$

$$x =_\alpha y = \begin{cases} x =_\beta y & \text{if } x \text{ and } y \text{ belong to } M_\beta \\ \bigcap\{(x(z) \leftrightarrow y(z)) | z \in M_\beta\} & \text{if } x \text{ and } y \text{ belong to } M_\alpha \setminus M_\beta \\ 0 & \text{otherwise.} \end{cases}$$

Thereby, $\langle M_\beta, L\rangle$ denotes the set of all mappings z from M_β into L satisfying the following two conditions

(1) For all x and y belonging to M_β,

$x =_\beta y \leq (z(x) \rightarrow z(y))$

(2) For any η with $0 \leq \eta < \beta$, there exists an element x of $M_\beta \setminus M_\eta$ such that $z(x) \neq 0$ holds.

Let F denote the union of all M_α over all ordinal numbers α.

<u>Theorem 1.21</u> [59]. The algebraic structure $\mathfrak{M} = (M, \{\varepsilon_{\mathfrak{M}}, \rho_{\mathfrak{M}}\})$ is an L-fuzzy model of the ε-theory if

(1) $M = F \cup \langle F, L\rangle$

(2) $$x \mathrel{\underset{\bullet}{\in}} y = \begin{cases} x \in_\eta y & \text{if } x \text{ and } y \text{ belong to } F \text{ and } \eta = \max\{\tau(x), \tau(y)\} \\ y(x) & \text{if belongs to } F \text{ and } y \text{ belongs to } M \setminus F \\ 0 & \text{otherwise} \end{cases}$$

$$(3)\quad x \doteq y = \begin{cases} x =_\eta y & \text{if x and y belong to F and } \eta = \max\{\tau(x),\tau(y)\} \\ \bigcap\{(x(z) \leftrightarrow y(z)) \mid z \in F\} & \text{if x and y belong to } M \setminus F \\ 0 & \text{otherwise.} \end{cases}$$

In order to define L-fuzzy sets, the derived predicate σ is introduced by

$$\sigma(X) = \exists Y(X \in Y)$$

which has the following property

$$\sigma_{\mathfrak{M}}(x) \neq 0 \quad \text{if and only if } x \text{ belongs to } F.$$

Assume that $\sigma_{\mathfrak{M}}(x) \neq 0$, then because of

$$\sigma_{\mathfrak{M}}(x) = \sum_{y \in M} x \in y$$

x must belong to F by definition. On the other hand, to each x of F there exists a mapping of $\langle F,L \rangle$ which assigns 1 to x and 0 to any other element of F. This implies $\sigma_{\mathfrak{M}}(x) = 1$. Evidently, $\sigma_{\mathfrak{M}}(x) = 0$ for all x of $M \setminus F$.

Definition 1.22. The elements of M resp. F are called L-fuzzy classes resp. L-fuzzy sets.

In [59] modifications of the L-fuzzy model introduced above are also studied in a detailed way. It has been shown that the axioms of Gödel-Bernays are valid in them. For instance, the W-formula

$$\bigwedge X \bigwedge Y \bigwedge Z(Z \in Y \Longleftrightarrow (\sigma(Z) \wedge \bigwedge U(U \in Z \Rightarrow U \in X)))$$

is valid in $\mathfrak{M}$. Let X,U,Z be interpreted by x,u,z, respectively. Then Y is interpretable by the mapping $\mathfrak{P}_L(X)$ from F into L defined as follows

$$\mathfrak{P}_L(X)(z) = \bigcap_{u \in M} (u \mathrel{\dot\in} z \rightarrow u \mathrel{\dot\in} x)$$

for all z of F. Thus the power set axiom is valid in $\mathfrak{M}$.

Remark. Special models of this kind for Lukasiewicz's truth value algebra (with a finite as well as an infinite number of elements) are investigated by D. Klaua [40,41], R. Giles [23] and S. Gottwald [30]. But these many-valued set theories are defined semantically without applying generalized model theory.

2. R-FUZZY AUTOMATA AND R-FUZZY GRAMMARS

This chapter deals with a generalization of the notions automaton and context-free grammar within the formalism of R-fuzzy sets. An appropriate calculus of R-fuzzy events will be developed in Section 2.1. Section 2.2 is devoted to solve the problems of analysis and synthesis for R-fuzzy automata. Context-free R-fuzzy grammars and R-fuzzy pushdown acceptors are investigated in Section 2.3. Besides an algebraic characterization of the set of all generated R-fuzzy events, the associated problems of analysis and synthesis are solved. Moreover, some closure properties will be derived.

2.1. R-fuzzy events

Considering usual events as mappings from the free monoid X^* generated by a finite set X into $\underline{2} = \{0,1\}$ permits the following generalization: R-fuzzy events are mappings from X^* into a po-semiring R, i.e. R-fuzzy events are R-fuzzy sets with support X^*. In [85] it has been shown that the substitution of X^* by a more general structure yields a unified calculus for investigating time-variant and controlled automata as well as usual ones.

Assume that T is the transition monoid of a control device generated by X and $\varkappa: X^* \to T$ is the associated homomorphism. Then $X^* \times T$ forms a partial semigroup by setting

$$(w,t)\cdot(w',t') = \begin{cases} (ww',t) & \text{if } t' = t\cdot\varkappa(w) \\ \text{undefined} & \text{otherwise} \end{cases}$$

for all pairs $(w,t),(w',t')$ of $X^* \times T$, where ww' denotes concatenation of w with w' in X^*. The partial semigroup obtained in this way is denoted by $X^*\varkappa T$.

Definition 2.1. Let X be a finite set, let T be a monoid and let $\varkappa: X^* \to T$ be a homomorphism. The partial semigroup $X^*\varkappa T$ is called input-semigroup over X with respect to $\varkappa$ (or, shortly, input-semigroup).

Examples. 1) X^* is an input-semigroup since X^* is isomorphic to $X^*\varkappa\{1\}$, where $\varkappa$ is the trivial homomorphism defined by $\varkappa(w) = 1$ for all $w \in X^*$.

2) Let $\mathbb{N}$ be the additive monoid of natural numbers. Consider the homomorphism λ assigning the length $|w|$ to each w of X^*. The input-semigroup $X^*\lambda\mathbb{N}$ describes the control mechanism of time-variant automata (cf. [84]).

Let H be an input-semigroup. By E_H (or, shortly, E) we mean the set of all left or right identities of H, whereby an element e of H is called left or right identity if e·h or h·e is defined and e·h = h or h·e = h holds, respectively, for each h of H. E is a non-empty set. A subset B of $H \setminus E$ is said to be a basis of H provided each h of $H \setminus E$ can exactly be represented as follows $h = b_1 \cdot b_2 \cdot \ldots b_k$ with $b_1, b_2, \ldots, b_k \in B$. The length of an element h of H, in symbols $|h|$, is the number of elements of B in h when each element is counted as many times as it occures. The length of elements of B equals 1 and that of identities is assumed to be 0. If H has a basis B, then to any mapping d from B in an arbitrary monoid M, there uniquely exists a homomorphism $d^{\#}: H \to M$, that is a mapping satisfying the following conditions:

(1) $d^{\#}(h \cdot h') = d^{\#}(h) \cdot d^{\#}(h')$ provided $h \cdot h'$ is defined in H

(2) $d^{\#}(e) = 1$ for all e of E,

where 1 is the unit of M.

Theorem 2.1. Any input-semigroup has a basis.

Definition 2.2. Let B be a basis of an input-semigroup H. Then R-fuzzy sets with support H are said to be R-fuzzy events (over B or, occasionally, over H). The set of all R-fuzzy events over B is denoted by $\mathfrak{E}_R B$.

Remark. Each element h of an input-semigroup H is to be identified with the corresponding R-fuzzy event $\bar{h}: H \to R$ defined by

$$\bar{h}(h') = \begin{cases} 1 & \text{if } h' = h \\ 0 & \text{otherwise.} \end{cases}$$

Next, we are going to introduce rational R-fuzzy events by means of rational operations in $\mathfrak{E}_R B$. Henceforth, H is always assumed to be an input-semigroup with basis B.

Definition 2.3. For two R-fuzzy events A and A', the product A·A' is defined as follows

$$A \cdot A' = \{h \in H \mid \exists h_1 \exists h_2 (h = h_1 \cdot h_2 \,\Delta\, h_1 \in A \,\Delta\, h_2 \in A')\}.$$

If an R-fuzzy set A is defined syntactically, that is $A = \{x \mid \alpha(x)\}$ in general, then we have to prove that the W-formula α satisfies the assumptions of Theorem 1.17. Otherwise, A does not exist.

Theorem 2.2. The product of R-fuzzy events is well defined.

Proof. Assume that A and A' are R-fuzzy events. Let $\alpha = \alpha(h)$ denote the following W-formula

$$\exists h_1 \exists h_2 (h = h_1 \cdot h_2 \wedge h_1 \in A \wedge h_2 \in A').$$

Then

$$\|\alpha(h)\| = \sum_{h_1 \in H} \sum_{h_2 \in H} \|h = h_1 \cdot h_2\| \cdot \|h_1 \in A\| \cdot \|h_2 \in A'\|$$
$$= \sum_{h_1 \cdot h_2 = h} A(h_1) \cdot A'(h_2).$$

Since each h of H possesses a finite number of factorizations $h = h_1 \cdot h_2$ only, the summation is well defined in R, i.e.

$$\|\alpha(h)\| \in R \qquad \text{for all } h \in H.$$

Consequently, by Theorem 1.17, $A \cdot A' = \{h | \alpha(h)\}$ does exist.

Theorem 2.3. The set $\mathfrak{E}_R B$ forms a po-semiring with respect to the sum and product of R-fuzzy events.

Proof. Evidently, $\mathfrak{E}_R B$ is a commutative monoid with respect to sum. Consider R-fuzzy events as mappings from H into R. The sum A + A' of two R-fuzzy events A and A' is, thus, defined by

$$(A + A')(h) = A(h) + A'(h) \qquad \text{for all } h \in H.$$

Now, the assertion follows from the fact that (R,+) is a commutative monoid.

$\mathfrak{E}_R B$ is a monoid with respect to product. Let A,A',A" be R-fuzzy events. Successively, we get

$$((A \cdot A') \cdot A'')(h) = \sum_{h_1 \cdot h_2 = h} (A \cdot A')(h_1) \cdot A''(h_2)$$
$$= \sum_{h_1 \cdot h_2 = h} \Big(\sum_{h_1' \cdot h_2' = h_1} A(h_1') \cdot A'(h_2') \Big) \cdot A''(h_2)$$
$$= \sum_{h_1' \cdot h_2'' = h} A(h_1') \cdot \Big(\sum_{h_2' \cdot h_2 = h_2''} A'(h_2') \cdot A''(h_2) \Big)$$
$$= (A \cdot (A' \cdot A''))(h)$$

for all h of H. Therefore, the product of R-fuzzy events is associative.

The validity of the distributivity laws can easily be verified. Thus, it only remains to prove the monotony of operations. But this can be done by a straightforward computation.

Remark. Any R-fuzzy event $A \in \mathfrak{E}_R B$ can equivalently be expressed as a formal power series

$$p_A = \sum_{h \in H} (p_A, h) h \qquad \text{with } (p_A, h) = A(h).$$

The set of all formal power series over B with coefficients in R is denoted by R[[B]]. Indeed, R[[B]] is a po-semiring with respect to the usual operations and is isomorphic to $\mathfrak{E}_R B$. Formal power series in several non commuting variables has been introduced and investigated by P. M. Schützenberger [74,75]. M. Fliess [18] has developed this approach and recently exhibited a new non-commutative symbolic calculus [20]. A review of formal power series can be found in [8,69].

In order to define the iteration of R-fuzzy events a metric on $\mathfrak{E}_R B$ will be introduced. For R-fuzzy events A and A', we set

$$\delta(A, A') = \{h \in H \mid A(h) \neq A'(h)\}.$$

Now, a metric is defined by

$$m(A, A') = \begin{cases} 0 & \text{if } A = A' \\ 2^{-\min\{|h| \in \mathbb{N} \mid h \in \delta(A,A')\}} & \text{if } A \neq A'. \end{cases}$$

Remark. This metric is a generalization of that one proposed for usual events by Bodnarčuk [12]. It coincides - up to isomorphism - with the metric for formal power series (cf. [18]).

Theorem 2.4. The set $\mathfrak{E}_R B$ forms a complete metric space.

Proof. (1) By definition, m is a metric on $\mathfrak{E}_R B$.
(2) $\mathfrak{E}_R B$ is a complete space since every Cauchy sequence $(A_n)_{n \in \mathbb{N}}$ converges to a limit A. The construction of A is based on the fact that $(A_n)_{n \in \mathbb{N}}$ is a Cauchy sequence if and only if, for each h of H, there exists a natural number n(h) such that $n \geq n(h)$ implies $A_n(h) = A_{n(h)}(h)$. Now, A is defined by

$$A = \{h \in H \mid h \in A_{n(h)}\}.$$

Let $\varepsilon > 0$ be arbitrary. Then there exists a natural number $n(\varepsilon)$ such that

$$m(A, A_n) < \varepsilon \qquad \text{for all } n \text{ of } \mathbb{N} \text{ with } n > n(\varepsilon),$$

where $n(\varepsilon) = \max\{n(h) \mid h \in H_\varepsilon\}$ with $H_\varepsilon = \{h \in H \mid \varepsilon \leq 2^{-|h|}\}$.

By Banach's fixed point principle, every contractive operator F on $\mathfrak{C}_R B$ has a fixed point $Z_o = F(Z_o)$ satisfying

$$Z_o = \lim_{n\to\infty} \sum_{k=1}^{n} F^k(Z)$$

with $F^k(Z) = F(F^{k-1}(Z))$ for $k > 1$ and $F^1(Z) = F(Z)$, where Z is an arbitrary R-fuzzy event of $\mathfrak{C}_R B$. Especially, Z can be chosen to be the empty R-fuzzy event $\emptyset$ assigning 0 to each h of H. As usually, we shall write

$$Z_o = \sum_{k=1}^{\infty} F^k(Z)$$

for the limit.

Assume that an R-fuzzy event A fulfils the condition $A \cap E = \emptyset$, i.e. $A(h) = 0$ for each identity $h \in E$. Then the operator F_A defined by

$$F_A(Z) = A\cdot Z + E .$$

is contractive. Hence, F_A has a fixed point A^*.

<u>Definition 2.4</u>. Let A be an R-fuzzy event of $\mathfrak{C}_R B$ satisfying $A \cap E = \emptyset$. Then

$$A^* = \sum_{k=0}^{\infty} A^k \qquad \text{with } A^o = E \text{ and } A^k = A^{k-1}\cdot A \text{ for } k > 1$$

is called the iteration of A.

<u>Theorem 2.5</u>. The iteration A^* of an R-fuzzy event A, if it exists, can be represented as follows.

$$A^*(h) = \begin{cases} 1 & \text{if } h \in E \\ \sum_{k=1}^{|h|} \sum_{h_1\cdot h_2\cdot\ldots\cdot h_k = h} A(h_1)\cdot A(h_2)\cdot\ldots\cdot A(h_k) & \text{if } h \in H \setminus E. \end{cases}$$

Proof. Let A be an R-fuzzy event of $\mathfrak{C}_R B$ satisfying $A \cap E = \emptyset$. Denote by $\bar{A}$ the R-fuzzy event defined as follows

$$\bar{A}(h) = 1 \qquad \text{for all } h \in E$$

$$\bar{A}(h) = \sum_{k=1}^{|h|} \sum_{h_1\cdot h_2\cdot\ldots\cdot h_k = h} A(h_1)\cdot A(h_2)\cdot\ldots\cdot A(h_k) \qquad \text{for all } h \in H \setminus E.$$

Since the fixed point of a contractive operator is unique, it is sufficient to show that $\bar{A}$ is the fixed point A^* of F_A, i.e. the equality

$$\bar{A} = A \cdot \bar{A} + E \qquad (*)$$

has to be verified. For $h \in E$, the equation (*) holds obviously. Now, let h be an arbitrary element of $H \setminus E$. Then it remains to prove that $\bar{A}(h) = (A \cdot \bar{A})(h)$ is valid. Successively, we derive

$$\begin{aligned}(A \cdot \bar{A})(h) &= \sum_{h' \cdot h'' = h} A(h') \cdot \bar{A}(h'') \\ &= \sum_{h' \cdot h'' = h} A(h') \cdot \Big(\sum_{k=1}^{|h''|} \sum_{h_1 \cdot h_2 \cdot \ldots \cdot h_k = h''} A(h_1) \cdot A(h_2) \cdot \ldots \cdot A(h_k) \Big) \\ &= \sum_{k=1}^{|h|} \sum_{h' \cdot h'' = h} \sum_{h_1 \cdot h_2 \cdot \ldots \cdot h_k = h''} A(h') \cdot A(h_1) \cdot A(h_2) \cdot \ldots \cdot A(h_k) \\ &= \sum_{k=1}^{|h|} \sum_{h_1 \cdot h_2 \cdot \ldots \cdot h_k = h} A(h_1) \cdot A(h_2) \cdot \ldots \cdot A(h_k) \\ &= \bar{A}(h) \qquad \text{for all } h \in H \setminus E.\end{aligned}$$

Definition 2.5. The subalgebra of $\mathfrak{C}_R B$ generated by $\{\bar{b} \mid b \in B\} \cup \{E\}$ with respect to the rational operations (scalar product, product, sum and iteration) is denoted by $\mathrm{Rat}_R B$. Its elements are called rational R-fuzzy events.

Therefore, an R-fuzzy event is rational if it is either

(1) an elementary R-fuzzy event, that is an element of the basis B (considered as R-fuzzy event) or the set E of identities or

(2) it can be obtained from elementary R-fuzzy events by applying finitely many times the rational operations.

We shall now be concerned with systems of linear equations in the algebra $\mathfrak{C}_R B$:

$$Z_i = \sum_{j=1}^{n} A_{ij} \cdot Z_j + A_i' \qquad \text{for } i = 1,2,\ldots,n,$$

where $Z_i, A_{ij}, A_i' \in \mathfrak{C}_R B$ for $i,j = 1,2,\ldots,n$. It is more convenient to write this system of equations in matrix form:

$$\underline{Z} = \underline{A} \cdot \underline{Z} + \underline{A}'$$

where $\underline{Z} = (Z_i)$ and $\underline{A}' = (A_i')$ are n-dimensional column vectors and $\underline{A} = (A_{ij})$ is an $n \times n$ matrix with coefficients in $\mathfrak{C}_R B$.

It may easily be seen that the product space $(\mathfrak{C}_R B)^n$ is a complete metric space with respect to the following distance

$$m(\underline{A}, \underline{A}') = \max\{m(A_i, A_i') \mid i = 1,2,\ldots,n\}$$

for $\underline{A} = (A_i)$ and $\underline{A}' = (A_i')$ of $(\mathfrak{C}_R B)^n$. Thus, the equation $\underline{Z} = \underline{A}\cdot\underline{Z} + \underline{A}'$ can be solved by successive iteration. Assuming $A_{ij} \cap E = \emptyset$ for all $i,j = 1,2,\ldots,n$, we get as the unique solution

$$\underline{Z}_o = \underline{A}^*\cdot\underline{A}'.$$

An important question is under what assumptions the components of $\underline{Z}_o$ are rational R-fuzzy events. In order to solve the question, some preparations are necessary. $(\mathfrak{C}_R B)_n$ denotes the semiring of all $n \times n$ matrices with coefficients in $\mathfrak{C}_R B$. Let $(\mathrm{Rat}_R B)_n$ be the subsemiring of those matrices whose coefficients are rational R-fuzzy events. Let $(B)_n$ be the subset of all matrices of $(\mathfrak{C}_R B)_n$ consisting of the unit matrix E_n defined by

$$(E_n)_{ij} = \begin{cases} E & \text{if } i = j \\ 0 & \text{if } i \neq j \end{cases}, \quad i,j = 1,2,\ldots,n$$

and all matrices whose coefficients are R-fuzzy events with support B.

<u>Theorem 2.6</u>. For any natural number $n \geq 1$, the following equality holds

$$(\mathrm{Rat}_R B)_n = \mathrm{Rat}_R((B)_n).$$

Proof. (1) By definition, $\mathrm{Rat}_R((B)_n)$ is the smallest subsemiring of $(\mathfrak{C}_R B)_n$ containing $(B)_n$ which is closed with respect to scalar product and iteration. Since $(B)_n$ is included in $(\mathrm{Rat}_R B)_n$, we have

$$\mathrm{Rat}_R((B)_n) \subseteq (\mathrm{Rat}_R B)_n$$

provided $(\mathrm{Rat}_R B)_n$ is also closed with respect to scalar product and iteration. Evidently, the scalar product $r\underline{A}$ of an arbitrary element r of R with a matrix $\underline{A}$ of $(\mathrm{Rat}_R B)_n$ belongs to $(\mathrm{Rat}_R B)_n$, that means $(\mathrm{Rat}_R B)_n$ is closed with respect to scalar product. It only remains to show that the iteration $\underline{A}^*$ of a matrix $\underline{A} = (A_{ij})$ of $(\mathrm{Rat}_R B)_n$ satisfying $A_{ij} \cap E = \emptyset$ for all $i,j = 1,2,\ldots,n$ is an element of $(\mathrm{Rat}_R B)_n$ too. By induction over n this assertion will be proved. For $n = 1$, the assertion is trivial. Assume that the assertion is already proved for all $k < n$. Then $\underline{A}$ is partitioned in submatrices

$$\underline{A} = \begin{vmatrix} \underline{A}_{11} & \underline{A}_{12} \\ \underline{A}_{21} & \underline{A}_{22} \end{vmatrix}$$

such that $\underline{A}_{11}$ and $\underline{A}_{22}$ are square. The iteration $\underline{A}^*$ represented by

$$\underline{A}^* = \begin{vmatrix} \underline{A}^*_{11} & \underline{A}^*_{12} \\ \underline{A}^*_{21} & \underline{A}^*_{22} \end{vmatrix}$$

fulfils the equation $\underline{A}^* = \underline{A}\cdot\underline{A}^* + \underline{E}_n$, where $\underline{E}_n$ is the n × n unit matrix. From this follows (cf. [15]):

$$\underline{A}^*_{11} = \underline{A}_{11}\cdot\underline{A}^*_{11} + \underline{A}_{12}\cdot\underline{A}^*_{21} + E$$
$$\underline{A}^*_{12} = \underline{A}_{11}\cdot\underline{A}^*_{12} + \underline{A}_{12}\cdot\underline{A}^*_{22}$$
$$\underline{A}^*_{21} = \underline{A}_{21}\cdot\underline{A}^*_{11} + \underline{A}_{22}\cdot\underline{A}^*_{21}$$
$$\underline{A}^*_{22} = \underline{A}_{21}\cdot\underline{A}^*_{12} + \underline{A}_{22}\cdot\underline{A}^*_{22} + E.$$

Using Banach's fixed point principle, we conclude

$$\underline{A}^*_{12} = (\underline{A}_{11})^*\cdot\underline{A}_{12}\cdot\underline{A}^*_{22}$$
$$\underline{A}^*_{21} = (\underline{A}_{22})^*\cdot\underline{A}_{21}\cdot\underline{A}^*_{11}.$$

By substituting both solutions in the first system, we obtain the following equations:

$$\underline{A}^*_{11} = (\underline{A}_{11} + \underline{A}_{12}\cdot(\underline{A}_{22})^*\cdot\underline{A}_{21})\cdot\underline{A}^*_{11} + E$$
$$\underline{A}^*_{22} = (\underline{A}_{22} + \underline{A}_{21}\cdot(\underline{A}_{11})^*\cdot\underline{A}_{12})\cdot\underline{A}^*_{22} + E.$$

Therefore, the remaining two solutions are given by

$$\underline{A}^*_{11} = (\underline{A}_{11} + \underline{A}_{12}\cdot(\underline{A}_{22})^*\cdot\underline{A}_{21})^*$$
$$\underline{A}^*_{22} = (\underline{A}_{22} + \underline{A}_{21}\cdot(\underline{A}_{11})^*\cdot\underline{A}_{12})^*.$$

Hence $\underline{A}^*$ belongs to $(\mathrm{Rat}_R B)_n$, because, by assumption, all submatrices $\underline{A}^*_{ij}$, $i,j = 1,2$, have rational coefficients. Consequently, $(\mathrm{Rat}_R B)_n$ contains $\mathrm{Rat}_R((B)_n)$.

(2) Statement: $(\mathrm{Rat}_R B)_n \subseteq \mathrm{Rat}_R((B)_n)$.

Let $\underline{A} = (A_{ij})$ be a matrix of $(\mathrm{Rat}_R B)_n$. Then $\underline{A}$ can be decomposed in a finite sum of n^2 matrices $\underline{A}_{ij}$, $i,j = 1,2,\ldots,n$, such that the only non-zero coefficient in $\underline{A}_{ij}$ is equal to A_{ij} at the place (i,j). Since A_{ij} is a rational R-fuzzy event, $\underline{A}_{ij}$ belongs to $\mathrm{Rat}_R((B)_n)$. Hence $\underline{A}$ is an element of $\mathrm{Rat}_R((B)_n)$, which proves the theorem.

As a conclusion we obtain

<u>Theorem 2.7</u>. If in the system of linear equations

$$\underline{Z} = \underline{A}\cdot\underline{Z} + \underline{A}'$$

the coefficients of $\underline{A}$ and $\underline{A}'$ are rational R-fuzzy events, so are the coefficients of the solution $\underline{Z}_0 = \underline{A}^* \cdot \underline{A}'$ provided it exists.

Proof. Let $\underline{A} = (A_{ij})$ be a matrix of $(Rat_R B)_n$ satisfying $A_{ij} \cap E = \emptyset$ for $i,j = 1,2,\ldots,n$. Then, by Theorem 2.6, $\underline{A}^*$ belongs to $(Rat_R B)_n$. Since the coefficients of $\underline{Z}_0$ are obtained from that of $\underline{A}^*$ and $\underline{A}'$ by means of rational operations, namely sum and product, they are rational R-fuzzy events.

Quotients of R-fuzzy events are a very powerful tool in the calculus of R-fuzzy events. If we proposed

$$A^{-1}A' = \{h \in H \mid \exists h'(h' \in A \,\Delta\, h' \cdot h \in A')\}$$

for R-fuzzy events A and A', then $A^{-1}A'$ would not always be defined. By interpreting the W-formula

$$\exists h'(h' \in A \,\Delta\, h' \cdot h \in A'),$$

$A^{-1}A'$ is represented as follows

$$(A^{-1}A')(h) = \sum_{h' \in H} A(h') \cdot A'(h' \cdot h).$$

Observe that this leads to an infinite summation which is not defined generally. Therefore, certain restrictions have to be formulated.

Let $H = X^* \varkappa T$ be an input-semigroup. With any element $w \in X^*$, an R-fuzzy event $\hat{w}$ is associated by

$$\hat{w}(w',t) = \begin{cases} 1 & \text{if } w' = w \\ 0 & \text{if } w' \neq w \end{cases}, \quad (w',t) \in H.$$

Definition 2.6. Let A be an R-fuzzy event. The quotient $w^{-1}A$ of A with respect to w of X^* is defined by

$$w^{-1}A = \{h \in H \mid \exists h'(h' \in \hat{w} \,\Delta\, h' \cdot h \in A)\}.$$

A monoid T is called locally finite [17] if each element t of T admits only a finite number of factorizations $t = t_1 \cdot t_2$.

Theorem 2.8. Let $H = X^* \varkappa T$ be an input-semigroup with a locally finite monoid T and let A be an R-fuzzy event. Then $w^{-1}A$ is well defined for all w of X^*.

Proof. By definition, we have

$$(w^{-1}A)(w',t') = \begin{cases} \sum\limits_{t\in[t']_w} A(ww',t) & \text{if } [t']_w \neq \emptyset \\ 0 & \text{otherwise} \end{cases}$$

for all $(w',t') \in X^* \times T$, where $[t']_w = \{t \in T | t\cdot\varkappa(w) = t'\}$. Since T is a locally finite monoid, the summation above is finite, i.e.

$$(w^{-1}A)(w',t') \in R \qquad \text{for all } (w',t') \in X^* \times T.$$

Consequently, by Theorem 1.17, the quotient $w^{-1}A$ is well defined.

Especially, for the time-variant case, we have (cf. [83]):

$$(w^{-1}A)(w',t') = \begin{cases} A(ww',t' - |w|) & \text{if } t' \geq |w| \\ 0 & \text{if } t' < |w| \end{cases}$$

for all $(w',t') \in X^* \times \mathbb{N}$.

It can easily be seen that the following properties are satisfied for all A of $\mathfrak{E}_R B$:

(1) $e^{-1}A = A$

(2) $(uv)^{-1}A = v^{-1}(u^{-1}A)$ for all $u,v \in X^*$.

If, further, $H = X^*\varkappa T$ is an input-semigroup with a locally finite monoid T which is left cancellative, i.e. $t_1\cdot t = t_2\cdot t$ implies $t_1 = t_2$ for all $t_1,t_2,t \in T$, then

(3) $(w^{-1}A)(e,t\cdot\varkappa(w)) = A(w,t)$ for all $w \in X^*$, $t \in T$

(4) $A = \sum\limits_{x\in X} x\cdot x^{-1}A + A_E$, where $A_E = A \cap E$.

<u>Theorem 2.9</u>. Let $H = X^*\varkappa T$ be an input-semigroup with a locally finite monoid T. For two R-fuzzy events A and A', the following properties are valid for all $w \in X^*$:

(1) $w^{-1}(rA) = r(w^{-1}A)$ for all $r \in R$

(2) $w^{-1}(A + A') = w^{-1}A + w^{-1}A'$

(3) $w^{-1}(A \cap A') = w^{-1}A \cap w^{-1}A'$

(4) $w^{-1}(A \mathbin{\pmb{\cap}} A') = w^{-1}A \mathbin{\pmb{\cap}} w^{-1}A'$

(5) $w^{-1}(A\cdot A') = (w^{-1}A)\cdot A' + (A^{-1}\hat{w})^{-1}A'$

(6) $w^{-1}A^* = (((A^*)^{-1}\hat{w})^{-1}A)\cdot A^*$ provided $A \cap E = \emptyset$

whereby, in (5) and (6), the definition of $A^{-1}\hat{w}$ as well as $(A^*)^{-1}\hat{w}$ is slightly modified as follows

- $A^{-1}\hat{w} = \{h \in H \setminus E \mid \exists h'(h' \in A \wedge h' \cdot h \in \hat{w})\}$.

Proof. Let A and A' be R-fuzzy events and let $w \in X^*$.

(1) For any $r \in R$, we have

$$w^{-1}(rA) = \{h \in H \mid \exists h'(h' \in \hat{w} \wedge h' \cdot h \in rA)\}$$

Since $h' \cdot h \in rA = (h' \cdot h \in A) \wedge r$, it follows

$$w^{-1}(rA) = \{h \in H \mid \exists h'(h' \in \hat{w} \wedge h' \cdot h \in A) \wedge r\} = r(w^{-1}A).$$

(2) may be proved successively as follows

$$\begin{aligned} w^{-1}(A + A') &= \{h \in H \mid \exists h'(h' \in \hat{w} \wedge h' \cdot h \in (A + A'))\} \\ &= \{h \in H \mid \exists h'(h' \in \hat{w} \wedge (h' \cdot h \in A \vee h' \cdot h \in A'))\} \\ &= \{h \in H \mid \exists h'((h' \in \hat{w} \wedge h' \cdot h \in A) \vee (h' \in \hat{w} \wedge h' \cdot h \in A'))\} \\ &= w^{-1}A + w^{-1}A'. \end{aligned}$$

(3) and (4) are proved in analogy to (2).

(5) In the W-formula defining

$$w^{-1}(A \cdot A') = \{h \in H \mid \exists h'(h' \in \hat{w} \wedge h' \cdot h \in (A \cdot A'))\},$$

the term $h' \cdot h \in (A \cdot A')$ can be replaced by

$$\begin{aligned} &\exists h_1 \exists h_2((h_1 \cdot h_2 = h \wedge h' \cdot h_1 \in A \wedge h_2 \in A') \vee \\ &\qquad (h_1 \cdot h_2 = h' \wedge h_2 \notin E \wedge h_1 \in A \wedge h_2 \cdot h \in A')). \end{aligned}$$

Thus

$$\begin{aligned} w^{-1}(A \cdot A') &= \{h \in H \mid \exists h_1 \exists h_2((h_1 \cdot h_2 = h \wedge h_1 \in w^{-1}A \wedge h_2 \in A') \vee \\ &\qquad (\exists h_2(h_2 \in A^{-1}\hat{w} \wedge h_2 \cdot h \in A'))\} \\ &= (w^{-1}A) \cdot A' + (A^{-1}\hat{w})^{-1}A'. \end{aligned}$$

(6) follows from (5) by successive application of $A^* = A \cdot A^* + E$:

$$\begin{aligned} w^{-1}A^* &= w^{-1}(A \cdot A^* + E) = (w^{-1}A) \cdot A^* + (A^{-1}\hat{w})^{-1}A^* = \ldots \\ &= ((E^{-1}\hat{w})^{-1}A + (A^{-1}\hat{w})^{-1}A + \ldots + ((A^k)^{-1}\hat{w})^{-1}A + \ldots) \cdot A^* \\ &= (((A^*)^{-1}\hat{w})^{-1}A) \cdot A^*. \end{aligned}$$

Definition 2.7. An R-fuzzy event A is said to be finitely closed with respect to quotients if there is a finite number of R-fuzzy events $A_o = A, A_1, \dots, A_k$ satisfying

$$w^{-1}A_i = \sum_{j=0}^{k} r_{ij}(w)\cdot A_j \qquad \text{for all } w \in X^* \text{ and } i = 0,1,\dots,k,$$

where $r_{ij}(w)$ are special R-fuzzy events with the property that $r_{ij}(w)(h) = 0$ for each h of $H \setminus E$

Theorem 2.10. Let $H = X^*\varkappa T$ be an input-semigroup with a locally finite monoid T. Then, any rational R-fuzzy event is finitely closed with respect to quotients.

Proof. (1) For an elementary R-fuzzy event $(x,t) \in B$, where $B = X \times T$, the quotient $w^{-1}(x,t)$ has the following property

$$w^{-1}(x,t) = \begin{cases} (e, t\cdot\varkappa(x)) & \text{if } w = x \\ 0 & \text{if } w \neq x \end{cases}$$

for all $w \in X^*$ and, especially, for E we have

$$w^{-1}E = \begin{cases} E & \text{if } w = e \\ 0 & \text{if } w \neq e \end{cases}$$

for all $w \in X^*$. Evidently, elementary R-fuzzy events are finitely closed with respect to quotients.

(2) It remains to prove that rA with $r \in R$, $A + A'$, $A\cdot A'$ and A^*, if it exists, are finitely closed with respect to quotients supposed A and A' are rational R-fuzzy events having the required property. In this case there are two sequences $A_o = A, A_1, \dots, A_k$ and $A'_o = A', A'_1, \dots, A'_{k'}$, of R-fuzzy events such that, for all $w \in X^*$, the following equations hold:

$$w^{-1}A_i = \sum_{j=0}^{k} r_{ij}(w)\cdot A_j \qquad \text{for } i = 0,1,\dots,k \qquad (*)$$

$$w^{-1}A'_i = \sum_{j=0}^{k'} r'_{ij}(w)\cdot A'_j \qquad \text{for } i = 0,1,\dots,k'. \qquad (**)$$

Consider the sequence $rA_o, A_o, A_1, \dots, A_k$. By Theorem 2.9 (1),

$$w^{-1}(rA_o) = r(w^{-1}A_o) = \sum_{j=0}^{k} r(r_{oj}(w)\cdot A_j) = \sum_{j=0}^{k} \bar{r}_{oj}(w)\cdot A_j .$$

From this, together with (*), it follows that rA is finitely closed with respect to quotients.

In order to show that $A + A'$ satisfies the assertion, the sequence $A_o + A_o', A_o, A_1, \ldots, A_k, A_o', A_1', \ldots, A_{k'}'$ is used. Because of Theorem 2.9 (2)

$$w^{-1}(A_o + A_o') = \sum_{j=0}^{k} r_{oj}(w) \cdot A_j + \sum_{j=0}^{k'} r'_{oj}(w) \cdot A_j'$$

is valid, which proves, together with (*) and (**), that $A + A'$ is finitely closed with respect to quotients.

To prove that $A \cdot A'$ fulfils the assertion, we choose the following sequence $A_o \cdot A', A_1 \cdot A', \ldots, A_k \cdot A', A_o', A_1', \ldots, A'_{k'}$. By means of Theorem 2.9.(5) we have

$$w^{-1}(A_i \cdot A') = \sum_{j=0}^{k} r_{ij}(w) \cdot (A_j \cdot A') + \sum_{j=0}^{k'} \bar{r}_{ij}(w) \cdot A_j' \qquad i = 0,1,\ldots,k,$$

where $\bar{r}_{ij}(w)$ is determined by

$$(A_i^{-1} w)^{-1} A' = \sum_{t \in T} \sum_{\substack{u,v \in X^* \\ uv=w, v \neq e}} A_i(u,t)(v^{-1}A')$$

$$= \sum_{t \in T} \sum_{uv=w, v \neq e} A_i(u,t)(\sum_{j=0}^{k'} r'_{oj}(v) \cdot A_j'$$

$$= \sum_{j=0}^{k'} \bar{r}_{oj}(w) \cdot A_j'.$$

Therefore,

$$\bar{r}_{ij}(w) = \sum_{t \in T} \sum_{uv=w, v \neq e} A_i(u,t) r'_{ij}(v) \qquad \text{for } i,j = 0,1,\ldots,k.$$

In view of (*) and (**), it is evident that $A \cdot A'$ is finitely closed with respect to quotients.

Assume that $A \cap E = \emptyset$ holds. For the sequence $A^*, A_o \cdot A^*, A_1 \cdot A^*, \ldots, A_k \cdot A^*$, one can show

$$w^{-1}A^* = \sum_{j=0}^{k} \bar{r}_{oj}(w) \cdot (A_j \cdot A^*)$$

$$w^{-1}(A_i \cdot A^*) = \sum_{j=0}^{k} \bar{\bar{r}}_{ij}(w) \cdot (A_j \cdot A^*) \qquad \text{for } i = 0,1,\ldots,k$$

for all $w \in X^*$ in analogy to the case considered above, where

$$\bar{r}_{oj}(w) = \sum_{t \in T} \sum_{uv=w, v \neq e} A^*(u,t) r_{oj}(v) \qquad j = 0,1,\ldots,k$$

$$\bar{\bar{r}}_{ij}(w) = r_{ij}(w) + \sum_{t \in T} \sum_{uv=w, v \neq e} A_i(u,t) \bar{r}_{oj}(v) \qquad i,j = 0,1,\ldots,k.$$

Hence, A^* is finitely closed with respect to quotients.

2.2. R-fuzzy automata

Since L. A. Zadeh [93] has formulated the notion of a fuzzy set, a growing number of papers have been engaged in the studies of fuzzy sets and applications to automata. Fuzzy automata were first defined by W. G. Wee and K. S. Fu [92] as learning automata and then fuzzy automata have been applied to the arears of learning control [32], interaction with random enviroments [92], and gaming [21]. Properties of fuzzy automata has been investigated by M. Mizumoto et al. [48,49,53] and E. S. Santos [70,71,72]. Especially, in [71] common features of probabilistic and fuzzy automata are shown. A further and more general development can be found in [91], where the phenomenon of indeterminancy, or say fuzziness, in the dynamic of automata is modelled by using po-semirings R. It turns out that the proposed concept of an R-fuzzy automaton includes the non-deterministic, fuzzy, (stationary) pseudo [70], and generalized probabilistic [78] or linear space automata [34]. Also concerning non-determinism generally, a categorical approach is presented by M. A. Arbib and E. G. Manes [3] with their theory of fuzzy machines in a category and by H. Ehrig et. al. [16] who studied automata in so-called pseudo-closed categories.

It has to be mentioned here that the use of semirings in the study of automata was originated by P. M. Schützenberger [74,75]. Although there are considered mostly the semiring of natural numbers, the ring of integers or commutative rings, the developed formalism is general enough to deal with arbitrary semirings as it was done by M. Fliess [18]. S. Eilenberg [17] motivates his introduction of so-called R-X-automata by means of the phenomenon of multiplicity which appears 'whenever any fact takes place for serveral reasons and we wish to study not only the fact itself but also the reasons for which it takes place.'

In the sequel it will be assumed that X is always a finite set (input alphabet), $H = X^* \ltimes T$ is an input-semigroup with a locally finite monoid T and B is basis of H.

Definition 2.8. An R-fuzzy automaton $\mathfrak{A}$ (over B) is a quadruple

$$\mathfrak{A} = (S, S_o, S_f, d)$$

where S is a finite set of internal states, $S_o, S_f \in \mathfrak{I}_R S$ are R-fuzzy subsets of initial and final states, respectively, and d is a mapping from $B \times S$ into $\mathfrak{I}_R S$ which describes the local transition behaviour of $\mathfrak{A}$.

Remark. The concept of an R-fuzzy automaton also includes the time-variant as well as controlled versions of different notions of automata (cf. [1,6,66,79]).

In order to define the global behaviour of an R-fuzzy automaton $\mathcal{A}$, the mapping d is regarded as a mapping from B into $Rel_R S$, where for each b of B, the R-fuzzy relation d(b) as value at b is defined by

$$d(b) = \{(s,s') \in S \times S \mid s' \in d(b,s)\}.$$

Since B is a basis of H, d admits a unique extension $d^{\#}: H \to Rel_R S$ with the properties:

(1) $d^{\#}(e,t) = id_S$ for all $t \in T$

(2) $d^{\#}(h \cdot b) = d^{\#}(h) \cdot d(b)$ for all $h \in H$, $b \in B$ provided $h \cdot b$ is defined in H.

Thereby, id_S denotes the identical R-fuzzy realtion on S defined as follows

$$id_S(s,s') = \begin{cases} 1 & \text{if } s = s' \\ 0 & \text{if } s \neq s' \end{cases} \quad \text{for all } s,s' \in S.$$

Now, we are in a position to define the global behaviour $[\mathcal{A}]$ of $\mathcal{A}$ as R-fuzzy event:

$$[\mathcal{A}] = \{h \in H \mid \exists s \exists s' (s \in S_o \wedge (s,s') \in d^{\#}(h) \wedge s' \in S_f)\},$$

i.e., for each h of H, we have

$$[\mathcal{A}](h) = \sum_{s,s' \in S} S_o(s) \cdot d^{\#}(h)(s,s') \cdot S_f(s').$$

Definition 2.9. An R-fuzzy event A is said to be recognizable if there exists an R-fuzzy automaton $\mathcal{A}$ such that $A = [\mathcal{A}]$. The set of all recognizable R-fuzzy events is denoted by $Rec_R B$.

Theorem 2.11 (Analysis of R-fuzzy automata). Any recognizable R-fuzzy event is rational.

Proof. Let A be a recognizable R-fuzzy event. Then there exists an R-fuzzy automaton $\mathcal{A} = (S, S_o, S_f, d)$ such that $A = [\mathcal{A}]$. By means of d, a matrix $\underline{D} \in (\mathfrak{E}_R B)_n$, where $n = card(S)$, is associated with $\mathcal{A}$ as follows

$$\underline{D} = \sum_{b \in B} \underline{D}(b) \quad \text{with } \underline{D}(b)_{s,s'} = d(b)(s,s') \text{ for } b \in B,\ s,s' \in S.$$

Clearly, $\underline{D}$ belongs to $(Rat_R B)_n$. Since for the coefficients $\underline{D}_{s,s'}$ of $\underline{D}$ the condition $\underline{D}_{s,s'} \cap E = \emptyset$ is satisfied, $\underline{D}^*$ exists and is an element of $(Rat_R B)_n$ by Theorem 2.6. If $\underline{D}(h)$ denotes that matrix whose coefficients are $\underline{D}_{s,s'}(h)$, then

$$\underline{D}^*(h) = d^{\#}(h) \quad \text{for all } h \in H$$

This statement can be proved by induction over the length of h using the fact

$$\underline{D}^*_{s,s'}(h) = D^{|h|}_{s,s'}(h) \qquad \text{for all } h \in H,\ s,s' \in S.$$

For $h = b_1 \cdot b_2 \cdot \ldots b_k$ with $k \geq 1$, we have

$$D^k_{s,s'}(h) = \sum_{s_1,s_2,\ldots,s_k \in S} D_{s,s_1}(b_1) \cdot D_{s_1,s_2}(b_2) \cdot \ldots D_{s_k,s'}(b_k)$$

for all $s,s' \in S$, consequently, $D^k_{s,s'}(h) = d^{\#}(h)(s,s')$. This implies $\underline{D}^*(h) = d^{\#}(h)$ for all $h \in H$. Thus

$$[A](h) = \sum_{s,s' \in S} S_o(s) \cdot \underline{D}^*_{s,s'}(h) \cdot S_f(s') \qquad \text{for all } h \in H.$$

Therefore,

$$[A] = \underline{S}_o \cdot \underline{D}^* \cdot \underline{S}_f,$$

where S_o and S_f are regarded as vectors $\underline{S}_o$ and $\underline{S}_f$, respectively. Since the coefficients of $\underline{S}_o$, $\underline{D}^*$ and $\underline{S}_f$ are rational, [A] is a rational R-fuzzy event

The proof of Theorem 2.11 gives an constructive method of computing the global behaviour of an R-fuzzy automaton. But there is a more algebraic and effective method. In the classical case such a method was proposed by D. N. Arden [4] and by M. A. Spivak (cf. [76]). Let $A = (S,S_o,S_f,d)$ be an R-fuzzy automaton with $S = \{1,2,\ldots,n\}$. Then a system of linear equations

$$Z_i = \sum_{j=1}^{n} A_{ij} \cdot Z_i + A'_i \qquad \text{for } i = 1,2,\ldots,n \qquad (*)$$

is associated with A by setting

$$A_{ij} = \sum_{b \in B} d(b)(i,j) = D_{ij} \qquad \text{for } i,j = 1,2,\ldots,n$$

$$A'_i = S_f(i) \qquad \text{for } i = 1,2,\ldots,n.$$

The system (*) may be expressed in matrix form

$$\underline{Z} = \underline{D} \cdot \underline{Z} + \underline{S}_f.$$

By successive iteration, we obtain the unique solution $\underline{Z}_o = \underline{D}^* \cdot \underline{S}_f$ and, therefore,

$$[A] = \underline{S}_o \cdot \underline{Z}_o = \underline{S}_o \cdot \underline{D}^* \cdot \underline{S}_f.$$

Example. Consider the $\mathbb{N}$-fuzzy automaton $\mathcal{A} = (\{s_o,s_f\},s_o,s_f,d)$ over $X = \{x,y\}$ given by

$$d(x) = \begin{vmatrix} 0 & 1 \\ 2 & 0 \end{vmatrix} \quad \text{and} \quad d(y) = \begin{vmatrix} 3 & 1 \\ 0 & 0 \end{vmatrix}.$$

The use of transition matrices is convenient and uniquely determined by definition. Their coefficients describe the multiplicity of the related transitions. The associated matrix $\underline{D}$ introduced in the proof of Theorem 2.11 can be represented by

$$\underline{D} = \begin{vmatrix} 3y & x + y \\ 2x & 0 \end{vmatrix}$$

whose coefficients may be regarded as formal power series. But they can also be thought of as R-fuzzy events. Applying the formulas used in the proof of Theorem 2.6, we derive for instance

$$\underline{D}^*_{12} = (3y)^* \cdot (x + y) \cdot (2x \cdot (3y)^* \cdot (x + y))^*.$$

From this follows

$$[\mathcal{A}](w) = \begin{cases} 2^n \cdot 3^{l + m \cdot n} & \text{if } w \in y^l X (xy^m X)^n \text{ for } l,m,n \geq 0 \\ 0 & \text{otherwise.} \end{cases}$$

Notice that any recognizable or rational R-fuzzy event has the following property

$$A = A' + rE \qquad \text{with } A' = A \cap (H \setminus E) \text{ and } r = A(e,1).$$

In general, an R-fuzzy event is called e-normalized if A is decomposable in the above mentioned form.

Theorem 2.12 [17]. An e-normalized R-fuzzy event A is recognizable if and only if $A' = A \cap (H \setminus E)$ is recognizable.

Proof. (1) Let A be recognizable. Then there exists an R-fuzzy automaton $\mathcal{A} = (S,S_o,S_f,d)$ such that $A = [\mathcal{A}]$. By adding a new internal state $s_o \notin S$ to S, an R-fuzzy automaton $\mathcal{A}' = (S \cup \{s_o\},s_o,S_f',d')$ is constructed as follows

$$S_f'(s) = \begin{cases} S_f(s) & \text{if } s \in S \\ 0 & \text{if } s = s_o \end{cases}$$

$$d'(b)(s,s') = \begin{cases} S_o(s') & \text{if } s = s_o,\ s' \in S \\ d(b)(s,s') & \text{if } s,s' \in S \\ 0 & \text{otherwise.} \end{cases}$$

It may easily be shown that $[\mathcal{A}'] = [\mathcal{A}] \cap (H \setminus E)$, that means A' is recognizable.

(2) Conversely, assume that A' is recognizable. Then there exists an R-fuzzy automaton $\mathcal{A}' = (S', S'_0, S'_f, d')$ satisfying $A' = [\mathcal{A}']$. Take $S = S' \cup \{s_0\}$ with $s_0 \notin S'$ and define $S_0, S_f \in \mathfrak{X}_R S$ as well as $d: B \to \mathrm{Rel}_R S$ by setting

$$S_0(s) = \begin{cases} A(e,1) & \text{if } s = s_0 \\ S'_0(s) & \text{if } s \in S' \end{cases}$$

$$S_f(s) = \begin{cases} 1 & \text{if } s = s_0 \\ S'_f(s) & \text{if } s \in S' \end{cases}$$

$$d(b)(s,s') = \begin{cases} d'(b)(s,s') & \text{if } s,s' \in S' \\ 0 & \text{otherwise.} \end{cases}$$

Clearly, the R-fuzzy automaton $\mathcal{A} = (S, S_0, S_f, d)$ has the following property

$$[\mathcal{A}] = [\mathcal{A}'] + A(e,1)E.$$

Since, by assumption, A is decomposable into $A = A' + A(e,1)E$ with $A' = [\mathcal{A}']$, A is recognizable.

An R-fuzzy automaton $\mathcal{A} = (S, S_0, S_f, d)$ is called normalized [17] if $S_0 = \{s_0\}$ and $S_f = \{s_f\}$ are distinct singletons and if, furthermore, d satisfies $d(b)(s,s_0) = 0$ and $d(b)(s_f,s) = 0$ for all $b \in B$ and $s \in S$.

Theorem 2.13 [17]. For any R-fuzzy automaton $\mathcal{A}$ there exists a normalized R-fuzzy automaton $\mathcal{A}'$ such that

$$[\mathcal{A}'] = [\mathcal{A}] \cap (H \setminus E).$$

Proof. Let $\mathcal{A} = (S, S_0, S_f, d)$ be an R-fuzzy automaton. Define $S' = S \cup \{s_0, s_f\}$ with $s_0, s_f \notin S$ and define the new transition mapping $d': B \to \mathrm{Rel}_R S'$ as follows

$$d'(b)(s,s') = \begin{cases} d(b)(s,s') & \text{if } s,s' \in S \\ \sum\limits_{s\in S} S_0(s)\cdot d(b)(s,s') & \text{if } s = s_0, s' \in S \\ \sum\limits_{s'\in S} d(b)(s,s')\cdot S_f(s') & \text{if } s \in S,\ s' = s_f \\ \sum\limits_{s,s'\in S} S_0(s)\cdot d(b)(s,s')\cdot S_f(s') & \text{if } s = s_0, s' = s_f \\ 0 & \text{otherwise.} \end{cases}$$

Obviously, the R-fuzzy automaton $\mathcal{A}' = (S', s_0, s_f, d)$ is normalized and a simple calculation shows that $[\mathcal{A}'] = [\mathcal{A}] \cap (H \setminus E)$ holds.

Theorem 2.14 [17]. The set $Rec_R B$ of all recognizable R-fuzzy events is closed under rational operations.

Proof. Let A and A' be recognizable R-fuzzy events. Then there are R-fuzzy automata $\mathcal{A} = (S, S_0, S_f, d)$ and $\mathcal{A}' = (S', S'_0, S'_f, d')$ such that $A = [\mathcal{A}]$ and $A' = [\mathcal{A}']$.

(1) Let r be an arbitrary element of R. Observe that $r\mathcal{A} = (S, rS_0, S_f, d)$ recognizes rA because

$$[r\mathcal{A}] = (r\underline{S}_0)\cdot\underline{D}^*\cdot\underline{S}_f = r(\underline{S}_0\cdot\underline{D}^*\cdot\underline{S}_f) = r[\mathcal{A}] = rA.$$

Hence $Rec_R B$ is closed under scalar product.

(2) In order to prove that $A + A' \in Rec_R B$, the direct sum $\mathcal{A} \oplus \mathcal{A}'$ of $\mathcal{A}$ and $\mathcal{A}'$ is constructed as follows

$$\mathcal{A} \oplus \mathcal{A}' = (S \oplus S', S_0 \oplus S'_0, S_f \oplus S'_f, d \oplus d'),$$

where $S \oplus S'$ denotes the disjoint union of S and S', the direct sum for fuzzy sets has already been defined in Section 1.2.3 and $d \oplus d'$ is a mapping from B into $Rel_R(S \oplus S')$ defined by $(d \oplus d')(b) = d(b) \oplus d'(b)$ for all $b \in B$. Observe that $d \oplus d'$ regarded as matrix coincides with the direct sum of the two matrices d and d'. A simple calculation shows

$$[\mathcal{A} \oplus \mathcal{A}'] = [\mathcal{A}] + [\mathcal{A}'].$$

Therefore, $A + A'$ is recognizable and, consequently, $Rec_R B$ is closed under sum.

(3) We know that any recognizable R-fuzzy event is e-normalized. Thus $A = A_1 + rE$ with $A_1 = A \cap (H \setminus E)$ and $r = A(e,1)$ as well as $A' = A'_1 + r'E$ with $A'_1 = A' \cap (H \setminus E)$ and $r' = A'(e,1)$. By Theorem 2.12, A_1 and A'_1 are recognizable. Now, consider the product

$$A\cdot A' = A_1\cdot A'_1 + rA'_1 + r'A_1 + rr'E.$$

In order to prove that $A\cdot A'$ is recognizable it sufficies to show that each component on the right hand side is recognizable by property (2). Evidently, rA'_1 and $r'A_1$ are recognizable by property (1). Since $rr'E$ is also recognizable, it only remains to verify that $A_1\cdot A'_1$ belongs to $Rec_R B$. Without loss of generality, we assume that there exist normalized R-fuzzy automata $\mathcal{A}_1 = (S, s_0, s_f, d)$ and $\mathcal{A}'_1 = (S', s'_0, s'_f, d')$ satisfying $A_1 = [\mathcal{A}_1]$ and $A'_1 = [\mathcal{A}'_1]$. Next, a normalized R-fuzzy automaton $\mathcal{A}_1\cdot\mathcal{A}'_1$ is constructed as follows

$$\mathfrak{A}_1 \cdot \mathfrak{A}_1' = (S \oplus (S' \setminus \{s_0'\}), s_0, s_f', \bar{d})$$

with

$$\bar{d}(b)(s_1,s_2) = \begin{cases} d(b)(s_1,s_2) & \text{if } s_1,s_2 \in S \\ d'(b)(s_1,s_2) & \text{if } s_1,s_2 \in S' \setminus \{s_0'\} \\ d'(b)(s_0',s_2) & \text{if } s_1 = s_f,\ s_2 \in S' \setminus \{s_0'\} \\ 0 & \text{otherwise.} \end{cases}$$

An easy consideration shows

$$[\mathfrak{A}_1 \cdot \mathfrak{A}_1'] = A_1 \cdot A_1',$$

which proves that $Rec_R B$ is closed under product.

(4) Assume that $A \cap E = \emptyset$. Then the iteration A^* exists. Let $\mathfrak{A}$ be a normalized R-fuzzy automaton recognizing A. Then merging the initial and final state into a single state which is both initial and final, we obtain an R-fuzzy automaton $\mathfrak{A}^*$. It is clear that

$$[\mathfrak{A}^*] = A^*.$$

Therefore, A^* is recognizable and, consequently, $Rec_R B$ is closed under iteration.

Theorem 2.15. If R is a commutative po-semiring, then $Rec_R B$ is closed under bold intersection.

Proof. Let A and A' be R-fuzzy events recognized by $\mathfrak{A} = (S,S_0,S_f,d)$ and $\mathfrak{A}' = (S',S_0',S_f',d')$, respectively. For the product $\mathfrak{A} \times \mathfrak{A}'$ of $\mathfrak{A}$ and $\mathfrak{A}'$ constructed as follows

$$\mathfrak{A} \times \mathfrak{A}' = (S \times S', S_0 \times S_0', S_f \times S_f', d \times d')$$

with $(d \times d')(b) = d(b) \times d'(b)$ for all $b \in B$, we conclude

$$[\mathfrak{A} \times \mathfrak{A}'] = [\mathfrak{A}] \cap [\mathfrak{A}']$$

supposed R is commutative. This implies the assertion.

Remark. As in the usual time-variant case, we can uniquely associate an R-fuzzy event A_1 over X with any R-fuzzy event A over B by setting $A_1(w) = A(w,1)$ for all $w \in X^*$. Let $Rec_R^1 B$ denotes the image of $Rec_R B$ under $f: \mathfrak{F}_R B \to \mathfrak{F}_R X$ given by $f(A) = A_1$. Then $Rec_R^1 B$ is not closed under product and iteration (cf. [90]). But it is closed under sum and bold intersection.

Theorem 2.16 (Synthesis of R-fuzzy automata). Any rational R-fuzzy event is recognizable.

Proof. By definition, $Rat_R B$ is the smallest set of R-fuzzy events containing the elementary R-fuzzy events which is closed under rational operations. Therefore, by Theorem 2.14, it suffices to show that $Rec_R B$ contains the elementary R-fuzzy events. But, in fact, any $\bar{b}$ with $b \in B$ is recognized by $\mathcal{A}_b = (\{s_o, s_f\}, s_o, s_f, d_b)$ with

$$d_b(b')(s,s') = \begin{cases} 1 & \text{if } b' = b \text{ and } s = s_o,\ s' = s_f \\ 0 & \text{otherwise} \end{cases}$$

for all $b' \in B$ and $s, s' \in \{s_o, s_f\}$. Since the trivial R-fuzzy automaton $\mathcal{A} = (\{s\}, s, s, \emptyset)$ without any local transition recognizes the set E of identities, $\{\bar{b} | b \in B\} \cup \{E\}$ is a subset of $Rec_R B$ and, consequently, $Rat_R B$ is included in $Rec_R B$.

Combining Theorem 2.11 and Theorem 2.16, we get the following Kleene characterization of recognizable R-fuzzy events.

Theorem 2.17. An R-fuzzy event is recognizable if and only if it is rational.

Remark. For time-variant (deterministic or non-deterministic) automata, a Kleene characterization has first been established by R. M. Baer and E. H. Spanier [6]. Also the Nerode criterion was investigated. But a generalization of it for R-fuzzy automata is not always possible.

Theorem 2.18 (Nerode criterion). Let $H = X^* \ltimes T$ be an input-semigroup with a locally finite monoid T which is left cancellative. An R-fuzzy event over H is recognizable if and only if it is e-normalized and finitely closed with respect to quotients.

Proof. (1) Let A be a recognizable R-fuzzy event. By Theorem 2.17, A is rational. Since any rational R-fuzzy event is finitely closed with respect to quotients, by Theorem 2.10, one direction is proved.

(2) In order to prove the opposite direction, assume A is an e-normalized R-fuzzy event which is finitely closed with respect to quotients. Then there is a finite number of R-fuzzy events $A_o = A, A_1, \ldots, A_k$ such that

$$w^{-1}A_i = \sum_{j=0}^{k} r_{ij}(w) \cdot A_j \qquad \text{for } w \in X^*,\ i = 0,1,\ldots,k.$$

Now, we define an R-fuzzy automaton $\mathcal{A} = (S, s_o, s_f, d)$ with $S = \{s_o, s_1, \ldots, s_k, s_f\}$ by

$$d(x,t)(s_i,s_j) = \begin{cases} r_{ij}(x)(e,t_x) & \text{for } i,j = 0,1,\dots,k \\ \sum_{\varkappa=0}^{k} r_{i\varkappa}(x)(e,t_x)\cdot A_\varkappa(e,t_x) & \text{for } i = 0,1,\dots,k \text{ and } j = f \\ 0 & \text{otherwise} \end{cases}$$

where $t_w = t\cdot\varkappa(w)$ for $t \in T$, $w \in X^*$. Obviously, $[\mathfrak{A}](e,t) = 0$ for all t of T. By Theorem 2.12, it is sufficient to show that

$$[\mathfrak{A}](w,t) = A(w,t) \qquad \text{for all } w \in X^* \setminus \{e\},\ t \in T.$$

For this purpose, we prove

$$d^{\#}(w,t)(s_i,s_f) = \sum_{j=0}^{k} r_{ij}(w)(e,t_w)\cdot A_j(e,t_w) \tag{*}$$

by induction over the length $|w|$ of $w \in X^*$. For words w of length 1, (*) is valid by definition. Assume assertion (*) has already been proved for all $w \in X^*$ with $|w| < n$. Let $x \in X$ and $w \in X^*$ with $|w| = n - 1$. Then, using that T is left cancellative, we derive successively

$$\begin{aligned} d^{\#}(xw,t)(s_i,s_f) &= \sum_{j=0}^{k} d(x,t)(s_i,s_j)\cdot d^{\#}(w,t_x)(s_j,s_f) \\ &= \sum_{j=0}^{k} \sum_{j'=0}^{k} r_{ij}(x)(e,t_x)\cdot r_{jj'}(w)(e,t_{xw})\cdot A_{j'}(e,t_{xw}) \\ &= \sum_{j=0}^{k} r_{ij}(x)(e,t_x)\cdot (w^{-1}A_j)(e,t_{xw}) \\ &= (w^{-1}(\sum_{j=0}^{k} r_{ij}(x)\cdot A_j))(e,t_{xw}) \\ &= (w^{-1}(x^{-1}A_i))(e,t_{xw}) = ((xw)^{-1}A_i)(e,t_{xw}) \\ &= \sum_{j=0}^{k} r_{ij}(xw)(e,t_{xw})\cdot A_j(e,t_{xw}). \end{aligned}$$

Now, from (*) follows $d^{\#}(w,t)(s_0,s_f) = (w^{-1}A_0)(e,t_w)$. Therefore, $[\mathfrak{A}](w,t) = (w^{-1}A)(e,t_w)$. Since T is left cancellative, we get $[\mathfrak{A}](w,t) = A(w,t)$ for all $w \in X^* \setminus \{e\}$, $t \in T$, which proves the theorem.

2.3. R-fuzzy grammars

In the last few years, there has been an increasing amount of research done on integrating the concept of fuzziness, randomness or general weights with formal grammars and languages. By extracting the basic properties common to these concepts, context-free R-fuzzy grammars [86] will be introduced in this section.

Fuzzy grammars were proposed by E. T. Lee and L. A. Zadeh [43], who consider the set of rewriting rules as a fuzzy set. Such grammars are utilized as models for natural languages (cf. [50,94]), which usually involve some indeterminancy and ambigiuty due to vagueness rather than randomness. An improvement in this direction was made by M. Mizumoto et al. [51] with their notion of an n-fold fuzzy grammar, where the grade of application of the rule to be used next is conditioned by the $n \geq 1$ rules used previous in a derivation.

In the case of context-free stochastic grammar (cf. [33]), probability distributions are assigned to all those subsets of rewriting rules which have a fixed non-terminal on the left hand side. An application of the generated languages to pattern recognition has been discussed by K. S. Fu et al. (cf. [22]).

So-called weighted grammars (cf. [67]) are constructed from ordinary ones by associating elements of a weighting space to every rewriting rule. Using an arbitrary semiring as weighting space, D. Stanat [77] exhibited a homomorphism theorem for context-free weighted grammars (in Greibach normal form). The weight of any word, as well as the set of derivations of the word, may be determined from the image under a homomorphism which maps each terminal to a polynomial, that is an R-fuzzy set with a finite support.

2.3.1. Context-free R-fuzzy events

In this section we intend to generalize the notion of a context-free grammar. To do this, certain restrictions on the set of rewriting rules must be stated in order to be able to define the R-fuzzy event generated by a context-free R-fuzzy grammar. Moreover, an algebraic characterization of the set of all R-fuzzy events generated by context-free R-fuzzy grammars shall be established.

Definition 2.10. A context-free R-fuzzy grammar G is a quadruple

$$G = (X, V_N, \alpha_0, P),$$

where X and V_N are disjoint finite sets of terminals and non-terminals, respectively, $\alpha_o \in V_N$ is the axiom and $P \in \mathcal{I}_R^f(V_N \times V^*)$ with $V = X \cup V_N$ is the R-fuzzy set of rewriting rules or productions. Especially, G is called regular if $P \in \mathcal{I}_R^f(V_N \times X^*(V_N \cup \{e\}))$.

Convention. In the sequel, context-free R-fuzzy grammars will shortly be called R-fuzzy grammars.

As usual, the notation $\alpha \underset{G}{\longrightarrow} v$ is used instead of $(\alpha,v) \in P$ for all $\alpha \in V_N$, $v \in V^*$. Consider the $\mathbb{N}$-fuzzy grammar $G = (\{x\},\{\alpha\},\alpha,P)$ with $P(\alpha,\alpha) = P(\alpha,x) = 1$. Then the set P of rewriting rules can be represented as follows

$$\alpha \underset{G}{\longrightarrow} \alpha = 1 \quad \text{and} \quad \alpha \underset{G}{\longrightarrow} x = 1.$$

Next, we define an R-fuzzy relation $\underset{G}{\Longrightarrow}$ on V^* by the rule

$$v_1 \underset{G}{\Longrightarrow} v_2 = \begin{cases} \alpha \underset{G}{\longrightarrow} v & \text{if there are words } u,u',v \in V^* \text{ and } \alpha \in V_N \text{ such that } v_1 = u\alpha u' \text{ and } v_2 = uvu' \\ 0 & \text{otherwise.} \end{cases}$$

We say v_1 generates directly v_2 with degree $v_1 \underset{G}{\Longrightarrow} v_2$. Instead of $\underset{G}{\Longrightarrow}$, we will shortly write $\Longrightarrow$.

The reflexive transitive closure

$$\Longrightarrow^* = \sum_{n=0}^{\infty} \Longrightarrow^n \quad \text{with } \Longrightarrow^0 = id_{V^*} \text{ and } \Longrightarrow^n = \Longrightarrow^{n-1} \cdot \Longrightarrow,\ n \geq 1$$

of $\Longrightarrow$ describes, if it exists, the R-fuzzy set of all derivations of G.

Before setting up restrictions ensuring the existence of $\Longrightarrow^*$, some motivations will be given. It can easily be seen that in the example above

$$\alpha \Longrightarrow^n v = \begin{cases} 1 & \text{if } v \in V^* \\ 0 & \text{otherwise} \end{cases}$$

for all $n \geq 1$. Therefore, $\alpha \Longrightarrow^* v$ does not exist for each v of V^* because there are infinitely many derivations.

Theorem 2.19. Let $G = (X,V_N,\alpha_o,P)$ be an R-fuzzy grammar such that $\Longrightarrow^n \cdot V^m = \emptyset$ provided there is a natural number $k > 1$ satisfying $n \geq k \cdot m$ for all $n \geq 1$ and $m \geq 0$. Then the reflexive transitive closure $\Longrightarrow^*$ of $\Longrightarrow$ exists.

Proof. For any R-fuzzy grammar $G = (X,V_N,\alpha_o,P)$, we have $v \Longrightarrow v' = 0$ for words v,v' of V^* with $|v| > |v'| + 1$. By induction over n, it may be proved that all powers $\Longrightarrow^n$ exist. The basis step $n = 1$ is trivial. It only remains to verify the induction step from n to n + 1. Consider

$$v_1 \Longrightarrow^{n+1} v_2 = \sum_{v \in V^*} (v_1 \Longrightarrow^{n} v) \cdot (v \Longrightarrow v_2).$$

Because of $v \Longrightarrow v_2 = 0$ for $|v| > |v_2| + 1$, it follows

$$v_1 \Longrightarrow^{n+1} v_2 = \sum_{\substack{v \in V^* \\ |v| \leq |v_2|+1}} (v_1 \Longrightarrow^{n} v) \cdot (v \Longrightarrow v_2).$$

Since the summation is finite, $v_1 \Longrightarrow^{n+1} v_2$ is defined for all v_1, v_2 of V^* by induction assumption.

By the premise of the theorem, there exists a constant $k > 1$ such that

$$v \Longrightarrow^* v' = \sum_{n=0}^{\infty} v \Longrightarrow^{n} v' = \sum_{n=0}^{k|v'|} v \Longrightarrow^{n} v'$$

for all $v, v' \in V^*$. Therefore, $\Longrightarrow^*$ exists.

<u>Theorem 2.20</u>. An R-fuzzy grammar G satisfies the condition $\Longrightarrow^{n} \cdot V^{m} = \emptyset$ for $n \geq 2 \cdot m$, where $n \geq 1$ and $m \geq 0$ are arbitrary natural numbers, if and only if $\underset{G}{\longrightarrow} \cdot (V_N \cup \{e\}) = \emptyset$.

Proof. (1) Let $G = (X, V_N, \alpha_o, P)$ be an R-fuzzy grammar such that the condition $\Longrightarrow^{n} \cdot V^{m} = \emptyset$ is fulfilled for all $n \geq 1$ and $m \geq 0$. Especially, $\Longrightarrow^{2} \cdot V = \emptyset$ and $\Longrightarrow \cdot V^{o} = \Longrightarrow \cdot \{e\} = \emptyset$ hold. This implies the assertion $\longrightarrow \cdot (V_N \cup \{e\}) = \emptyset$.

(2) Let $G = (X, V_N, \alpha_o, P)$ be an R-fuzzy grammar satisfying $\longrightarrow \cdot (V_N \cup \{e\}) = \emptyset$. If V_{ij} denotes the set of all those words v of V^* in which exactly i terminals and j non-terminals occur, then the following statement may be proved by induction:

$$\Longrightarrow^{2i+j} \cdot V_{ij} = \emptyset \qquad \text{for } i, j = 0, 1, \ldots, n \text{ with } i + j \neq 0.$$

The basis step is valid because $\Longrightarrow \cdot V_{01} = \longrightarrow \cdot V_N = \emptyset$ (for $i = 0$ and $j = 1$) as well as $\Longrightarrow^{2} \cdot V_{10} = \Longrightarrow^{2} \cdot X = \emptyset$ (for $i = 1$ and $j = 0$). The induction step from $n = 2i + j$ to $n + 1 = 2i + (j + i)$ and $n + 2 = 2(i + 1) + j$ can be verified as follows

$$\text{(i)} \quad \Longrightarrow^{2i+j+1} \cdot V_{i,j+1} = \Longrightarrow^{2i+j} \cdot \Longrightarrow \cdot V_{i,j+1}$$
$$\subseteq \Longrightarrow^{2i+j} \cdot (V_{i-1,j+1} \cup V_{ij})$$
$$= \Longrightarrow \cdot \Longrightarrow^{2(i-1)+(j+1)} \cdot V_{i-1,j+1} \cup$$
$$\Longrightarrow^{2i+j} \cdot V_{ij} = \emptyset$$

$$\text{(ii)}\quad \Longrightarrow^{2(i+1)+j}\cdot V_{i+1,j} = \Longrightarrow^{2i+j+1}\cdot\Longrightarrow\cdot V_{i+1,j}$$
$$\subseteq \Longrightarrow^{2i+j+1}\cdot(V_{i,j+1} \cup V_{i+1,j-1})$$
$$= \Longrightarrow^{2i+(j+1)}\cdot V_{i,j+1} \cup$$
$$\Longrightarrow^{2(i+1)+(j-1)}\cdot V_{i+1,j-1} = \emptyset.$$

Immediately, the statement above yields $\Longrightarrow^{n}\cdot V^{m} = \emptyset$ provided $n \geq 2\cdot m$ for $n \geq 1$ and $m \geq 0$.

Theorem 2.21. If the R-fuzzy set P of rewriting rules of a given R-fuzzy grammar $G = (X,V_N,\alpha_o,P)$ can be decomposed into $P = P_o + P_1$ such that

(1) $\underset{G_o}{\Longrightarrow}\cdot\underset{G_o}{\Longrightarrow} = \underset{G_1}{\Longrightarrow}\cdot\underset{G_1}{\Longrightarrow} = \emptyset$

(2) $\underset{G_1}{\longrightarrow}\cdot(V_N \cup \{e\}) = \emptyset$

hold, where $G_o = (X,V_N,\alpha_o,P_o)$ and $G_1 = (X,V_N,\alpha_o,P_1)$. Then the reflexive transitive closure $\underset{G}{\Longrightarrow}^{*}$ of $\underset{G}{\Longrightarrow}$ exists.

Proof. By assumption (2), all powers $\underset{G_1}{\Longrightarrow}^{n}, n \geq 1$, are well defined. Since

$$\underset{G}{\Longrightarrow}^{n} = \underset{G_o}{\Longrightarrow}\cdot\underset{G_1}{\Longrightarrow}^{n-1} + \underset{G_1}{\Longrightarrow}^{n} \qquad \text{for } n \geq 1,$$

all powers $\underset{G}{\Longrightarrow}^{n}$ are well defined too. Furthermore,

$$\underset{G}{\Longrightarrow}^{*} = \sum_{n=0}^{\infty} \underset{G_o}{\Longrightarrow}\cdot\underset{G_1}{\Longrightarrow}^{n} + \sum_{n=0}^{\infty} \underset{G_1}{\Longrightarrow}^{n} = \underset{G_o}{\Longrightarrow}\cdot\underset{G_1}{\Longrightarrow}^{*} + \underset{G_1}{\Longrightarrow}^{*}$$

Consequently, the reflexive transitive closure $\underset{G}{\Longrightarrow}^{*}$ of $\underset{G}{\Longrightarrow}$ exists.

Remark. Let $G = (X,V_N,\alpha_o,P)$ be an R-fuzzy grammar satisfying the premises of Theorem 2.21. Without loss of generality, it may be assumed that P_o contains at most rewriting rules of the form $\alpha_o \longrightarrow e$ and $\alpha_o \longrightarrow \alpha_1$. We call $|G| = (X,V_N,\alpha_o,|P|)$, where $|P|$ is the support of P (see Section 1.3.1), the underlying context-free grammar of G. Then the decomposition of P into $P = P_o + P_1$ corresponds to the well-known procedure (cf. [68]) by which to any context-free grammar an equivalent context-free grammar is constructed such that the only rewriting rule with e on the right hand side starts with α_o and, furthermore, α_o does not occur on the right hand side of another rewriting rule. Premise (2) of Theorem 2.21, however, confines the class of all possible context-free grammars. But observe that an R-fuzzy grammar G whose underlying context-free grammar $|G|$ is in Chomsky normal form, satisfies premise (2) of Theorem 2.21. Since any e-free context-free language can be generated by a context-free grammar in Chomsky normal form, the premises of Theorem 2.21 are, in fact, not restrictive from the point of view of generating context-free languages. •

<u>General assumption</u>. Henceforth, for any considered R-fuzzy grammar, the premises of Theorem 2.21 shall be fulfilled.

Let $G = (X, V_N, \alpha_0, P)$ be an R-fuzzy grammar. Then $L(G,\alpha)$ denotes the R-fuzzy set of all words of X^* derived from $\alpha \in V_N$, that is

$$L(G,\alpha) = \{w \in X^* | \alpha \Longrightarrow^* w\}$$

$L(G,\alpha)$ is called the R-fuzzy event generated by G.

<u>Definition 2.11</u>. An R-fuzzy event $A \in \mathfrak{E}_R X$ is said to be context-free if there exists an R-fuzzy grammar $G = (X, V_N, \alpha_0, P)$ such that $A = L(G,\alpha_0)$. Especially, A is called regular if G is a regular R-fuzzy grammar.

In the sequel, we are going to determine $L(G,\alpha)$. For this purpose, two mappings

$$\tau: \mathfrak{E}_R V \to \mathfrak{E}_R X \qquad \text{and} \qquad \delta_G: \mathfrak{E}_R V \to \mathfrak{E}_R V$$

are introduced by $\tau(A) = A \cap X^*$ and $\delta_G(A) = \tau(A) + A \cdot \Longrightarrow$ for each A of $\mathfrak{E}_R V$. The following properties can easily be concluded

$$\tau^2(A) = \delta_G(\tau(A)) = \tau(A)$$

$$\delta_G^n(A) = \tau(A) + \tau(A \cdot \Longrightarrow) + \ldots + \tau(A \cdot \Longrightarrow^{n-1}) + A \cdot \Longrightarrow^n \qquad n \geq 1$$

By setting $D_G^{(n)} = \tau \cdot \delta_G^n$, it follows

$$D_G^{(n)}(A) = \tau(\sum_{\nu=1}^{n} A \cdot \Longrightarrow^\nu) \qquad \text{for } n \geq 1.$$

Therefore, $D_G^{(n)}(A)$ is the R-fuzzy event of all those words of X^* derivable from elements of A in at most n steps. In particular, for $\alpha \in V_N$

$$D_G^{(n)}(\alpha) = \{w \in X^* | \exists\nu(\nu \in \{1,2,\ldots,n\} \wedge \alpha \Longrightarrow^\nu w)\}$$

or, by fuzzy interpreting

$$D_G^{(n)}(\alpha)(w) = \sum_{\nu=1}^{n} \alpha \Longrightarrow^\nu w \qquad \text{for all } w \in X^*,$$

that means

$$D_G^{(n)}(\alpha) = \{\alpha\}\cdot(\sum_{\nu=1}^{n} \Longrightarrow^{\nu}) \cap X^*.$$

In order to solve the problem whether or not the sequence $D_G^{(n)}(\alpha)$ is convergent, it sufficies to restrict ourselves on R-fuzzy grammars without rewriting rules having e on the right hand side. Otherwise, let $G = (X,V_N,\alpha_o,P)$ be an R-fuzzy grammar with rewriting rules $\alpha_o \longrightarrow e$ and $\alpha_o \longrightarrow \alpha_1$. Then we compute

$$D_G^{(1)}(\alpha_o) = \{e|\alpha_o \longrightarrow e\}$$

$$D_G^{(n)}(\alpha_o) = \alpha_o \longrightarrow \alpha_1\cdot D_G^{(n-1)}(\alpha_1) \qquad \text{for } n > 1$$

$$D_G^{(n)}(\alpha) = D_{G_1}^{(n)}(\alpha) \qquad \text{for } n \geq 1,\ \alpha \in V_N \setminus \{\alpha_o\},$$

where $G_1 = (X,V_{1N},\alpha_1,P_1)$ with $V_{1N} = V_N \setminus \{\alpha_o\}$, $V_1 = X \cup V_{1N}$ and $P_1 = \{(\alpha,v) \in V_{1N} \times V_1^*|\alpha \longrightarrow v\}$. Clearly, the sequence $D_G^{(n)}(\alpha)$ is convergent if and only if the sequence $D_{G_1}^{(n)}(\alpha)$ is convergent.

Now, we assume that $G = (X,V_N,\alpha_1,P)$ is an R-fuzzy grammar with $V_N = \{\alpha_1,\alpha_2,\ldots,\alpha_n\}$ satisfying $\longrightarrow\cdot(V_N \cup \{e\}) = \emptyset$. With G, we associate an operator F_G on $(\mathfrak{C}_R^! X)^n$, where $\mathfrak{C}_R^! X = \mathfrak{C}_R X$ is the complete subspace of all e-free R-fuzzy events, that is $\mathfrak{C}_R^! X = \{A \in \mathfrak{C}_R X|e \in A = 0\}$. Let f_v be a mapping from $(\mathfrak{C}_R^! X)^n$ into $\mathfrak{C}_R^! X$ defined by

$$f_v(Z_1,Z_2,\ldots,Z_n) = v[^{\alpha}j/Z_j],$$

that means, first any α_j is substituted by $Z_j \in \mathfrak{C}_R^! X$, $j = 1,2,\ldots,n$, in $v \in V^*$ and then the R-fuzzy events are multiplied, whereby the elements of X are considered as R-fuzzy events. The i-th component of $F_G(\underline{Z})$, $\underline{Z} = (Z_1,Z_2,\ldots,Z_n) \in (\mathfrak{C}_R^! X)^n$, is now defined as R-fuzzy event of all words of X^* derivable from α_i if any non-terminal α_j is replaced by an arbitrary word of the related R-fuzzy event Z_j:

$$F_G(\underline{Z})_i = \{w \in X^*|\exists v(\alpha_i \longrightarrow v \wedge w \in v[^{\alpha}j/Z_j])\}.$$

By means of fuzzy interpretation, we obtain

$$F_G(\underline{Z})_i = \sum_{v \in V^*} (\alpha_i \longrightarrow v)\cdot v[^{\alpha}j/Z_j] \qquad \text{for } i = 1,2,\ldots,n.$$

If G is a regular R-fuzzy grammar, then F_G is a linear operator given by

$$F_G(\underline{Z}) = \underline{A}\cdot\underline{Z} + \underline{A}',$$

where the matrix $\underline{A} = (A_{ij})$ and the column vector $\underline{A}' = (A_i')$ are defined as follows

$$A_{ij} = \{w \in X^* | \alpha_i \longrightarrow w\alpha_j\}$$
$$A_i^! = \{w \in X^* | \alpha_i \longrightarrow w\}$$

for all non-terminals $\alpha_i, \alpha_j \in V_N$.

Examples. 1) Let $G = (X, V_N, \alpha_1, P)$ be an R-fuzzy grammar, where R is the following po-semiring $R = \{0, r, r', 1\}$ whose operations and partial order are defined by

+	0	r	r'	1
0	0	r	r'	1
r	r	r	1	1
r'	r'	1	r'	1
1	1	1	1	1

•	0	r	r'	1
0	0	0	0	0
r	0	r	0	r
r'	0	0	r'	r'
1	0	r	r'	1

and $0 \leq r, r' \leq 1$. We put $X = \{x, y, z\}$, $V_N = \{\alpha_1, \alpha_2, \alpha_3, \alpha_4, \alpha_5\}$ and define

$\alpha_1 \longrightarrow \alpha_2\alpha_3 = r$ $\quad\quad$ $\alpha_1 \longrightarrow \alpha_4\alpha_5 = r'$

$\alpha_2 \longrightarrow xy = 1$ $\quad\quad$ $\alpha_2 \longrightarrow x\alpha_2 y = 1$

$\alpha_3 \longrightarrow z = 1$ $\quad\quad$ $\alpha_3 \longrightarrow z\alpha_3 = 1$

$\alpha_4 \longrightarrow x = 1$ $\quad\quad$ $\alpha_4 \longrightarrow x\alpha_4 = 1$

$\alpha_5 \longrightarrow yz = 1$ $\quad\quad$ $\alpha_5 \longrightarrow y\alpha_5 z = 1.$

The corresponding operator F_G is determined as follows

$$F_G(\underline{Z})_1 = rZ_2 \cdot Z_3 + r'Z_4 \cdot Z_5$$
$$F_G(\underline{Z})_2 = xy + x \cdot Z_2 \cdot y$$
$$F_G(\underline{Z})_3 = z + z \cdot Z_3$$
$$F_G(\underline{Z})_4 = x + x \cdot Z_4$$
$$F_G(\underline{Z})_5 = yz + y \cdot Z_5 \cdot z$$

ith $\underline{Z} = (Z_1, Z_2, Z_3, Z_4, Z_5) \in (\mathfrak{C}_R X)^5$. The fixed point $\underline{Z}_o$ can easily be alculated

$$Z_1^o = r\{x^m y^m z^n | m \neq n,\ m,n \geq 1\} + r'\{x^m y^n z^n | m \neq n,\ m,n \geq 1\}$$
$$Z_2^o = \{x^m y^m | m \geq 1\}$$
$$Z_3^o = \{z^n | n \geq 1\}$$
$$Z_4^o = \{x^m | m \geq 1\}$$
$$Z_5^o = \{y^n z^n | n \geq 1\}.$$

2) Consider the regular $\mathbb{N}$-fuzzy grammar $G = (\{x,y\},\{\alpha_1,\alpha_2\},\alpha_1,P)$ with

$$\alpha_1 \longrightarrow y\alpha_1 = 3 \qquad \alpha_2 \longrightarrow x\alpha_1 = 2$$
$$\alpha_1 \longrightarrow x\alpha_2 = 1 \qquad \alpha_2 \longrightarrow e = 1$$
$$\alpha_1 \longrightarrow y\alpha_2 = 1.$$

The related linear operator F_G given by $F_G(\underline{Z}) = \underline{A}\cdot\underline{Z} + \underline{A}'$ is determined as follows

$$\underline{A} = \begin{vmatrix} 3y & x + y \\ 2x & 0 \end{vmatrix} \quad \text{and} \quad \underline{A}' = \begin{vmatrix} 0 \\ 1 \end{vmatrix}.$$

Comparing the example of Section 2.2, we get for the first component of the solution $\underline{Z}_o = \underline{A}^*\cdot\underline{A}'$

$$Z_1^o = (3y)^*\cdot(x + y)\cdot(2x\cdot(3y)^*\cdot(x + y))^*.$$

Theorem 2.22. If $G = (X,V_N,\alpha_o,P)$ is an R-fuzzy grammar satisfying the condition $\longrightarrow\cdot(V_N \cup \{e\}) = \emptyset$, then the sequence $(L(G,\alpha))_{\alpha\in V_N}$ of R-fuzzy events generated by G is fixed point of F_G.

Proof. (1) Statement: F_G is contractive.

Let $V_N = \{\alpha_o,\alpha_1,\ldots,\alpha_{n-1}\}$. Assume that the distance $m(\underline{Z},\underline{Z}')$ of two vectors $\underline{Z} = (Z_o,Z_1,\ldots,Z_{n-1})$ and $\underline{Z}' = (Z_o',Z_1',\ldots,Z_{n-1}')$ of $(\mathbb{C}_R'X)^n$ is 2^{-m}, where $m \geq 0$ is an arbitrary natural number. From this follows

$$Z_i(w) = Z_i'(w) \qquad i = 0,1,\ldots,n-1 \qquad (*)$$

for all $w \in X^*$ with $|w| < m$. To prove statement (1), it is sufficient to show that (*) implies

$$F_G(\underline{Z})_i(w) = F_G(\underline{Z}')_i(w) \qquad i = 0,1,\ldots,n-1$$

for all $w \in X^*$ with $|w| \leq m$. At first, take the R-fuzzy events $f_v(\underline{Z}) = v[^{\alpha}j/Z_j]$ for all $v \in V^*$ with $\alpha_i \longrightarrow v \neq 0$. Suppose that v contains at least one terminal x of X. Therefore, there are $u_1,u_2 \in V^*$ such that $v = u_1xu_2$ and we get

$$f_v(\underline{Z}) = f_{u_1}(\underline{Z})\cdot x\cdot f_{u_2}(\underline{Z}).$$

Consequently, for all $w \in X^*$

$$f_v(\underline{Z})(w) = \sum_{\substack{w_1,w_2\in X^*\\ w_1xw_2=w}} f_{u_1}(\underline{Z})(w_1)\cdot f_{u_2}(\underline{Z})(w_2)$$

Because of (*), it follows

$$f_v(\underline{Z})(w) = f_v(\underline{Z}')(w) \qquad (**)$$

for all $w \in X^*$ with $|w| \leq m$. Analogously, the equation (**) may be proved for an arbitrary v of V^* whose length is greater than 1. For this case, we have

$$f_v(\underline{Z})(w) = \sum_{\substack{w_1,w_2 \in X^* \setminus \{e\} \\ w_1 w_2 = w}} f_{u_1}(\underline{Z})(w_1) \cdot f_{u_2}(\underline{Z})(w_2)$$

Since $Z_i(e) = 0$ for $i = 0,1,\ldots,n-1$, the equation (*) implies (**).

By the general assumption, P only contains rewriting rules $\alpha_i \longrightarrow v$ with $|v| \geq 2$ or $v \in X$. Therefore, equation (**) always holds for v of V^* with $\alpha_i \longrightarrow v \neq 0$ and, consequently,

$$F_G(\underline{Z})_i(w) = F_G(\underline{Z}')_i(w) \qquad i = 0,1,\ldots,n-1$$

for all $w \in X^*$ with $|w| \leq m$. Hence $\min\{|w| \mid F_G(\underline{Z})_i(w) \neq F_G(\underline{Z}')_i(w)\}$ is greater than m for all $i = 0,1,\ldots,n-1$. Thus there exists a constant c satisfying $0 \leq c < 1$ such that

$$m(F_G(\underline{Z}),F_G(\underline{Z}')) \leq c \cdot m(\underline{Z},\underline{Z}'),$$

that means F_G is a contractive operator.

(2) Statement: $(L(G,\alpha))_{\alpha \in V_N}$ is fixed point of F_G.

If we choose $\underline{Z} = (\alpha_0,\alpha_1,\ldots,\alpha_{n-1})$, by induction over k we will prove

$$F_G^k(\alpha_0,\alpha_1,\ldots,\alpha_{n-1})_i = D_G^{(k)}(\alpha_i) \qquad \text{for } i = 0,1,\ldots,n-1.$$

Basis step:

$$F_G^1(\alpha_0,\alpha_1,\ldots,\alpha_{n-1})_i = \{w \in X^* \mid \exists v(\alpha_i \longrightarrow v \wedge w = v)\} = D_G^{(1)}(\alpha_i).$$

Induction step:

$$\begin{aligned} F_G^{k+1}(\alpha_0,\alpha_1,\ldots,\alpha_{n-1})_i &= F_G(D_G^{(k)}(\alpha_0),D_G^{(k)}(\alpha_1),\ldots,D_G^{(k)}(\alpha_{n-1}))_i \\ &= \{w \in X^* \mid \exists v(\alpha_i \longrightarrow v \wedge w \in v[{}^{\alpha_j}/D_G^{(k)}(\alpha_j)])\} \\ &= D_G^{(k+1)}(\alpha_i). \end{aligned}$$

Therefore, the limit of the sequence $F_G^k(\alpha_0,\alpha_1,\ldots,\alpha_{n-1})$, $k \geq 1$, is $(D_G(\alpha_0),D_G(\alpha_1),\ldots,D_G(\alpha_{n-1}))$ with $D_G(\alpha_i) = \{w \in X^* \mid \alpha_i \Longrightarrow^* w\}$. Hence

$$(L(G,\alpha_0),L(G,\alpha_1),\ldots,L(G,\alpha_{n-1}))$$

is fixed point of F_G.

Theorem 2.23. Let $G = (X,V_N,\alpha_o,P)$ be an R-fuzzy grammar. The sequence $D_G^{(k)}(\alpha)$, $k \geq 1$, converges to the limit $L(G,\alpha)$ for each α of V_N.

At the end of this section, we intend to establish an algebraic characterization of context-free R-fuzzy events which generalizes that of usual context-free languages presented by Letičevskiĭ [44]. For this purpose, specially generated subalgebras of $\mathfrak{E}_R X$ are needed. Their elements are determined by so-called R-polynomials p. Let $U = \{u_1,u_2,\dots,u_n\}$ be a finite set (of variables). An R-polynomial p is represented as follows

$$p = \sum_{u \in U^*} r(u)u \qquad \text{with } r(u) \in R,$$

where only finitely many coefficients r(u) are not equal to zero. The substitution of R-fuzzy events $A_1,A_2,\dots,A_n$ into p, denoted by $p(A_1,A_2,\dots,A_n)$, is defined as usual

$$p(A_1,A_2,\dots,A_n) = \sum_{u \in U^*} r(u)u[^{u}i/A_i].$$

Definition 2.12. A subalgebra of $\mathfrak{E}_R X$ is said to be R-polynomially generated by a subset $\mathcal{A}$ of $\mathfrak{E}_R X$ if for each element A of it, there are finitely many R-fuzzy events $A_1,A_2,\dots,A_n$ of $\mathcal{A}$ such that A equals $p(A_1,A_2,\dots,A_n)$ for some R-polynomial p. The subalgebra is denoted by $R[\mathcal{A}]$.

Theorem 2.24. An R-fuzzy event over X is context-free if and only if it belongs to a finitely R-polynomially generated subalgebra of $\mathfrak{E}_R X$ which is closed under quotients.

Proof. (1) For the proof of necessity, let A be an R-fuzzy event over X generated by $G = (X,V_N,\alpha_o,P)$ with $V_N = \{\alpha_o,\alpha_1,\dots,\alpha_n\}$.

(i) Construction of a finite subset $\mathcal{A} \subseteq \mathfrak{E}_R X$ so that $A \in R[\mathcal{A}]$.

Without loss of generality, it is assumed that P can be decomposed into $P = P_o + P_1$ such that P_o only contains rewriting rules of the form $\alpha_o \dashrightarrow e$ and $\alpha_o \dashrightarrow \alpha_1$ and $G_1 = (X,V_{1N},\alpha_1,P_1)$ with $V_{1N} = V_N \setminus \{\alpha_o\}$ fulfils the condition $\dashrightarrow\cdot(V_{1N} \cup \{e\}) = \emptyset$. With G_1 we associate a linear operator F_{G_1} on $(\mathfrak{E}_R V)^n$ by setting

$$F_{G_1}(\underline{Z})_i = \sum_{j=1}^{n} A_{ij}\cdot Z_j + A_i' \qquad i = 1,2,\dots,n$$

where

$$A_{ij} = \{v \in V^* \mid \alpha_i \underset{G_1}{\dashrightarrow} v\alpha_j\} \qquad \text{and} \qquad A_i' = \{v \in V^* \mid \alpha_i \underset{G_1}{\dashrightarrow} v\}$$

for arbitrary $\underline{Z} = (Z_1, Z_2, \ldots, Z_n)$ of $(\mathbb{C}_R V)^n$. In matrix form, we get

$$F_{G_1}(\underline{Z}) = \underline{A} \cdot \underline{Z} + \underline{A}'$$

where $\underline{A} = (A_{ij})$ and $\underline{A}' = (A_i')$. The iteration $\underline{A}^*$ of $\underline{A}$ exists because of $A_{ij}(e) = 0$ for $i,j = 1,2,\ldots,n$. Observe that P_1 has not rewriting rules of the form $\alpha_i \longrightarrow \alpha_j$. By construction, the i-the component Z_i^o of the fixed point $\underline{Z}_o = \underline{A}^* \cdot \underline{A}'$ consists of all those words which are derivable from α_i in such a way that only the rightmost symbol is successively substituted in according to rewriting rules. Therefore, it is in general not possible to derive each word of $L(G_1,\alpha_i)$. Thus the non-terminals α_j different from the rightmost one must be replaced by words of $L(G_1,\alpha_j)$:

$$L(G_1,\alpha_i) = Z_i^o[\alpha_j / L(G_1,\alpha_j)].$$

By Theorem 2.7, every component Z_i^o of $\underline{Z}_o$ is a rational R-fuzzy event over V since A_{ij} and A_i' are rational for $i,j = 1,2,\ldots,n$. Hence, by Theorem 2.10, there are n families of finitely many R-fuzzy events $Z_{i0}, Z_{i1}, \ldots, Z_{ik_i}$ over V such that $Z_{i0} = Z_i^o$ and

$$v^{-1} Z_{ij} = \sum_{\varkappa=0}^{k_i} r_\varkappa^{ij}(v) \cdot Z_{i\varkappa} \qquad i = 1,2,\ldots,n, \; j = 0,1,\ldots,k_i \qquad (*)$$

for all v of V^*. Writing Z_{ij}^ν instead of $\alpha_\nu^{-1} Z_{ij}$ and setting $\overline{Z}_{ij} = Z_{ij}[\alpha_\varkappa / L(G_1,\alpha_\varkappa)]$ as well as $\overline{Z}_{ij}^\nu = Z_{ij}^\nu[\alpha_\varkappa / L(G_1,\alpha_\varkappa)]$, we define the finite set $\mathcal{A}$ as follows

$$\mathcal{A} = \{\overline{Z}_{ij} \mid i = 1,2,\ldots,n, \; j = 0,1,\ldots,k_i\} \cup$$
$$\{\overline{Z}_{ij}^\nu \mid i,\nu = 1,2,\ldots,n, \; j = 0,1,\ldots,k_i\} \cup \{e\}$$

Evidently, we have $L(G_1,\alpha_i) \in \mathcal{A}$ for $i = 1,2,\ldots,n$. Thus, $L(G,\alpha_o) \in R[\mathcal{A}]$ because of $L(G,\alpha_o) = (\alpha_o \longrightarrow e) \cdot \{e\} + (\alpha_o \longrightarrow \alpha_1) \cdot L(G_1,\alpha_1)$.

(ii) Statement: $R[\mathcal{A}]$ is closed under quotients.

Since each element A' of $R[\mathcal{A}]$ is obtained by finitely many applications of addition, multiplication or scalar multiplication of elements of $\mathcal{A}$, the quotient $x^{-1}A'$ belongs to $R[\mathcal{A}]$ if the quotients of all generating elements are in $R[\mathcal{A}]$ by Theorem 2.9.

By means of (*), the following representation can be derived

$$Z_{ij} = \sum_{x \in X} x \cdot \Big(\sum_{\varkappa=0}^{k_i} r_\varkappa^{ij}(x) \cdot Z_{i\varkappa} \Big) + \sum_{\nu=1}^{n} \alpha_\nu \cdot Z_{ij}^\nu + Z_{ij}^e$$

with $Z_{ij}^e(e) = Z_{ij}(e)$ and $Z_{ij}^e(v) = 0$ for all $v \neq e$ of V^*. Now, the elements of $\mathcal{A}$ have the following representation:

$$Z_{ij} = \sum_{x\in X} x\cdot(\sum_{\varkappa=0}^{k_i} r_{\varkappa}^{ij}(x)\cdot Z_{i\varkappa}) + \sum_{\nu=1}^{n} L(G_1,\alpha_\nu)\cdot Z_{ij}^{\nu} + z_{ij}^{e}$$

and

$$Z_{ij}^{\nu} = \sum_{\varkappa=0}^{k} r_{\varkappa}^{ij}(\alpha_\nu)\cdot Z_{i\varkappa}$$

for $i,\nu = 1,2,\ldots,n$, $j = 0,1,\ldots,k_i$. Because of the last formula, it suffices to show that $x^{-1}Z_{ij} \in R[\mathcal{A}]$ holds for $i = 1,2,\ldots,n$ and $j = 0, 1,\ldots,k_i$. Since $Z_{\nu o} = L(G_1,\alpha_\nu)$, we have

$$Z_{ij} = \sum_{x\in X} x\cdot((\sum_{\varkappa=0}^{k_i} r_{\varkappa}^{ij}(x)\cdot Z_{i}) + \sum_{\nu=1}^{n} \sum_{\varkappa=0}^{k_i} r_{\varkappa}^{\nu o}(x)\cdot Z_{\nu\varkappa}\cdot Z_{ij}^{\nu}) + z_{ij}^{e}$$

Therefore, the quotients have the following form:

$$x^{-1}Z_{ij} = \sum_{\varkappa=0}^{k_i} r_{\varkappa}^{ij}(x)\cdot Z_{i\varkappa} + \sum_{\nu=1}^{n} \sum_{\varkappa=0}^{k_i} r_{\varkappa}^{\nu o}(x)\cdot Z_{\nu\varkappa}\cdot Z_{ij}^{\nu}$$

for $i = 1,2,\ldots,n$ and $j = 0,1,\ldots,k_i$. Hence all quotients of elements of $\mathcal{A}$ belong to $R[\mathcal{A}]$.

(2) Statement: Let $\mathcal{A}$ be a finite subset of $\mathfrak{C}_R X$. If $R[\mathcal{A}]$ is closed under quotients, then each A of $R[\mathcal{A}]$ is context-free.

Let $\mathcal{A}$ be a finite subset of $\mathfrak{C}_R X$ and let A_o be an arbitrary element of $R[\mathcal{A}]$. Without loss of generality, it is assumed that $\mathcal{A} = \{\{e\},A_o,A_1,\ldots, A_n\}$, whereby $A_o = A_1 + A_o^e$. We have to construct an R-fuzzy grammar $G = (X,V_N,\alpha_o,P)$ with $V_N = \{\alpha_o,\alpha_1,\ldots,\alpha_n\}$ so that $L(G,\alpha_o) = A_o$ holds. In order to determine P, the quotients $x^{-1}A_i$ are represented by R-polynomials $p_{x,i}$ for all x of X and $i = 1,2,\ldots,n$. By assumption, such a representation is possible:

$$x^{-1}A_i = p_{x,i}(A_1,A_2,\ldots,A_n).$$

Suppose that $p_{x,i} = \sum_{v\in V_N^*} r_{x,i}(v)v$. Then we define

$\alpha_o \longrightarrow e = A_o(e)$ $\qquad$ $\alpha_o \longrightarrow \alpha_1 = 1$

$\alpha_i \longrightarrow xv = r_{x,i}(v)$ $\qquad$ for $x \in X$, $v \in V_N^*$ and $i = 1,2,\ldots,n$.

Obviously, G fulfils the general assumption. Thus $\Longrightarrow^*$ exists. It only remains to show that G generates A_o. Consider the R-fuzzy grammar $G_1 = (X,V_{1N},\alpha_1,P_1)$ with $V_{1N} = \{\alpha_1,\alpha_2,\ldots,\alpha_n\}$ and P_1 contains the rewriting rules $\alpha_i \longrightarrow xv = r_{x,i}(v)$ only. The fixed point of F_{G_1} is the vector $\underline{A} = (A_1,A_2,\ldots,A_n)$ because

$$F_{G_1}(\underline{A})_i = \sum_{v\in V^*} (\alpha_i \longrightarrow v)\cdot v[^{\alpha}j/A_j]$$
$$= \sum_{x\in X} \sum_{v\in V_N^*} r_{x,i}(v)(xv)[^{\alpha}j/A_j]$$
$$= \sum_{x\in X} x\cdot(\sum_{v\in V_N^*} r_{x,i}(v)v[^{\alpha}j/A_j])$$
$$= \sum_{x\in X} x\cdot p_{x,i}(\underline{A})$$
$$= \sum_{x\in X} x\cdot x^{-1}A_i = A_i \qquad \text{for } i = 1,2,\ldots,n.$$

By Theorem 2.22, it follows $L(G_1,\alpha_i) = A_i$. Since $A_o = A_1 + A_o^e = L(G_1,\alpha_1) + \{e|A_o(e)\}$, we get $A_o = L(G,\alpha_o)$, which proves Statement (2).

Remark. Using an appropriate Banach space of finite measure, H. W. Pohl [61] exhibited an analogous treatment of context-free stochastic grammars introduced by T. Huang and K. S. Fu [33].

The existence of normal forms for R-fuzzy grammars will briefly be discussed now. An R-fuzzy grammar $G = (X,V_N,\alpha_o,P)$ is said to be in Chomsky normal form if the underlying context-free grammar $|G|$ only has rewriting rules of the type $\alpha \longrightarrow \beta\gamma$ and $\alpha \longrightarrow x$ with $\alpha,\beta,\gamma \in V_N$ and $x \in X$. G is called in Greibach normal form if $|G|$ has rewriting rules of the type $\alpha \longrightarrow xv$ with $\alpha \in V_N$, $x \in X$ and $v \in V^*$ only (cf. [68]). Two R-fuzzy grammars are called equivalent if they generate the same R-fuzzy event. By the general assumption, the rewriting rules of an R-fuzzy grammar $G = (X,V_N,\alpha_o,P)$ are of the type $\alpha \longrightarrow x$ or $\alpha \longrightarrow v$ with $\alpha \in V_N$, $x \in X$ and $v \in V^*$, whereby $|v| \geq 2$. It may easily be seen that there exists an equivalent R-fuzzy grammar in Chomsky normal form. From the proof of Theorem 2.24, it follows that also an equivalent R-fuzzy grammar in Greibach normal form can be constructed whose rewriting rules even have the special form $\alpha \longrightarrow xv$ with $\alpha \in V_N$, $x \in X$ and $v \in V_N^*$. Chomsky and Greibach normal forms are also studied in [39,77].

2.3.2. R-fuzzy pushdown automata

This section deals with generalized models of acceptors for context-free R-fuzzy events and investigates some closure properties of cf-$Gen_R X$.

Definition 2.13. An R-fuzzy pushdown automaton $\mathfrak{K}$ over X is a quintuple

$$\mathfrak{K} = (S,K,s_o,k_o,d),$$

where S and K are disjoint finite sets of internal states and pushdown symbols, respectively, $s_o \in S$ is the start state, $k_o \in K$ is the start pushdown symbol and d is a mapping from $(X \cup \{e\}) \times S \times K$ into $\mathfrak{I}_R^f(S \times K^*)$

satisfying the following conditions

(1) $\{e\} \cup K \nsubseteq \langle s,k\rangle$ for $(s,k) \in S \times (K \setminus \{k_0\})$

(2) $k_0 \notin \langle s,k_0\rangle$ for $s \in S$,

where $\langle s,k\rangle = \{\varkappa \in K^* \mid \exists s'(s' \in S \wedge (s',\varkappa) \in d(e,s,k))\}$. d determines the local transition behaviour of $\mathfrak{R}$.

Remark. The local transition function must be restricted so that the global behaviour of $\mathfrak{R}$ can also be defined in the case R is not a complete po-semiring.

Given an R-fuzzy pushdown automaton $\mathfrak{R} = (S,K,s_0,k_0,d)$ over X, let $\underset{\mathfrak{R}}{|\!\!===}$ be the R-fuzzy relation on $X^* \times S \times K^*$ defined as follows

$$\sigma \underset{\mathfrak{R}}{|\!\!===} \sigma' = \begin{cases} d(x,s,k)(s',\varkappa') & \text{if } \sigma = (xw,s,k\varkappa) \text{ and } \sigma' = (w,s',\varkappa'\varkappa) \\ 0 & \text{otherwise} \end{cases}$$

for $x \in X \cup \{e\}$, $w \in X^*$, $s,s' \in S$ and $\varkappa,\varkappa' \in K^*$. In the sequel, we will shortly write $|\!\!===$ instead of $\underset{\mathfrak{R}}{|\!\!===}$.

Clearly, the set $\{\sigma \in X^* \times S \times K^* \mid \sigma \;|\!\!===\; \sigma' \neq 0\}$ is finite for each situation σ' of $X^* \times S \times K^*$. Therefore, all powers $|\!\!===^n$, $n \geq 1$, exist as the following calculation shows:

$$\sigma \;|\!\!===^{n+1}\; \sigma' = \sum_{\sigma'' \in X^* \times S \times K^*} (\sigma \;|\!\!===\; \sigma'')\cdot(\sigma'' \;|\!\!===^n\; \sigma').$$

By assumption, we have $(X^m \times S \times K^*)\cdot|\!\!===^n\cdot(X^* \times S \times K^{m'}) = \emptyset$ provided $n > 2\cdot m + m'$ for all $n > 1$, $m,m' \geq 0$. Let us consider the case $m' = 0$ at first. The longest sequences $\sigma = \sigma_1,\sigma_2,\ldots,\sigma_n = \sigma'$ of situations appear if $\sigma = (w,s_0,k_0)$ with $w \in X^m$ and $\sigma' = (e,s,e)$ with $s \in S$. Then $n = 2\cdot m - 1$ is possible because the pushdown store may be filled up with m symbols erasable in $|w|$ steps when the input head reads $w \in X^m$. But these m pushdown symbols are generated in at most $m - 1$ steps. The case $m' \neq 0$ only differs from the privous one in such a way that m' pushdown symbols can be generated additionally, that means the length of sequences $\sigma_1,\sigma_2,\ldots,\sigma_n$ is at most $n = 2\cdot m + m' - 1$.

Consequently, the reflexive transitive closure

$$|\!\!===^* = \sum_{n=0}^{\infty} |\!\!===^n$$

exists. By means of $|\!\!===^*$, we define the global behaviour $[\mathfrak{R}]$ of an R-fuzzy pushdown automaton $\mathfrak{R}$ as follows

$$[\mathfrak{R}] = \{w \in X^* \mid \exists s(s \in S \wedge (w,s_0,k_0) \;|\!\!===^*\; (e,s,e))\}$$

<u>Definition 2.14</u>. An R-fuzzy event A over X is said to be pd-recognizable if there exists an R-fuzzy pushdown automaton $\mathfrak{R}$ over X such that $A = [\mathfrak{R}]$. The set of all pd-recognizable R-fuzzy events over X is denoted by pd-$\mathrm{Rec}_R X$.

<u>Theorem 2.25</u> (Analysis of R-fuzzy pushdown automata). The behaviour of an R-fuzzy pushdown automaton over X is a context-free R-fuzzy event over X.

Proof. Let $\mathfrak{R} = (S,K,s_0,k_0,d)$ be an R-fuzzy pushdown automaton over X. By Theorem 2.24, it is sufficient to show that there exists a finite subset $\mathcal{A}$ of $\mathfrak{C}_R X$ such that $[\mathfrak{R}] \in R[\mathcal{A}]$ and, moreover, $R[\mathcal{A}]$ is closed under quotients. First, we define

$$\mathcal{A} = \{k(s,s') \mid k \in K \text{ and } s,s' \in S\},$$

where $k(s,s') = \{w \in X^* \mid (w,s,k) \overset{*}{\Longrightarrow} (e,s',e)\}$. Since $[\mathfrak{R}] = \sum_{s \in S} k_0(s_0,s)$, $[\mathfrak{R}]$ belongs to $R[\mathcal{A}]$.

Next, we are going to prove that $x^{-1}k(s,s') \in R[\mathcal{A}]$ for all $k(s,s') \in \mathcal{A}$. For this purpose, some preparations are necessary. Let $n = \mathrm{card}(S)$. We introduce matrices $(\varkappa) \in (\mathfrak{C}_R X)_n$ whose coefficients are defined by

$$\varkappa(s,s') = \{w \in X^* \mid (w,s,\varkappa) \overset{*}{\Longrightarrow} (e,s,e)\}.$$

The corresponding mapping from K^* into $(\mathfrak{C}_R X)_n$ is a homomorphism since

$$e(s,s') = \begin{cases} \{e\} & \text{if } s = s' \\ 0 & \text{if } s \neq s' \end{cases}, \quad s,s' \in S$$

and, furthermore, for all $\varkappa,\varkappa' \in K^*$ and $s,s' \in S$

$$\begin{aligned} (\varkappa\varkappa')(s,s') &= \{w \in X^* \mid (w,s,\varkappa\varkappa') \overset{*}{\Longrightarrow} (e,s',e)\} \\ &= \{w \in X^* \mid \exists s'' \exists u\, v(s'' \in S \land u,v \in X^* \land w = uv \land \\ &\qquad (u,s,\varkappa) \overset{*}{\Longrightarrow} (e,s\ \ ,e) \land (v,s\ \ ,\varkappa') \overset{*}{\Longrightarrow} (e,s,e))\} \\ &= \sum_{s'' \in S} \varkappa(s,s'') \cdot \varkappa'(s'',s'). \end{aligned}$$

In view of this fact, it is evident that the coefficients $\varkappa(s,s')$ of a matrix $(\varkappa)$ are elements of $R[\mathcal{A}]$ for all $\varkappa \in K^*$. Now, take the quotient

$$\begin{aligned} x^{-1}k(s,s') &= \{w \in X^* \mid (xw,s,k) \overset{*}{\Longrightarrow} (e,s',e)\} \\ &= \{w \in X^* \mid \exists s' \exists \varkappa(s'' \in S \land \varkappa \in K^* \land (s'',\varkappa) \in d(x,s,k) \land \\ &\qquad (w,s'',\varkappa) \overset{*}{\Longrightarrow} (e,s',e))\}. \end{aligned}$$

Then every quotient $x^{-1}k(s,s')$ can be represented as follows

$$x^{-1}k(s,s') = \{w \in X^* \mid (xw,s,k) \models\!=\!=^* (e,s',e)\}$$
$$= \{w \in X^* \mid \exists s'' \exists \varkappa (s'' \in S \wedge \varkappa \in K^* \wedge (s'',\varkappa) \in d(x,s,k) \wedge (w,s'',\varkappa) \models\!=\!=^* (e,s',e))\}$$

Therefore, we get

$$x^{-1}k(s,s') = \sum_{(s'',\varkappa)\in S\times K^*} d(x,s,k)(s,\varkappa)\varkappa(s'',s')$$

yielding the fact that $\varkappa(s'',s') \in R[\mathcal{A}]$ implies $x^{-1}k(s,s') \in R[\mathcal{A}]$ for all $k \in K$ and $s,s' \in S$. Hence $[\mathfrak{R}]$ is context-free.

Theorem 2.26 (Synthesis of R-fuzzy pushdown automata). Any context-free R-fuzzy event is pd-recognizable by an R-fuzzy pushdown automaton with one internal state.

Proof. Let $G = (X,V_N,\alpha_0,P)$ be an R-fuzzy grammar. By the general assumption, P is decomposable into $P = P_0 + P_1$, where P_0 only contains rewriting rules of the type $\alpha_0 \dashrightarrow e$ and $\alpha_0 \dashrightarrow \alpha_1$. Furthermore, the R-fuzzy grammar $G_1 = (X,V_{1N},\alpha_1,P_1)$ with $V_{1N} = V \setminus \{\alpha_0\}$ satisfies the condition $\longrightarrow\cdot(V_1 \cup \{e\}) = \emptyset$. By Theorem 2.23, there exists a finite subset $\mathcal{A}$ of $\mathfrak{C}_R X$ such that $L(G_1,\alpha_1)$ belongs to $R[\mathcal{A}]$, which is closed under quotients. Without loss of generality, it may be supposed that all A of $\mathcal{A}$ are e-free R-fuzzy events.

Define an R-fuzzy pushdown automaton $\mathfrak{R} = (\{s\},K,s,k_0,d)$ by setting

$$K = \mathcal{A} \cup \{k_0,k_1\}$$

with $k_0 = (\alpha_0 \longrightarrow e)\{e\} + (\alpha_0 \dashrightarrow \alpha_1)L(G_1,\alpha_1)$ and $k_1 = L(G_1,\alpha_1)$,

$$d(x,s,k)(s,\varkappa) = (x^{-1}k)(\varkappa) \qquad \text{for } x \in X \cup \{e\},\ k \in K \text{ and } \varkappa \in K^*.$$

By Theorem 2.9, we derive

$$x^{-1}(k\varkappa) = (x^{-1}k)\varkappa + k(e)(x^{-1}\varkappa) = (x^{-1}k)\varkappa$$

for all $k \in K$ and $\varkappa \in K^*$ since $k(e) = 0$. For R-polynomials, it follows

$$x^{-1}\Big(\sum_{\varkappa\in K^*} r(\varkappa)\varkappa\Big) = \sum_{\varkappa\in K^*} r(\varkappa)x^{-1}\varkappa.$$

Now, we prove the following statement by induction

$$(w,s,\varkappa) \models\!=\!=^* (e,s,e) = (w^{-1}\varkappa)(e)$$

for all $w \in X^*$ and $\varkappa \in K^*$. Let $w = e$, then

$$(e,s,e) \;|\!\!===^* (e,s,e) = 1 = (e^{-1}\{e\})(e)$$
$$(e,s,k_o) \;|\!\!===^* (e,s,e) = d(e,s,k_o)(s,e) = k_o(e) = (e^{-1}k_o)(e)$$
$$(e,s,\varkappa) \;|\!\!===^* (e,s,e) = 0 = \varkappa(e) = (e^{-1}\varkappa)(e) \qquad \text{for } \varkappa \neq e,\ \varkappa \neq k_o.$$

Induction step:

$$\begin{aligned}(xw,s,\varkappa) \;|\!\!===^* (e,s,e) &= \sum_{\varkappa' \in K^*} (x^{-1}\varkappa)(\varkappa')((w,s,\varkappa') \;|\!\!===^* (e,s,e)) \\ &= \sum_{\varkappa' \in K^*} (x^{-1}\varkappa)(\varkappa')(w^{-1}\varkappa')(e) \\ &= ((xw)^{-1}\varkappa)(e).\end{aligned}$$

Notice that $x^{-1}\varkappa$ can be represented as R-polynomial since $R[A]$ is closed under quotients:

$$x^{-1}\varkappa = \sum_{\varkappa' \in K^*} (x^{-1}\varkappa)(\varkappa')\varkappa'.$$

Hence

$$w^{-1}(x^{-1}\varkappa) = \sum_{\varkappa' \in K^*} (x^{-1}\varkappa)(\varkappa')(w^{-1}\varkappa').$$

Therefore, we obtain

$$[\mathfrak{R}](w) = (w,s,k_o) \;|\!\!===^* (e,s,e) = (w^{-1}k_o)(e) = k_o(w).$$

Since $k_o = L(G,\alpha_o)$, the assertion $[\mathfrak{R}] = L(G,\alpha_o)$ holds, that means $L(G,\alpha_o)$ is accepted by an R-fuzzy pushdown automaton with one internal state.

Theorem 2.27. The set pd-$Rec_R X$ of all pd-recognizable R-fuzzy events over X equals the set cf-$Gen_R X$ of all context-free R-fuzzy events over X. In particular, the set $Rec_R X$ of all recognizable R-fuzzy events over X is equal to the set r-$Gen_R X$ of all regular R-fuzzy events over X.

Proof. (1) Combining Theorem 2.25 and Theorem 2.26, the equality

$$\text{pd-}Rec_R X = \text{cf-}Gen_R X$$

follows immediately.

(2) Statement: $Rec_R X = \text{r-}Gen_R X$.

(i) Assume that A is a recognizable R-fuzzy event over X. By Theorem 2.10, there are finitely many R-fuzzy events $A_o = A, A_1, \dots, A_n$ such that

$$w^{-1}A_i = \sum_{j=0}^{n} r_{ij}(w) \cdot A_j \qquad i = 0,1,\dots,n$$

for all $w \in X^*$. Define a regular R-fuzzy grammar $G = (X, V_N, \alpha_o, P)$ by

$V_N = \{\alpha_o,\alpha_1,\ldots,\alpha_n\}$ and

$$\alpha_i \longrightarrow e = A_i(e) \qquad \text{for } i = 0,1,\ldots,n$$

$$\alpha_i \longrightarrow x\alpha_j = r_{ij}(x) \qquad \text{for } i,j = 0,1,\ldots,n \text{ and } x \in X.$$

Now, we show that $\underline{A} = (A_o,A_1,\ldots,A_n)$ is fixed point of the associated operator F_G:

$$F_G(\underline{A})_i = \sum_{x\in X}\sum_{j=0}^{n} (\alpha_i \longrightarrow x\alpha_j)\cdot(x\alpha_j)[^{\alpha}k/A_k] + (\alpha_i \longrightarrow e)\cdot\{e\}$$

$$= \sum_{x\in X}\sum_{j=0}^{n} r_{ij}(x)\cdot A_j + A_i(e)\{e\}$$

$$= \sum_{x\in X} x\cdot x^{-1}A_i + A_i(e)\{e\} = A_i \qquad \text{for } i = 0,1,\ldots,n.$$

Thus, by Theorem 2.22, $A = L(G,\alpha_o)$, which implies $\mathrm{Rec}_R X \subseteq \text{r-Gen}_R X$.

(ii) Let $G = (X,V_N,\alpha_o,P)$ be a regular R-fuzzy grammar with $V_N = \{\alpha_o,\alpha_1,\ldots,\alpha_n\}$. Since the associated operator F_G is linear, all components $L(G,\alpha_i)$, $i = 0,1,\ldots,n$, of the fixed point are rational R-fuzzy events provided the coefficients A_{ij} and $A_i^!$ of the corresponding system of equations

$$Z_i = \sum_{j=0}^{n} A_{ij} + A_i^! \qquad i = 0,1,\ldots,n$$

are rational R-fuzzy events by Theorem 2.7. But, in fact

$$A_{ij} = \{w \in X^* \mid \alpha_i \longrightarrow w\alpha_j\}$$

$$A_i^! = \{w \in X^* \mid \alpha_i \longrightarrow w\}$$

are rational. By Theorem 2.17, $L(G,\alpha_o)$ is recognizable and, thus, $\text{r-Gen}_R X \subseteq \mathrm{Rec}_R X$.

Remark. In literature, other conditions of acception are also studied (cf. [24,47,68]). By selecting final states, a word w is accepted by a pushdown automaton if it enters a final state after reading w independent of the content of the pushdown store. Let $\mathfrak{R} = (S,K,s_o,k_o,d)$ be an R-fuzzy pushdown automaton and let $S_f \in \mathfrak{I}_R S$ be a fuzzy set of final states. Then

$$\mathfrak{R}(S_f) = \{w \in X^* \mid \exists s \exists \varkappa (s \in S_f \wedge \varkappa \in K^* \wedge (w,s_o,k_o) \mid\!\!=\!=\!=^* (e,s,\varkappa))\}$$

denotes the accepted R-fuzzy event. The proof of equivalence of both conditions of accepting in the usual case (cf. [47]) can be generalized in a straightforward way.

Theorem 2.28. Let $\mathfrak{R}$ be an R-fuzzy pushdown automaton. Then there exists another R-fuzzy pushdown automaton $\mathfrak{R}'$ with an R-fuzzy set S_f' of final states such that $[\mathfrak{R}] = \mathfrak{R}'(S_f')$ and vice versa.

Proof. (1) Let $\mathfrak{R} = (S,K,s_0,k_0,d)$ be an R-fuzzy pushdown automaton over X. A new R-fuzzy pushdown automaton $\mathfrak{R}' = (S',K',s_0',k_0',d')$ over X is constructed by setting

$$S' = S \cup \{s_f\}, \qquad \text{where } s_f \notin S$$
$$K' = K \cup \{k_0',k'\}, \qquad \text{where } k_0',k' \notin K$$

and

$$d'(x,s,k) = \begin{cases} \{(s_0,k_0k')\} & \text{if } x = e,\ s = s_0\ \ k = k_0' \\ \{(s_f,k')\} & \text{if } x = e,\ s \in S,\ \ k = k' \\ d(x,s,k) & \text{if } (x,s,k) \in (X \cup \{e\}) \times S \times K. \end{cases}$$

Obviously, for all $w \in X^*$:

$$(w,s_0,k_0') \mathrel{\underset{\mathfrak{R}'}{|\!\!=\!=\!=^*}} (e,s_f,k') = (w,s_0,k_0) \mathrel{\underset{\mathfrak{R}}{|\!\!=\!=\!=^*}} (e,s_f,e).$$

Therefore, we get $\mathfrak{R}'(\{s_f\}) = [\mathfrak{R}]$.

(2) Let $\mathfrak{R}' = (S,K,s_0,k_0,d')$ be an R-fuzzy pushdown automaton over X and let $S_f' \in \mathfrak{I}_R S$. It can easily be shown that the R-fuzzy pushdown automaton $\mathfrak{R}$ defined as follows satisfies $[\mathfrak{R}] = \mathfrak{R}'(S_f')$:

$$\mathfrak{R} = (S \cup \{s_e\},K,s_0,k_0,d),$$

where $s_e \notin S$ and for $(x,s,k) \in (X \cup \{e\}) \times S \times K^*$

$$d(x,s,k) = \begin{cases} d'(x,s,k) & \text{if } d'(x,s,k) \cap (S_f' \times K^*) = \emptyset \\ d'(x,s,k) + \{(s_e,e)\} & \text{otherwise} \end{cases}$$

and for $k \in K$

$$d(e,s_e,k) = \{(s_e,e)\}.$$

Remark. In order to study closure properties of cf-$Gen_R X$, an acceptor model proposed by A. A. Letičevskiĭ [44] is very suitable. It is based on the fact that internal states of pushdown automata are not necessary and, furthermore, the manipulation on pushdown stores can be described in analogy to sequential machines.

Definition 2.15. An R-fuzzy acceptor $\mathcal{P}$ over X is a triple $\mathcal{P} = (P, p_o, d)$ consisting of a finite set P of pushdown symbols, an initial pushdown symbol p_o and a mapping $d\colon X \times P \to \mathfrak{T}_R^f(P^*)$ which describes the local transition behaviour.

We define a mapping $\delta\colon X \to \mathrm{Rel}_R P^*$ by

$$\delta(x)(\pi_1, \pi_2) = \begin{cases} d(x,p)(\pi') & \text{if there exists } p \in P \text{ and } \pi \in P^* \\ & \text{such that } \pi_1 = p\pi \text{ and } \pi_2 = \pi'\pi \\ 0 & \text{otherwise} \end{cases}$$

for all $x \in X$ and $\pi_1, \pi_2 \in P^*$. δ admits a unique extension $\delta^*\colon X^* \to \mathrm{Rel}_R P^*$ which is a homomorphism:

$$\delta^*(e) = \mathrm{id}_{P^*}$$

$$\delta^*(ww') = \delta^*(w) \cdot \delta^*(w') \qquad \text{for } w, w' \in X^*.$$

Observe that the product $\delta^*(w) \cdot \delta^*(w')$ is well defined although P^* is an infinite set. But, for a given $\pi \in P^*$, the condition $\delta^*(w)(\pi, \pi') \neq 0$ is only fulfilled for finitely many $\pi' \in P^*$. The global behaviour of an R-fuzzy acceptor $\mathcal{P} = (P, p_o, d)$ over X is the following R-fuzzy event

$$[\mathcal{P}] = \{w \in X^* \mid (p_o, e) \in \delta^*(w)\}.$$

Theorem 2.29. The global behaviour of an R-fuzzy acceptor is an e-free and context-free R-fuzzy event and vice versa.

Proof. (1) Let $\mathcal{P} = (P, p_o, d)$ be an R-fuzzy acceptor over X. By Theorem 2.24, it sufficies to show that there exists a finite subset $\mathcal{A}$ of $\mathfrak{E}_R X$ such that $[\mathcal{P}]$ belongs to $R[\mathcal{A}]$ and $R[\mathcal{A}]$ is closed under quotients.

Define $\mathcal{A} = \{\langle p \rangle \mid p \in P\}$, where $\langle \pi \rangle = \{w \in X^* \mid (\pi, e) \in \delta^*(w)\}$ for all $\pi \in P^*$. Clearly, $[\mathcal{P}] = \langle k_o \rangle$. Thus it remains to prove that $R[\mathcal{A}]$ is closed under quotients. By induction over the length of w, we verify the following statement:

$$\delta^*(w)(\pi\pi', \pi'') = \sum_{\substack{u,v \in X^* \\ w=uv,\, u \neq e}} \sum_{\substack{\pi_1, \pi_2 \in P^* \\ \pi'' = \pi_1\pi_2}} \delta^*(u)(\pi, \pi_1) \cdot \delta^*(v)(\pi', \pi_2)$$

for each $w \neq e$ of X^* and each $\pi \neq e, \pi', \pi'' \in P^*$. Evidently, the basis step is valid:

$$\delta^*(x)(\pi\pi', \pi'') = \delta^*(x)(\pi, \pi_1) \qquad \text{with } \pi'' = \pi_1\pi'.$$

Induction step:

$$\delta^*(xw)(\pi\pi', \pi'') = \sum_{\pi_1 \in P^*} \delta^*(x)(\pi\pi', \pi_1) \cdot \delta^*(w)(\pi_1, \pi'').$$

Considering the factor $\delta^*(x)(\pi\pi',\pi_1)$, we see that at least an element $\bar{\pi}$ of P^* with $\pi_1 = \bar{\pi}\pi'$ must exist . Otherwise, $\delta^*(x)(\pi\pi',\pi_1)$ equals zero. Therefore, we have

$$\begin{aligned}\delta^*(xw)(\pi\pi',\pi'') &= \sum_{\bar{\pi}\in P^*} \delta^*(x)(\pi,\bar{\pi})\cdot\delta^*(w)(\bar{\pi}\pi',\pi'') \\ &= \sum_{\substack{\bar{\pi}\in P^* \\ \bar{\pi}\neq e}} \delta^*(x)(\pi,\bar{\pi})\cdot\Big(\sum_{\substack{w=uv \\ u\neq e}} \sum_{\pi''=\pi_1\pi_2} \delta^*(u)(\bar{\pi},\pi_1)\cdot\delta^*(v)(\pi',\pi_2)\Big) \\ &\quad + \delta^*(x)(\pi,e)\cdot\delta^*(w)(\pi',\pi'') \\ &= \sum_{\substack{u,v\in X^* \\ xw=uv,\,u\neq e}} \sum_{\substack{\pi_1,\pi_2\in P^* \\ \pi''=\pi_1\pi_2}} \delta^*(u)(\pi,\pi_1)\cdot\delta^*(v)(\pi',\pi_2).\end{aligned}$$

The statement proved now implies that the mapping from P^* into $\mathfrak{C}_R X$ assigning $\langle\pi\rangle$ to π is a homomorphism. Consequently, any $\langle\pi\rangle$ belongs to $R[\mathcal{A}]$. Since

$$\begin{aligned}x^{-1}\langle p\rangle &= \{w \in X^* \mid (p,e) \in \delta^*(xw)\} \\ &= \{w \in X^* \mid \exists\pi(\pi \in P^* \wedge (p,\pi) \in \delta^*(x) \wedge (\pi,e) \in \delta^*(w))\} \\ &= \sum_{\pi\in P^*} d(x,p)(\pi)\langle\pi\rangle\end{aligned}$$

for all $x \in X$ and $p \in P$, the quotients $x^{-1}\langle p\rangle$ are elements of $R[\mathcal{A}]$, [illegible] means $R[\mathcal{A}]$ is closed under quotients.

(2) Let A be an e-free context-free R-fuzzy event over X. By Theorem 2.25, there exists an R-fuzzy pushdown automaton $\mathfrak{K} = (\{s\},K,s,k_0,d)$ over X such that $A = [\mathfrak{K}]$. With the data of $\mathfrak{K}$, an R-fuzzy acceptor $\mathfrak{P} = (K,k_0,d_{\mathfrak{P}})$ can be defined by setting

$$d_{\mathfrak{P}}(x,k)(\varkappa) = (x,s,k) \models\!\!= (e,s,\varkappa)$$

for $x \in X$, $k \in K$ and $\varkappa \in K^*$. The extended transition function fulfils the following condition

$$\delta^*_{\mathfrak{P}}(w)(\varkappa,\varkappa') = (w,s,\varkappa) \models\!\!=^* (e,s,\varkappa') \qquad (*)$$

for $w \in X^*$ and $\varkappa,\varkappa' \in K^*$. We are going to prove (*) by induction over the length of w. Since A is e-free, it can be assumed that $d(e,s,k) = \emptyset$ for all k of K. Thus

$$\delta^*_{\mathfrak{P}}(e)(\varkappa,\varkappa') = id_{K^*}(\varkappa,\varkappa') = (e,s,\varkappa) \models\!\!=^* (e,s,\varkappa').$$

Induction step:

$$\delta^*_{\mathfrak{P}}(wx)(\varkappa,\varkappa') = \sum_{\varkappa''\in K^*} \delta^*(w)(\varkappa,\varkappa'')\cdot\delta^*(x)(\varkappa'',\varkappa')$$

Therefore, we have

$$\delta^*(wx)(\varkappa,\varkappa') = \sum_{\varkappa''\in K^*} ((w,s,\varkappa) \mid\!\!\equiv\!\equiv^* (e,s,\varkappa''))\cdot((x,s,\varkappa'') \mid\!\!\equiv\!\equiv (e,s,\varkappa'))$$
$$= (wx,s,\varkappa) \mid\!\!\equiv\!\equiv^* (e,s,\varkappa').$$

In view of (*), it follows $[\mathcal{P}] = [\mathcal{R}]$. Hence A is accepted by $\mathcal{P}$.

At the end of this section, closure properties of cf-$Gen_R X$ will be investigated. For special po-semirings, closure properties are also studied by H. H. Kim [39].

Theorem 2.30. The set of all context-free R-fuzzy events over X is closed under the rational operations.

Proof. Let $A,A' \in$ cf-$Gen_R X$. By Theorem 2.24, there are two finite subsets $\mathcal{A}$ and $\mathcal{A}'$ of $\mathfrak{E}_R X$ satisfying $A \in R[\mathcal{A}]$ as well as $A' \in R[\mathcal{A}']$ and both subalgebras $R[\mathcal{A}]$ and $R[\mathcal{A}']$ are closed under quotients.

(1) Let r be an arbitrary element of R. Then $rA \in R[\mathcal{A}]$ since $R[\mathcal{A}]$ is a subalgebra. Thus, by Theorem 2.24 again, rA is context-free.

(2) Evidently, $A + A' \in R[\mathcal{A} \cup \mathcal{A}']$. It only remains to show that $R[\mathcal{A} \cup \mathcal{A}']$ is closed under quotients. But this follows from

$$R[\mathcal{A}] \cup R[\mathcal{A}'] = R[\mathcal{A} \cup \mathcal{A}']$$

immediately. Thus $A + A' \in$ cf-$Gen_R X$.

(3) Since $A\cdot A' \in R[\mathcal{A} \cup \mathcal{A}']$, from (2) follows $A\cdot A' \in$ cf-$Gen_R X$.

(4) Assume that A is e-free. Then A^* exists and belongs to $R[\mathcal{A} \cup \{A^*\}]$. By Theorem 2.9 (6), we have

$$x^{-1}A^* = (x^{-1}A)\cdot A^* \qquad \text{provided } A(e) = 0.$$

Since $x^{-1}A \in R[\mathcal{A}]$, we conclude $x^{-1}A^* \in R[\mathcal{A} \cup \{A^*\}]$. Thus, by Theorem 2.24, A^* is context-free, i.e. $A^* \in$ cf-$Gen_R X$.

Theorem 2.31. If R is a commutative po-semiring, then cf-$Gen_R X$ is closed under bold intersection with rational R-fuzzy events.

Proof. Let $A \in$ cf-$Gen_R X$ and let $A' \in Rat_R X$. Then there exists an R-fuzzy grammar $G = (X,V_N,\alpha_0,P)$ with $V_N = \{\alpha_0,\alpha_1,\ldots,\alpha_n\}$ such that $A = L(G,\alpha_0)$. By the general assumption, P can be decomposed into $P = P_0 + P_1$ such that $A = (\alpha_0 \longrightarrow e)\{e\} + (\alpha_0 \longrightarrow \alpha_1)L(G_1,\alpha_1)$ and $G_1 = (X,V_{1N},\alpha_1,P_1)$ with $V_{1N} = V \setminus \{\alpha_0\}$ fulfils the premise of Theorem 2.20. Without loss of generality, we suppose that G_1 is in Chomsky normal form. Moreover, A' is recognizable. In particular, there is a normalized R-fuzzy automaton $\mathcal{A} = (S, s_o, s_f, d)$ satisfying $A' \cap (X^* \setminus \{e\}) = [\mathcal{A}]$ by Theorem 2.13. Now, we are in a position to construct an R-fuzzy grammar $\overline{G} = (X, \overline{V}_N, \overline{\alpha}_o, \overline{P})$ generating $A \cap A'$. Put $\overline{V}_N = S \times V \times S$, $\overline{\alpha}_o = (s_o, \alpha_o, s_f)$ and define

$$(s_o,\alpha_o,s_f) \longrightarrow e = (\alpha_o \longrightarrow e)\cdot A'(e)$$

$$(s_o,\alpha_o,s_f) \longrightarrow (s_o,\alpha_1,s_f) = \alpha_o \longrightarrow \alpha_1$$

$$(s,\alpha_i,s') \longrightarrow x = (\alpha \longrightarrow x)\cdot d(x)(s,s')$$

$$(s,\alpha_i,s') \longrightarrow (s,\alpha_j,s\ )(s\ ,\alpha_k,s') = \alpha_i \longrightarrow \alpha_j\alpha_k$$

for $x \in X$, $s,s',s'' \in S$ and $i,j,k = 1,2,\ldots,n$. If R is commutative, then

$$(s_o,\alpha_1,s_f) \longrightarrow w = (\alpha_1 \longrightarrow w)\cdot d^{\#}(w)(s_o,s_f).$$

Hence $L(\overline{G},(s_o,\alpha_1,s_f)) = L(G_1,\alpha_1) \cap A'$. Because of $L(\overline{G},\overline{\alpha}_o)(e) = A(e)\cdot A'(e)$, we get $L(\overline{G},\overline{\alpha}_o) = A \cap A'$, i.e. $A \cap A' \in$ cf-Gen$_R X$.

3. CLOSURE PROPERTIES AND ACCEPTANCE POWER

In Section 3.1 the theory of abstract families of languages developed by S. Ginsburg et al. (cf. [24]) shall be generalized for families of R-fuzzy events. At first the basic operations between languages have to be defined for R-fuzzy events. After that closure properties can be studied in an axiomatic manner. For this reason the basic concept is that of an R-fuzzy trio which is a family of R-fuzzy events closed under three (elementary) operations.

Section 3.2 deals with R-fuzzy languages which are ordinary languages defined by R-fuzzy events with respect to cut-points. For instance, stochastic languages are $\mathbb{R}_+$-fuzzy languages (cf. [80]). It is known [82] that the family $\mathcal{L}_{stoch}$ of all stochastic languages is not closed under homomorphism. Therefore, $\mathcal{L}_{stoch}$ does not form a trio in the sense of S. Ginsburg [24]. Consequently, closure properties of $\mathcal{L}_{stoch}$ cannot be investigated within the formalism of abstract families of languages. In order to avoid this difficulty a more general notion will be proposed. A family $\mathcal{L}$ of languages is said to be semitrio if it contains all rational (regular) languages and is closed under inverse gsm mapping, intersection and union with rational languages. It will be shown that any semitrio is a family of R-fuzzy languages for some po-semiring R with a top element and vice versa. Since every trio is a semitrio (cf. [24]), new families of acceptors for trios can be obtained. These families are essentially determined by the underlying po-semiring. Thus, families of languages may be algebraically characterized in a way analogous to that by syntactic monoids.

Section 3.3 is devoted to the acceptance power of R-fuzzy automata for different po-semirings R. We shall say that two po-semirings R and R' are equivalent if the related families $\mathcal{L}_R$ of R-fuzzy languages and $\mathcal{L}_{R'}$ of R'-fuzzy languages are equal. In this context the following problems arise:

(1) How can equivalent po-semirings be classified?

(2) Is the index of the equivalence relation infinite?

Concerning problem (1) an interesting task is the characterization of all po-semirings which are equivalent to the Boolean semiring $\underline{2} = \{0,1\}$. If R is equivalent to $\underline{2}$, then each R-fuzzy language is rational. For instance, every $\mathbb{N}$-fuzzy language is rational. Some necessary finiteness conditions for po-semirings R are established so that R is equivalent to $\underline{2}$. It is an open problem whether these conditions are even sufficient.

We mainly focus our attention on problem (2). It will be shown that the equivalence relation has an infinite index by exhibiting an infinite hierarchy of special R-fuzzy languages. In [87] it has been demonstrated that the family $\mathcal{L}_{rat}$ of all rational languages is properly included in $\mathcal{L}_R$ if the multiplicative monoid (R,·) of R contains a non-trivial subgroup. For example, the po-semiring $\mathbb{Q}_+$ of all positive rational numbers has such a non-trivial subgroup. Thus, $\mathcal{L}_{rat}$ is properly included in the family of all $\mathbb{Q}_+$-fuzzy languages which equals the family of all rational stochastic languages. This known fact is the starting point for the above mentioned hierarchy of so-called n-rational languages. A language L is said to be n-rational if L is a $\mathbb{Q}_+^n$-fuzzy language, where $\mathbb{Q}_+^n$ is the n-times direct product of $\mathbb{Q}_+$.

It shall be remarked that this approach is regarded as a first attempt at characterizing the degree of non-rationality, or say non-regularity, of a family $\mathcal{L}_R$ in dependence on the algebraic structure of R, where the degree of non-rationality could be defined as the depth of $\mathcal{L}_R$ in an appropriate hierarchy beginning with $\mathcal{L}_{rat}$.

3.1. Families of R-fuzzy events

In analogy to [24] closure properties of families of R-fuzzy events are derived axiomatically.

Definition 3.1. Let R be a po-semiring and let $\mathfrak{X}$ be an infinite set. A non-empty set $\mathfrak{E}$ is called a family of R-fuzzy events (over $\mathfrak{X}$) if, for each A of $\mathfrak{E}$, there is a finite subset X of $\mathfrak{X}$ such that $A \in \mathfrak{E}_R X$.

Examples. 1) Consider

$$\mathfrak{E}_{rat} = \{A \mid A \in \mathrm{Rat}_R X \text{ for some finite subset } X \text{ of } \mathfrak{X}\}$$

which is called family of rational R-fuzzy events.

2) Consider

$$\mathfrak{E}_{cf} = \{A \mid A \in \text{cf-Gen}_R X \text{ for some finite subset } X \text{ of } \mathfrak{X}\}$$

which is called family of context-free R-fuzzy events.

A family $\mathfrak{E}$ of R-fuzzy events is said to be closed under an n-ary operation f provided f is a mapping from $\mathfrak{E} \times \mathfrak{E} \times \dots \times \mathfrak{E}$ (n-times) into $\mathfrak{E}$. Besides the rational operations, some others shall be introduced now.

Let $A \in \mathfrak{C}_R X$ and let $h: X^* \to Y^*$ be a homomorphism, where X and Y are finite sets. The homomorphic image h(A) of A under f is the following R-fuzzy event over Y:

$$h(A) = \{v \in Y^* | \exists u(u \in A \wedge v = h(u))\}.$$

In accordance with the fuzzy interpretation of W-formulas (see Section 1.2), we obtain

$$h(A)(v) = \sum_{\substack{u \in X^* \\ v=h(u)}} A(u) \qquad \text{for all } v \in Y^*.$$

Obviously, h(A) exists unless the summation is well defined. Since R is not complete in general, an appropriate restriction on h has to be stated. If e.g. h is e-free, that is $h^{-1}(e) = \{e\}$, then $h^{-1}(v)$ is a finite subset of X^* for all $v \in Y^*$. In this case, h(A) is well defined.

Now, assume that h is a homomorphism from Y^* into X^*. The inverse homomorphic image $h^{-1}(A)$ of A under f is the following R-fuzzy event over Y:

$$h^{-1}(A) = \{v \in Y^* | h(v) \in A\}$$

which yields

$$h^{-1}(A)(v) = A(h(v)) \qquad \text{for all } v \in Y^*.$$

Besides homomorphisms the mappings determined by generalized sequential machines play an important rule. A generalized sequential machine $\mathfrak{M}$ (cf. [24]) is a 6-tuple $\mathfrak{M} = (X,Y,Z,z_0,\delta,\lambda)$ consisting of finite sets X of inputs, Y of outputs and Z of states, $z_0 \in Z$ (the starting state), and mappings $\delta: Z \times X \to Z$ and $\lambda: Z \times X \to Y^*$ (transition and output function, respectively). The mappings δ and λ are extended to $Z \times X^*$ by $\delta(z,e) = z$, $\delta(z,wx) = \delta(\delta(z,w),x)$, $\lambda(z,e) = e$, and $\lambda(z,wx) = \lambda(z,w)\lambda(\delta(z,w),x)$ for for all $z \in Z$, $x \in X$ and $w \in X^*$. $\mathfrak{M}$ is called e-free if $\lambda(z,x) \neq e$ for all $z \in Z$ and $x \in X$. For any generalized sequential machine $\mathfrak{M} = (X,Y,Z,z_0,\delta,\lambda)$, the mapping M from X^* into Y^* defined by $M(w) = \lambda(z_0,w)$ for each w of X^* is called a gsm mapping. The inverse of a gsm mapping is called an inverse gsm mapping. Clearly, any homomorphism is a gsm mapping. But, on the other hand, the image M(A) of each $A \in \mathfrak{C}_R X$ under a gsm mapping, if it exists, as well as the inverse image $M^{-1}(A)$ can be represented by means of suitable homomorphisms.

<u>Theorem 3.1</u>. Let $\mathfrak{M} = (X,Y,Z,z_0,\delta,\lambda)$ be a generalized sequential machine. Then there exist a rational R-fuzzy event D over a certain alphabet V and two homomorphisms $h_1: V^* \to Y^*$ and $h_2: V^* \to X^*$ such that

(1) $M(A) = h_1(h_2^{-1}(A) \cap D)$ for $A \in \mathfrak{E}_R X$ provided $\mathfrak{M}$ is e-free.

(2) $M^{-1}(A) = h_1(h_2^{-1}(A) \cap D)$ for $A \in \mathfrak{E}_R Y$.

Proof. The alphabet V is given by

$$V = \{(z,x,\lambda(z,x),z') \mid z,z' \in Z \text{ and } x \in X\}.$$

The two homomorphisms h_1 and h_2 are defined in such a way that an arbitrary element $(z,x,\lambda(z,x),z')$ of V is mapped into $\lambda(z,x)$ and x, respectively. By means of the rational R-fuzzy event D, the behaviour of $\mathfrak{M}$ will be simulated. It turns out that it sufficies to choose a (crisp) subset D of V^*:

$$D = \bigcup_{n=0}^{\infty} D_n \qquad \text{with } D_n = V^n \text{ for } n \geq 0,$$

where D_n contains all those words of V^* which are generated by $\mathfrak{M}$ in n steps, that is $D_o = \{e\}$ and for $n \geq 1$:

$$D_n = \{(z_o,x_1,\lambda(z_o,x_1),z_1)(z_1,x_2,\lambda(z_1,x_2),z_2)\ldots (z_{n-1},x_n,\lambda(z_{n-1},x_n),z_n) \mid z_i = \delta(z_{i-1},x_i) \text{ for } i = 1,2,\ldots,n\}.$$

D is a rational (regular) subset of V^* (see Lemma 3.2.1 [24]) and can, thus, be considered as a rational R-fuzzy event over V.

Statement (1) will be proved as follows. Assume that $\mathfrak{M}$ is e-free. Then h_1 is an e-free homomorphism. Successively, we get

$$\begin{aligned}(h_1(h_2^{-1}(A) \cap D))(v) &= \sum_{u \in h_1^{-1}(v)} (h_2^{-1}(A) \cap D)(u) \\ &= \sum_{u \in h_1^{-1}(v)} A(h_2(u)) \cdot D(u) \\ &= \sum_{u \in (h_1^{-1}(v) \cap D)} A(h_2(u)) \\ &= \sum_{w \in M^{-1}(v)} A(w) \\ &= M(A)(v) \qquad \text{for all } v \in Y^*.\end{aligned}$$

Therefore, $M(A) = h_1(h_2^{-1}(A) \cap D)$.

(2) may be proved analogously.

<u>Definition 3.2.</u> A family of R-fuzzy events is said to be R-fuzzy trio if it is closed under e-free homomorphism, inverse homomorphism and bold intersection with rational R-fuzzy events.

Theorem 3.2. The family $\mathfrak{E}_{rat}$ of all rational R-fuzzy events forms an R-fuzzy trio provided R is a commutative po-semiring.

Proof. Let A be a rational R-fuzzy event over X. Then, by Theorem 2.17, there exists an R-fuzzy automaton $\mathcal{A} = (S,S_o,S_f,d)$ over X recognizing A.

(1) Suppose that $h: X^* \to Y^*$ is an e-free homomorphism. Now, construct an R-fuzzy automaton $\mathcal{A}' = (S',S_o,S_f,d')$ over Y so that $[\mathcal{A}'] = h(A)$. In analogy to a procedure presented by S. Eilenberg [17], S' is obtained by an extension of S as follows. For an arbitrary element x of X, let $h(x) = y_1y_2\dots y_n$. Then, for $n > 1$, $S_x = \{\overline{x}_2,\overline{x}_3,\dots,\overline{x}_n\}$ is a set of $n - 1$ new distinct states adjoint to S. If $n = 1$, put $S_x = \emptyset$. Hence

$$S' = \bigcup_{x\in X} S_x \cup S.$$

The definition of $d': X \times S \to \mathfrak{T}_R S$ is given in two steps. First assume that there is an element x of X such that $h(x) = y$ with $y \in Y$, then

$$d'(y,s_1)(s_2) = \begin{cases} \sum\limits_{\substack{u\in X^* \\ h(u)=y}} d(u,s_1)(s_2) & \text{if } s_1,s_2 \in S \\ 0 & \text{otherwise.} \end{cases}$$

Second assume that $h(x) = y_1y_2\dots y_n$ with $n > 1$, then

$$d'(y_i,s_1)(s_2) = \begin{cases} 1, & \text{if } s_1 = \overline{x}_i,\ s_2 = \overline{x}_{i+1} \text{ (where } \overline{x}_1 \text{ is an arbitrary state of S)} \\ 0 & \text{otherwise} \end{cases}$$

for $i = 1,2,\dots,n - 1$, and

$$d'(y_n,s_1)(s_2) = \begin{cases} \sum\limits_{\substack{u\in X^* \\ h(u)=y_1y_2\dots y_n}} d(u,\overline{x}_1)(s_2) & \text{if } s_1 = \overline{x}_n,\ s_2 \in S \\ 0 & \text{otherwise.} \end{cases}$$

It is manifest that

$$[\mathcal{A}'](v) = \sum_{u\in h^{-1}(v)} [\mathcal{A}](u) = h(A)(v)$$

for all $v \in Y^*$. Hence h(A) is recognizable and, consequently, rational.

(2) Let $h: Y^* \to X^*$ be a homomorphism. It can easily be seen that the R-fuzzy automaton $\mathcal{A}' = (S,S_o,S_f,d')$ with $d'(y,s)(s') = d(h(y),s)(s')$ for $y \in Y$ and $s,s' \in S$ recognizes the inverse homomorphic image $h^{-1}(A)$ since

$$[\mathfrak{A}'](v) = [\mathfrak{A}](h(v)) \qquad \text{for all } v \in Y^*.$$

Therefore, $h^{-1}(A)$ is a rational R-fuzzy event by Theorem 2.17.

(3) By Theorem 2.15, $\mathfrak{E}_{rat}$ is closed under bold intersection with rational R-fuzzy events.

Theorem 3.3. The family $\mathfrak{E}_{cf}$ of all context-free R-fuzzy events forms an R-fuzzy trio provided R is a commutative po-semiring.

Proof. Without loss of generality, it is assumed that A is an e-free and context-free R-fuzzy event over X. Then, by Theorem 2.29, there is an R-fuzzy acceptor $\mathfrak{P} = (P, p_o, d)$ over X satisfying $A = [\mathfrak{P}]$.

(1) Let $h: X^* \to Y^*$ be an e-free homomorphism. In analogy to the proof of Theorem 3.2 (1), an R-fuzzy acceptor $\mathfrak{P}' = (P', p_o, d')$ over Y is constructed by setting

$$P' = \bigcup_{x \in X} P_x \cup P,$$

where $P_x = \{\bar{x}_2, \bar{x}_3, \ldots, \bar{x}_n\}$ if $h(x) = y_1 y_2 \ldots y_n$ for $n > 1$ and $P_x = \emptyset$ for $n = 1$. The definition of d' is also divided in two cases. First suppose that there is an element x of X with $h(x) = y$, then

$$d'(y,p)(\pi) = \begin{cases} \sum\limits_{\substack{u \in X^* \\ h(u)=y}} d(u,p)(\pi) & \text{if } p \in P,\ \pi \in P^* \\ 0 & \text{otherwise.} \end{cases}$$

In the second case, we assume that $h(x) = y_1 y_2 \ldots y_n$ with $n > 1$, then

$$d'(y_i,p)(\pi) = \begin{cases} 1 & \text{if } p = \bar{x}_i,\ \pi = \bar{x}_{i+1} \text{ (where } \bar{x}_1 \text{ is an arbitrary element of P)} \\ 0 & \text{otherwise} \end{cases}$$

for $i = 1,2,\ldots,n-1$ and

$$d'(y_n,p)(\pi) = \begin{cases} \sum\limits_{\substack{u \in X^* \\ h(u)=y_1 y_2 \ldots y_n}} d(u,p)(\pi) & \text{if } p = \bar{x}_n,\ \pi \in P^* \\ 0 & \text{otherwise.} \end{cases}$$

Thus, we have

$$[\mathfrak{P}'](v) = \delta^*_{\mathfrak{P}'}(v)(p_o,e) = \sum_{u \in h^{-1}(v)} \delta^*_{\mathfrak{P}}(u)(p_o,e) = \sum_{u \in h^{-1}(v)} [\mathfrak{P}](u)$$

for all $v \in Y^*$, which implies that h(A) is accepted by $\mathfrak{P}'$. Hence h(A) is a context-free R-fuzzy event by Theorem 2.29.

(2) Let $h: Y^* \to X^*$ be a homomorphism. The R-fuzzy acceptor $\mathfrak{P}' = (P,p_0,d')$ over Y with $d'(y,p)(\pi) = d(h(y),p)(\pi)$ for $y \in Y$, $p \in P$ and $\pi \in P^*$ accepts $h^{-1}(A)$. Therefore, $\mathfrak{E}_{cf}$ is closed under inverse homomorphism.

(3) From Theorem 2.31 follows that $\mathfrak{E}_{cf}$ is closed under bold intersection with rational R-fuzzy events.

Some properties of trios (cf. [24]) can be generalized in a straightforward way for R-fuzzy trios.

Theorem 3.4. Let $\mathfrak{E}$ be an R-fuzzy trio containing an R-fuzzy event A with $A(e) = 1$. Then $\mathfrak{E}$ includes $\mathfrak{E}_{rat}$.

Proof. Let $\mathfrak{E}$ be an R-fuzzy trio. Since $\{e\}$ is a rational R-fuzzy event, the bold intersection $A \cap \{e\} = \{e\}$ belongs to $\mathfrak{E}$ for each A of $\mathfrak{E}$. Notice that $\mathfrak{E}$ is non-empty. Now, let A' be an arbitrary rational R-fuzzy event over X and let $h: X^* \to X^*$ be a homomorphism defined by $h(w) = e$ for all $w \in X^*$. Then

$$h^{-1}(\{e\}) \cap A' = X^* \cap A' = A'.$$

Therefore, A' is an element of $\mathfrak{E}$, which implies $\mathfrak{E}_{rat} \subseteq \mathfrak{E}$.

Theorem 3.5. Any R-fuzzy trio is closed under products with rational R-fuzzy events.

Proof. Let $\mathfrak{E}$ be an R-fuzzy trio and let $A \in \mathfrak{E}$ be an R-fuzzy event over X. Furthermore, let A' be a rational R-fuzzy event over X'. Without loss of generality (cf. [24]), it is assumed that $X \cap X' = \emptyset$. (Otherwise, for each x' of X' let $\bar{x}'$ be a new symbole. Let h be the e-free homomorphism mapping each x' of X' onto $\bar{x}'$. Let h' be the e-free homomorphism which is the identity for $x \in X$ and which maps $\bar{x}'$ onto x'. Then h(A') is rational, $X \cap \bar{X}' = \emptyset$, where $\bar{X}' = \{\bar{x}' \mid x' \in X'\}$, $h'(A \cdot h(A')) = A \cdot A'$, and $A \cdot A'$ is in $\mathfrak{E}$ if $A \cdot h(A')$ is in $\mathfrak{E}$.) By means of the homomorphism $h: (X \cup X')^* \to X^*$ which is the identity for $x \in X$ and maps each x' of X' onto e, the products $A \cdot A'$ and $A' \cdot A$ can be represented as follows

$$A \cdot A' = h^{-1}(A) \cap X^* \cdot A' \qquad \text{and} \qquad A' \cdot A = A' \cdot X^* \cap h^{-1}(A).$$

We only prove the first representation. The second one may be shown analogously.

$$(A \cdot A')(w) = \sum_{\substack{u,v \in (X \cup X')^* \\ uv = w}} A(u) \cdot A'(v)$$

Since X and X' are disjoint, we conclude

$$(A\cdot A')(w) = A(h(w))\cdot \sum_{uv=w} X^*(u)\cdot A'(v)$$
$$= (h^{-1}(A))(w)\cdot (X^*\cdot A')(w)$$
$$= (h^{-1}(A) \cap X^*\cdot A')(w)$$

for all $w \in (X \cup X')^*$. In view of these representations, it follows that $A\cdot A'$ as well as $A'\cdot A$ belong to $\mathfrak{C}$.

<u>Theorem 3.6.</u> Any R-fuzzy trio is closed under gsm and inverse gsm mapping.

Proof. Conclusion of Theorem 3.1.

<u>Theorem 3.7.</u> Any R-fuzzy trio is closed under quotients.

Proof. Let $\mathfrak{C}$ be an R-fuzzy trio and let $A \in \mathfrak{C}$ be an R-fuzzy event over X. Consider $y^{-1}A$ with $y \in X$. Now, we construct a generalized sequential machine $\mathfrak{M} = (X,X,\{z_0,z_1\},z_0,\delta,\lambda)$ by setting

$$\delta(z,x) = z_1 \qquad \text{for } z = z_0 \text{ or } z = z_1 \text{ and all } x \in X$$

and

$$\lambda(z_0,y) = e$$
$$\lambda(z,x) = x \qquad \text{for all } (z,x) \in (\{z_0,z_1\} \times X) \setminus \{(z_0,y)\}.$$

Then M has the following property

$$M(yw) = M(w) = w \qquad \text{for all } w \in X^*.$$

Although $\mathfrak{M}$ is not e-free, the image $M(A \cap yX)$ exists. Moreover, we get

$$M(A \cap yX)(w) = \sum_{u\in M^{-1}(w)} (A \cap yX)(u)$$
$$= \sum_{yv\in M^{-1}(w)} A(yv).$$

The special property of M yields

$$M(A \cap yX)(w) = A(yw) = (y^{-1}A)(w)$$

for all $w \in X^*$. Consequently, $y^{-1}A = M(A \cap yX)$ belongs to $\mathfrak{C}$ by Theorem 3.6.

3.2. Families of R-fuzzy languages

In this section we intend to study closure properties of R-fuzzy languages which are accepted by R-fuzzy automata with respect to given cut-points. Moreover, a characterization of families of R-fuzzy languages will be presented by means of closure properties. This leads to the notion of a semitrio.

Definition 3.3. Let R be a po-semiring and let $\mathcal{A}$ be an R-fuzzy automaton over X. The set

$$L(\mathcal{A},c) = \{w \in X^* \mid [\mathcal{A}](w) \geq c\}$$

is said to be the language accepted by $\mathcal{A}$ with respect to the cut-point $c \in R$. A subset L of X^* is called an R-fuzzy language if there are an R-fuzzy automaton $\mathcal{A}$ over X and a cut-point $c \in R$ such that $L = L(\mathcal{A},c)$. The family of all R-fuzzy languages is denoted by $\mathcal{L}_R$.

Examples. 1) The family $\mathcal{L}_{rat}$ of all rational (regular) languages is a family of R-fuzzy languages because $\mathcal{L}_{rat}$ equals $\mathcal{L}_{\underline{2}}$, where $\underline{2} = \{0,1\}$ is the Boolean semiring.

2) The family $\mathcal{L}_{stoch}$ of all stochastic languages forms a family of R-fuzzy languages since $\mathcal{L}_{stoch}$ is equal to the family of all $\mathbb{R}_+$-fuzzy languages, where $\mathbb{R}_+$ is the po-semiring of all non-negative real numbers (cf. [80]).

Remark. Since every po-semiring R possesses a zero and a unit element, any (non-deterministic) automaton can be considered as an R-fuzzy automaton. Therefore, $\mathcal{L}_{rat}$ is included in every family of R-fuzzy languages.

As already mentioned, $\mathcal{L}_{stoch}$ is not closed under homomorphism. Thus, in general, $\mathcal{L}_R$ is also not closed under homomorphism. But this is a necessary assumption for investigating closure properties within the formalism proposed by S. Ginsburg et al. (cf. [24]). Therefore, a suitable generalization of the notion trio must be established. For this purpose some closure properties of $\mathcal{L}_R$ will be listed now. Among them the 'elementary' ones may be found out.

Theorem 3.8. Any family of R-fuzzy languages is closed under inverse gsm mapping and intersection with rational languages.

Proof. Let $\mathcal{L}_R$ be a family of R-fuzzy languages. By definition, for any R-fuzzy language L over X_L, there exist an R-fuzzy automaton $\mathcal{A}$ over X_L and a cut-point $c \in R$ such that $L = L(\mathcal{A},c)$.

(1) Assume that $\mathfrak{M} = (X, X_L, Z, z_0, \delta, \lambda)$ is a generalized sequential machine. We have to construct an R-fuzzy automaton $\mathcal{A}_{\mathfrak{M}}$ over X satisfying the condition $M^{-1}(L) = L(\mathcal{A}_{\mathfrak{M}}, c')$ for some $c' \in R$. Since, however,

$$M^{-1}(L) = \{w \in X^* \mid M(w) \in L(\mathcal{A}, c)\}$$
$$= \{w \in X^* \mid [\mathcal{A}](M(w)) \geq c\},$$

it is sufficient to construct $\mathcal{A}_{\mathfrak{M}}$ so that

$$[\mathcal{A}_{\mathfrak{M}}](w) = [\mathcal{A}](M(w)) \qquad \text{for all } w \in X^*$$

is fulfilled. Define $\mathcal{A}_{\mathfrak{M}} = (S \times Z, S_0 \times z_0, S_f \times Z, d_{\mathfrak{M}})$ by

$$d_{\mathfrak{M}}(x)((s_1,z_1),(s_2,z_2)) = \begin{cases} d(\lambda(z_1,x))(s_1,s_2) & \text{if } z_2 = \delta(z_1,x) \\ 0 & \text{otherwise} \end{cases}$$

for all $x \in X$, $s_1, s_2 \in S$ and $z_1, z_2 \in Z$. Consequently,

$$M^{-1}(L) = L(\mathcal{A}_{\mathfrak{M}}, c),$$

which proves that $\mathcal{L}_R$ is closed under inverse gsm mapping.

(2) Let A' be a rational language over X. The deterministic automaton $\mathcal{A}'$ over X accepting A' can be regarded as an R-fuzzy automaton such that

$$[\mathcal{A}'](w) = \begin{cases} 1 & \text{if } w \in L' \\ 0 & \text{if } w \notin L' \end{cases}$$

for all $w \in X^*$. Clearly, the product $\mathcal{A} \times \mathcal{A}'$ has the following property

$$[\mathcal{A} \times \mathcal{A}'](w) = \begin{cases} [\mathcal{A}](w) & \text{if } w \in L' \\ 0 & \text{if } w \notin L'. \end{cases}$$

for all $w \in (X_L \cup X)^*$. Therefore, $L \cap L'$ is accepted by $\mathcal{A} \times \mathcal{A}'$ with respect to c. Hence $\mathcal{L}_R$ is closed under intersection with rational languages.

<u>Conclusion</u>. Any family of R-fuzzy languages is closed under relative complements with respect to rational languages.

Proof. Let L be an R-fuzzy language over X and let L' be a rational language over X'. Because of $L \setminus L' = L \cap (X'^* \setminus L')$, the assertion holds by Theorem 3.8. Observe that $X'^* \setminus L'$ is a rational language.

Now, we are going to investigate marked products. Let L and L' be languages over X and X', respectively. Assume that a is a new symbol belonging neither to X nor to X'. Then $L \cdot a \cdot L'$ is called the marked product of L and L'.

Theorem 3.9. Any family of R-fuzzy languages is closed under marked products with rational languages.

Proof. Let L be an R-fuzzy language over X and let L' be a rational language over X'. Then there exist an R-fuzzy automaton $\mathfrak{A} = (S, S_o, S_f, d)$ over X accepting L with respect to $c \in R$ as well as a deterministic automaton $\mathfrak{A}' = (S', s_o', S_f', d')$ over X' accepting L'. At first, we construct the direct sum

$$\bar{\mathfrak{A}} \oplus \bar{\mathfrak{A}}' = (S \oplus S', S_o \oplus 0, 0 \oplus S_f', d \oplus d')$$

of $\bar{\mathfrak{A}} = (S, S_o, 0, d)$ and $\bar{\mathfrak{A}}' = (S', 0, S_f', d')$, whereby d and d' are considered as mappings from $X \cup X'$ into $\mathrm{Rel}_R S$ and $\mathrm{Rel}_R S'$, respectively. Assume that a is a new symbol belonging neither to X nor to X'. Now, define

$$(d \oplus d')(a)(s_1, s_2) = \begin{cases} S_f(s_1) & \text{if } s_1 \in S \text{ and } s_2 = s_o' \\ 0 & \text{otherwise.} \end{cases}$$

An easy calculation shows

$$[\bar{\mathfrak{A}} + \bar{\mathfrak{A}}'](w) = \begin{cases} [\mathfrak{A}](u) & \text{if there are } u \in X^* \text{ and } v \in L' \text{ such that } w = uav \text{ holds} \\ 0 & \text{otherwise} \end{cases}$$

for all $w \in (X \cup X')^*$. Hence

$$L \cdot a \cdot L' = L(\bar{\mathfrak{A}} \oplus \bar{\mathfrak{A}}', c).$$

Consequently, $L \cdot a \cdot L'$ is an R-fuzzy language. In analogy to it, we may prove that $L' \cdot a \cdot L$ also is an R-fuzzy language.

Theorem 3.10. Any family of R-fuzzy languages is closed under quotients.

Proof. Let L be an R-fuzzy language over X accepted by $\mathfrak{A} = (S, S_o, S_f, d)$ with respect to $c \in R$. Consider the quotient $v^{-1}L$ for a given $v \in X^*$. Constructing an R-fuzzy automaton $\mathfrak{A}' = (S, S_o, S_f, d')$ over X by setting $d'(x) = d^*(vx)$, we have

$$\begin{aligned} L(\mathfrak{A}', c) &= \{w \in X^* \mid [\mathfrak{A}'](w) \geq c\} \\ &= \{w \in X^* \mid vw \in L(\mathfrak{A}, c)\}. \end{aligned}$$

Evidently, $v^{-1}L = L(\mathfrak{A}', c)$. Thus $\mathcal{L}_R$ is closed under quotients.

Theorem 3.11. If R is a po-semiring with a greatest element, then $\mathcal{L}_R$ is closed under union with rational languages.

Proof. If R is a po-semiring with a greatest element ω, then, by axioms, we conclude

$$r + \omega = \omega + r = \omega + \omega = \omega \quad \text{and} \quad r\cdot\omega = \omega\cdot r = \omega\cdot\omega = \omega, \text{ if } r \neq 0$$

for all r of R. Now, let L be an R-fuzzy language over X accepted by $\mathcal{A} = (S,S_0,S_f,d)$ with respect to $c \in R$. Furthermore, let L' be a rational language over X' accepted by the deterministic automaton $\mathcal{A}' = (S',s_0',S_f',d')$ over X'. Clearly, $\mathcal{A}'$ can be regarded as an R-fuzzy automaton satisfying

$$d'(x)(s_1,s_2) = \begin{cases} \omega & \text{if } s_2 = d'(x,s_1) \\ 0 & \text{otherwise} \end{cases}$$

for all $x \in X$ and $s_1,s_2 \in S'$. The direct sum $\mathcal{A} \oplus \mathcal{A}'$ has the following property:

$$[\mathcal{A} \oplus \mathcal{A}'](w) = \begin{cases} \omega & \text{if } w \in L' \\ [\mathcal{A}](w) & \text{if } w \notin L' \end{cases}$$

for all $w \in (X \cup X')^*$. Hence

$$L \cup L' = L(\mathcal{A} \oplus \mathcal{A}',c).$$

Therefore, $\mathcal{L}_R$ is closed under union with rational languages.

We are now going to generalize the notion of a trio introduced by S. Ginsburg [24] so that closure properties of R-fuzzy languages can be dealt with. Taking into account that some interesting families of languages are not closed under homomorphism, Boasson et al. (cf. [5,11]) proposed the concept of a cylinder which is a family closed under inverse homomorphism and intersection with rational languages. For our aim, however, cylinders are not suitable. In particular, the requirement of closure under union with rational languages is necessary.

Definition 3.4. A semitrio is a family of languages containing $\mathcal{L}_{rat}$ which is closed under inverse gsm mapping, intersection and union with rational languages.

Examples. 1) $\mathcal{L}_{rat}$ and $\mathcal{L}_{stoch}$ are semitrios. In general, every family of R-fuzzy languages is a semitrio provided R has a greatest element.

2) Any trio is a semitrio (cf. [24]).

In the sequel, the semitrio $\langle L\rangle_{ST}$ generated by a language L will be represented as a family of R-fuzzy languages for some R.

<u>Theorem 3.12</u>. Let L be an arbitrary language. Then the semitrio $\langle L\rangle_{ST}$ generated by L is the following set

$$\langle L\rangle_{ST} = \{(M^{-1}(L) \cap L_r) \cup L'_r \mid M \text{ is a gsm mapping, } L_r \text{ and } L'_r \text{ are rational languages}\}$$

Proof. (1) The set $\mathfrak{L} = \{(M^{-1}(L) \cap L_r) \cup L'_r \mid M$ is a gsm mapping, L_r and L'_r are rational languages$\}$ is a semitrio.

Obviously, $\mathfrak{L}$ contains $\mathcal{L}_{rat}$ and is closed under intersection as well as union with rational languages. Therefore, it only remains to show that $\mathfrak{L}$ is closed under inverse gsm mapping. Let $L' \in \mathfrak{L}$, then there are a gsm mapping M_1 and two rational languages L_r and L'_r such that

$$L' = (M^{-1}(L) \cap L_r) \cup L'_r.$$

Take an arbitrary gsm mapping M_2. We have to prove that $M_2^{-1}(L')$ belongs to $\mathfrak{L}$. Assume that $\mathfrak{M}_i = (X_i, Y_i, Z_i, z_{i,o}, \delta_i, \lambda_i)$ are generalized sequential machines producing M_i, $i = 1,2$, whereby $Y_1 = X$ and $Y_2 = X_2$. Because of

$$M_2^{-1}(L') = (M_2^{-1}(M_1^{-1}(L)) \cap M_2^{-1}(L_r)) \cup M_2^{-1}(L'_r),$$

$M_2^{-1}(L')$ is in $\mathfrak{L}$ if there exists a generalized sequential machine $\mathfrak{M} = (X_2, Y_1, Z, z_o, \delta, \lambda)$ satisfying $M = M_1 \cdot M_2$. Observe that $M_2^{-1}(L_r)$ and $M_2^{-1}(L'_r)$ are rational languages [24]. Put $Z = Z_1 \times Z_2$ and define

$$\delta(z_1, z_2, x) = (\delta_1(z_1, x), \delta_2(z_2, \lambda_1(z_1, x)))$$

and

$$\lambda(z_1, z_2, x) = \lambda_2(z_2, \lambda_1(z_1, x))$$

for all $z_1 \in Z_1$, $z_2 \in Z_2$ and $x \in X$. It is manifest that

$$M(w) = \lambda_2(z_{2,o}, \lambda_1(z_{1,o}, w)) = M_2(M_1(w))$$

for all $w \in X_2^*$. Therefore, $M_2^{-1}(L')$ is an element of $\mathfrak{L}$. Since $\langle L\rangle_{ST}$ is the smallest semitrio containing L, it follows

$$\langle L\rangle_{ST} \subseteq \mathfrak{L}.$$

(2) Evidently, each language of $\mathfrak{L}$ belongs to $\langle L\rangle_{ST}$. Hence the converse inclusion

$$\langle L\rangle_{ST} \supseteq \mathfrak{L}$$

holds true.

Definition 3.5. Let L be a language over X. Then a po-semiring R_L is associated with L as follows

$$R_L = \{0,1,\omega\} \cup \{w^{-1}L \mid w \in X^*\} \cup X^*$$

whose operations and partial order are defined by

(1) 0 is zero and 1 is unit element.

(2) $r + r' = \omega$ for $r,r' \in R_L \setminus \{0\}$

(3) $r \cdot r' = \begin{cases} rr' & \text{if } r,r' \in X^* \\ (wr')^{-1}L & \text{if } r = w^{-1}L \text{ for some } w \in X^*,\ r' \in X^* \\ \omega & \text{otherwise} \end{cases}$

(4) 0 is bottom and ω is top element.

(5) $v \leq (wv)^{-1}L$ if and only if $w \in L$ for all $v,w \in X^*$.

Theorem 3.13. The semitrio $\langle L\rangle_{ST}$ generated by a language L is equal to the family of all R_L-fuzzy languages.

Proof. Let L be an arbitrary language over X_L.

(1) Statement: Any R_L-fuzzy language belongs to $\langle L\rangle_{ST}$.

At first, we investigate all possible 'structure' of R_L-fuzzy automata $\mathcal{A}$ over X. By the definition of R_L, $[\mathcal{A}](w) \neq \omega$ if and only if there is at most a path in $\mathcal{A}$ associated with w. Thus a 'deterministic' R_L-fuzzy automaton $\mathcal{A}_d = (S,s_o,S_f,d)$ with $s_o \in S$ and $S_f \subseteq S$ must exist such that

$$L(\mathcal{A},c) = L(\mathcal{A}_d,c) \cup \{w \in X^* \mid [\mathcal{A}](w) = \omega\}$$

for each cut-point c of R. Thereby, 'deterministic' means that for all pairs (x,s) of $X \times S$

$$d(x,s)(s') \neq 0 \quad \text{holds for exact one state } s' \in S.$$

Next, we show that $L_r' = \{w \in X^* \mid [\mathcal{A}](w) = \omega\}$ is a rational language. For this purpose, an auxiliary po-semiring $R' = \{0,1,\omega,\partial,\varepsilon\}$ is introduced by

+	0	1	ω	∂	ε
0	0	1	ω	∂	ε
1	1	ω	ω	ω	ω
ω	ω	ω	ω	ω	ω
∂	∂	ω	ω	ω	ω
ε	ε	ω	ω	ω	ω

•	0	1	ω	∂	ε
0	0	0	0	0	0
1	0	1	ω	∂	ε
ω	0	ω	ω	ω	ω
∂	0	∂	ω	ω	∂
ε	0	ε	ω	ω	ε

and $0 \leq 1 \leq \omega$, $0 \leq \partial \leq \omega$, $0 \leq \varepsilon \leq \omega$ and $\varepsilon \leq \partial$. R' is the homomorphic image of R_L with respect to the following homomorphism $h: R_L \to R'$ which is the identity of $\{0,1,\omega\}$ and is defined by $h(w^{-1}L) = \partial$ and $h(w) = \varepsilon$ for all $w \in X^*$. Therefore, L_r' can also be accepted by an R'-fuzzy automaton with respect to ω. Since R' is a finite po-semiring, L_r' is a rational language (see Section 3.3 or [87]).

It remains to show that $L(\mathfrak{A}_d,c)$ is representable as intersection of $M^{-1}(L)$ for a suitable gsm mapping M and a rational language. First we consider the case $c = e$. The required generalized sequential machine $\mathfrak{M} = (X,X_L,S,s_o,\delta,\lambda)$ is defined by $\delta(s,x) = s'$, where s' is determined by the condition $d(x,s)(s') \neq 0$, and $\lambda(s,x) = w$, where w is determined by $d(x,s)(\delta(s,x)) = w^{-1}L$ or $d(x,s)(\delta(s,x)) = w$ (1 and e are identified for this reason) for $s,s' \in S$ and $x \in X$. Thus

$$[\mathfrak{A}_d](w) = \begin{cases} M(w)^{-1}L & \text{if } \delta(s_o,w) \in S_f \\ 0 & \text{if } \delta(s_o,w) \notin S_f. \end{cases}$$

Put $L_r = \{w \in X^* | \delta(s_o,w) \in S_f\}$, so we have

$$\begin{aligned} L(\mathfrak{A}_d,e) &= \{w \in X^* | M(w) \in L\} \cap L_r \\ &= M^{-1}(L) \cap L_r. \end{aligned}$$

Since L_r is accepted by the deterministic automaton $\mathfrak{M}' = (S,s_o,S_f,d)$, L_r is a rational language. Hence the assertion is proved for $c = e$. The cases $c = 0$ and $c = \omega$ are trivial because $L(\mathfrak{A},0)$ and $L(\mathfrak{A},\omega)$ are rational languages. It can easily be seen that the language $L(\mathfrak{A},w^{-1}L)$ is rational for all $w \in X^*$. Therefore, the case $c = v$ with $v \neq e$ of X^* only remains to prove. For this purpose, it is sufficient to change the definition of λ as follows: $\lambda(s,x) = w$ must be replaced by $\lambda(s,x) = vw$ for those states s which satisfy $d(x,s)(\delta(s,x)) = w^{-1}L$ for some $x \in X$. Obviously, the assertion is also true in this case.

(2) Statement: Each element of $\langle L\rangle_{ST}$ is an R_L-fuzzy language.

Let $L' \in \langle L\rangle_{ST}$ be a language over X. Then, by Theorem 3.12, there exist a generalized sequential machine $\mathfrak{M} = (X,X_L,Z,z_o,\delta,\lambda)$ and two rational languages L_r and L_r' over X such that

$$L' = (M^{-1}(L) \cap L_r) \cup L_r'.$$

Assume that L_r and L_r' are accepted by the deterministic automata $\mathfrak{A}_r = (S,s_o,S_f,d)$ and $\mathfrak{A}_r' = (S',s_o',S_f',d')$ over X, respectively, where

$$[\mathfrak{A}_r](w) = \begin{cases} 1 & \text{if } w \in L_r \\ 0 & \text{if } w \notin L_r \end{cases}$$

and

$$[\mathcal{A}'_r](w) = \begin{cases} \omega & \text{if } w \in L'_r \\ 0 & \text{if } w \notin L'_r. \end{cases}$$

We have to construct an R_L-fuzzy automaton $\mathcal{A}$ over X so that $L' = L(\mathcal{A},c)$ for some cut-point c of R. To do this, an R_L-fuzzy automaton $\mathcal{A}_{\mathfrak{M}}$ is first defined as follows: $\mathcal{A}_{\mathfrak{M}} = (Z,z_o,Z,d_{\mathfrak{M}})$ with

$$d_{\mathfrak{M}}(x,z)(z') = \begin{cases} w^{-1}L & \text{if } z = z_o,\ z' = \delta(z_o,x) \text{ and } w = \lambda(z_o,x) \\ w & \text{if } z \neq z_o,\ z' = \delta(z,x) \text{ and } w = \lambda(z,x) \\ 0 & \text{otherwise.} \end{cases}$$

Regarding both deterministic automata $\mathcal{A}_r$ and $\mathcal{A}'_r$ as R_L-fuzzy automata, we compose $\mathcal{A}$ as follows

$$\mathcal{A} = (\mathcal{A}_{\mathfrak{M}} \times \mathcal{A}_r) \oplus \mathcal{A}'_r.$$

Since for all $w \in X^*$:

$$[\mathcal{A}](w) = ([\mathcal{A}_{\mathfrak{M}}](w)\cdot[\mathcal{A}_r](w)) + [\mathcal{A}'_r](w),$$

we conclude

$$L(\mathcal{A},e) = (M^{-1}(L) \cap L_r) \cup L'_r = L'.$$

Observe that $[\mathcal{A}_{\mathfrak{M}}](w) = M(w)^{-1}L$ for all $w \in X^*$ implies $[\mathcal{A}_{\mathfrak{M}}] = M^{-1}(L)$. Therefore, each language L' of $\langle L \rangle_{ST}$ is an R_L-fuzzy language.

Theorem 3.14. Any language is an R-fuzzy language.

Proof. We will show that any language L over X is an R_L-fuzzy language. The idea is based on the fact that L can be accepted by the following (infinite) deterministic automaton $\mathcal{A}_d = (Z,z_o,Z_f,\delta)$ over X (cf. [17]):

$$Z = \{w^{-1}L \mid w \in X^* \text{ and } w^{-1}L = \emptyset\}$$

$$z_o = L$$

$$Z_f = \{w^{-1}L \mid w \in L\}$$

and the transition function δ is determined by

$$\delta(x,w^{-1}L) = (wx)^{-1}L \qquad \text{for all } x \in X \text{ and } w \in X^*.$$

Now, we 'simulate' $\mathcal{A}_d$ by a (finite) R_L-fuzzy automaton $\mathcal{A} = (S,S_o,S_f,d)$. First assume that L is e-free. Then we define due to M. Karpinski

$$S = \{s_o,s_f\},\ S_o = \{s_o\},\ S_f = \{s_f\}$$

and for all $x \in X$

$$d(x) = \begin{vmatrix} 0 & x^{-1}L \\ 0 & x \end{vmatrix} .$$

Obviuosly, the behaviour of $\mathfrak{A}$ is given by

$$[\mathfrak{A}](w) = \begin{cases} 0 & \text{if } w = e \\ w^{-1}L & \text{if } w \neq e \end{cases}, \quad w \in X^*.$$

Hence $L = L(\mathfrak{A},e)$. In the case $e \in L$, we choose S_f as follows

$$S_f(s) = \begin{cases} e & \text{if } s = s_0 \\ 1 & \text{if } s = s_f. \end{cases}$$

Thus $[\mathfrak{A}](e) = e$ and, consequently, $L = L(\mathfrak{A},e)$ holds true for any language L over X, that means any language L is an R_L-fuzzy language.

In order to generalize the assertion of Theorem 3.13 for a given family $\mathcal{L}$ of languages, we introduce the corresponding po-semiring $R_{\mathcal{L}}$.

Definition 3.6. For a family $\mathcal{L}$ of languages, a po-semiring $R_{\mathcal{L}}$ is defined as follows

$$R_{\mathcal{L}} = \{0,1,\omega\} \cup \{w^{-1}L \mid w \in X_L^* \text{ and } L \in \mathcal{L}\} \cup \{X_L^* \mid L \in \mathcal{L}\}$$

whose operations and partial order are given by

(1) 0 is zero and 1 is unit element.

(2) $r + r' = \omega$ for $r,r' \in R \setminus \{0\}$

(3) $r \cdot r' = \begin{cases} rr' & \text{if } r,r' \in X_L^* \text{ for some } L \in \mathcal{L} \\ (wr')^{-1}L & \text{if } r = w^{-1}L \text{ for some } w \in X_L^* \text{ and } r' \in X_L^* \\ \omega & \text{otherwise} \end{cases}$

(4) 0 is bottom and 1 is top element

(5) $v \leq (wv)^{-1}L$ if and only if $w \in L$ for all $v,w \in X_L^*$.

Thereby, X_L denotes the alphabet of a language $L \in \mathcal{L}$.

Remarks. 1) If in the definitions of R_L and $R_{\mathcal{L}}$ the unit elements are deleted, then $R_{\mathcal{L}}$ can be represented as coproduct of all R_L, $L \in \mathcal{L}$. Let $\mathcal{R}_{pos,\omega}$ be the class of all positive po-semirings (without unit element) having a top element. The coproduct of a family $(R_i)_{i \in I}$ of po-semirings $R_i \in \mathcal{R}_{pos,\omega}$ is the following disjoint union

$$\bigsqcup_{i\in I} R_i = \{0,\omega\} \cup \bigcup_{i\in I} (R_i \setminus \{0_i,\omega_i\}),$$

where 0_i is the bottom and ω_i is the top element of R_i. If $+_i$ and $\cdot_i$ denote the operations of R_i and $\leq_i$ the partial order on R_i, then the addition $+$ and multiplication $\cdot$ as well as partial order $\leq$ of $\bigsqcup R_i$ are defined by

(1) 0 is zero as well as bottom element

(2) $r + r' = \begin{cases} r +_i r' & \text{if } r,r' \in R_i \text{ for some } i \in I \\ \omega & \text{otherwise} \end{cases}$

(3) $r \cdot r' = \begin{cases} r \cdot_i r' & \text{if } r,r' \in R_i \text{ for some } i \in I \\ \omega & \text{otherwise} \end{cases}$

(4) ω is top element

(5) $r \leq r'$ if and only if $r,r' \in R_i$ for some $i \in I$ and $r \leq_i r'$.

The family $(in_i)_{i\in I}$ of injections is defined by $in_i(0_i) = 0$, $in_i(\omega_i) = \omega$ and $in_i(r) = r$ for $r \in R_i \setminus \{0_i,\omega_i\}$.

2) R-fuzzy automata and thus R-fuzzy languages may also be defined for po-semirings R without unit element. Only the definition of the global behaviour $[A]$ of an R-fuzzy automaton $A = (S,S_o,S_f,d)$ has to be changed as follows

$$[A](e) = S_o \cdot S_f = \sum_{s\in S} S_o(s) \cdot S_f(s)$$

for the empty word e. Let $(R_i)_{i\in I}$ be a family of po-semirings, then

$$\mathcal{L}_{\bigsqcup_{i\in I} R_i} = \bigcup_{i\in I} \mathcal{L}_{R_i}$$

holds true (cf. [89]). One part of this statement is based on the fact that any R_i-fuzzy language is a $\bigsqcup R_i$-fuzzy language since R_i is subsemiring of $\bigsqcup R_i$ for all $i \in I$, that is

$$\mathcal{L}_{\bigsqcup_{i\in I} R_i} \supseteq \bigcup_{i\in I} \mathcal{L}_{R_i}.$$

In order to prove the opposite inclusion, let $L \subseteq X^*$ be a $\bigsqcup R_i$-fuzzy language accepted by $A = (S,S_o,S_f,d)$ with respect to a cut-point c. If c equals 0, then L is rational and belongs to each family $\mathcal{L}_{R_j}$ of R_j-fuzzy languages. Suppose that $c \notin \{0,\omega\}$. Clearly, there exactly exists an element j of I such that $c \in R_j$. By means of A, an R_j-fuzzy automaton $A_j = (S,S_{j,o},S_{j,f},d_j)$ over X is constructed as follows

$$S_{j,o}(s) = \begin{cases} S_o(s) & \text{if } S_o(s) \in R_j \\ 0 & \text{otherwise} \end{cases}$$

$$S_{j,f}(s) = \begin{cases} S_f(s) & \text{if } S_f(s) \in R_j \\ 0 & \text{otherwise} \end{cases}$$

and

$$d_j(x,s)(s') = \begin{cases} d(x,s)(s') & \text{if } d(x,s)(s') \in R_j \\ 0 & \text{otherwise.} \end{cases}$$

for $x \in X$ and $s,s' \in S$. Clearly, we get

$$L(\mathcal{A},c) = L(\mathcal{A}_j,c) \cup L_\omega$$

with $L_\omega = \{w \in X^* | [\mathcal{A}](w) = \omega\}$. Hence L is an R_j-fuzzy language provided L_ω is rational. Since, furthermore, $L(\mathcal{A},\omega) = L_\omega$ holds, it only remains to show that L_ω is rational. For this purpose, an auxiliary commutative po-semiring $R = \{0,\omega\} \cup \{\rho_i | i \in I\}$ is introduced whose operations and partial order are given by

(1) 0 is zero element

(2) $r + r' = \begin{cases} r & \text{if } r = r' \\ \omega & \text{otherwise} \end{cases}, \quad r,r' \in R \setminus \{0\}$

(3) $r \cdot r' = \begin{cases} r & \text{if } r = r' \\ \omega & \text{otherwise} \end{cases}, \quad r,r' \in R \setminus \{0\}$

(4) $0 \leq \rho_i \leq \omega$ for all $i \in I$.

R is the homomorphic image of $\sqcup R_i$ under $h: \sqcup R_i \to R$, which is defined by $h(0) = 0$, $h(\omega) = \omega$ and $h(r) = \rho_i$ for all $r \in R_i \setminus \{0_i, \omega_i\}$. Moreover, the homomorphic image of any finitely generated subsemiring of $\sqcup R_i$ is a finite subsemiring of R. Denote by $D_\mathcal{A}$ the set of all coefficients in S_o, S_f and all matrices $d(x)$ of $\mathcal{A}$, then the homomorphic image of the subsemiring generated by $D_\mathcal{A}$ is a finite subsemiring $R_\mathcal{A}$ of R. Consider the $R_\mathcal{A}$-fuzzy automaton $\mathcal{A}' = (S, S_o', S_f', d')$ over X defined by

$$S_o'(s) = h(S_o(s))$$

$$S_f'(s) = h(S_f(s))$$

$$d'(x,s)(s') = h(d(x,s)(s'))$$

for all $s,s' \in S$ and $x \in X$. Obviously, we get $L_\omega = L(\mathcal{A},\omega)$. Since $R_\mathcal{A}$ is finite, L_ω is rational. Thus

$$\mathcal{L}_{\bigsqcup_{i\in I} R_i} \subseteq \bigcup_{i\in I} \mathcal{L}_{R_i},$$

which proves the assertion.

Theorem 3.15. Let $\mathcal{L}$ be a family of languages, then

$$\langle\mathcal{L}\rangle_{ST} = \mathcal{L}_{R_{\mathcal{L}}}.$$

Proof. (1) For any family $\mathcal{L}$ of languages, $\bigcup_{L\in\mathcal{L}} \langle L\rangle$ is a semitrio containing $\mathcal{L}$. Thus

$$\langle\mathcal{L}\rangle_{ST} \subseteq \bigcup_{L\in\mathcal{L}} \langle L\rangle_{ST}.$$

(2) The opposite inclusion

$$\langle\mathcal{L}\rangle_{ST} \supseteq \bigcup_{L\in\mathcal{L}} \langle L\rangle_{ST}$$

is trivial. Consequently, we have $\langle\mathcal{L}\rangle_{ST} = \bigcup_{L\in\mathcal{L}} \langle L\rangle_{ST} = \bigcup_{L\in\mathcal{L}} \mathcal{L}_{R_L}$. Because of Remark 2), it follows

$$\langle\mathcal{L}\rangle_{ST} = \mathcal{L}_{\bigsqcup_{L\in\mathcal{L}} R_L}.$$

Since $\bigsqcup_{L\in\mathcal{L}} R_L$ is a po-semiring, by Remark 1), the theorem is proved.

Theorem 3.16. Any family of languages is included in a family of R-fuzzy languages for some po-semiring R.

Proof. Let $\mathcal{L} = \{L_i \mid i \in I\}$ be a family of languages L_i over X_i. By Theorem 3.14, there exist a family $\mathcal{R} = \{R_i \mid i \in I\}$ of po-semirings and a family $\{c_i \mid i \in I\}$ of cut-points such that L_i is an R_i-fuzzy language. By means of $\mathcal{R}$ we construct an po-semiring R as disjoint union

$$R = (\bigcup_{i\in I} R_i) \cup \{0, c, 1, \omega\}.$$

If $+_i$ and $\cdot_i$ denote addition and multiplication in R_i, respectively, and $\leq_i$ denotes the partial order on R_i, then the operations and partial order of R are defined by

(1) 0 is zero and 1 is unit element

$$(2)\quad r + r' = \begin{cases} r +_i r' & \text{if } r, r' \in R_i \\ \omega & \text{otherwise} \end{cases}$$

$$(3)\quad r \cdot r' = \begin{cases} r \cdot_i r' & \text{if } r, r' \in R_i \\ 0 & \text{if either } (r = c,\ r' \in R) \text{ or } (r \in R,\ r' = c) \\ \omega & \text{otherwise} \end{cases}$$

(4) 0 is bottom and ω is top element

(5) $r \leq r'$ if and only if either $r, r' \in R_i$ for some i of I and $r \leq_i r'$ or $r = c$ and $c_i \leq_i r'$.

Since any $R_i \in \mathcal{R}$ can be embedded in R, every R_i-fuzzy language is an R-fuzzy language. Hence $\mathcal{L}$ is included in $\mathcal{L}_R$.

Now, the following characterization of semitrios can be concluded.

Theorem 3.17. Any semitrio is a family of R-fuzzy languages for some po-semiring R with a greatest element and vice versa.

Proof. (1) Let $\mathcal{L}$ be a semitrio, then $\mathcal{L} = \langle\mathcal{L}\rangle_{ST}$. Therefore, by Theorem 3.15, $\mathcal{L}$ is a family of $R_{\mathcal{L}}$-fuzzy languages.

(2) By Theorem 3.8 and Theorem 3.11, any family of R-fuzzy languages forms a semitrio provided R has a greatest element.

Theorem 3.18. Any semitrio is closed under marked product with rational languages and under quotients.

Proof. Conclusions of Theorem 3.9 and Theorem 3.10.

3.3. Acceptance power

In this section we intend to compare the global behaviour of R-fuzzy automata for different kinds of po-semirings R. Our first problem is the characterization of all those po-semirings R which have the same 'finite-state computational' complexity as the Boolean semiring, that means, the related R-fuzzy automata have the same acceptance power as deterministic automata. But up to now only some necessary finiteness conditions for po-semirings R can be established so that the family of all R-fuzzy languages equals $\mathcal{L}_{rat}$. Secondly, we are concerned with the question whether there is an infinite hierarchy of po-semirings with different complexity.

Theorem 3.19. If R is a finite po-semiring, then $\mathcal{L}_R$ equals $\mathcal{L}_{rat}$.

Proof. Let L be a language accepted by an R-fuzzy automaton $\mathcal{A} = (S, S_o, S_f, d)$ over X with respect to $c \in R$. In analogy to Myhill's subset construction we define a deterministic automaton $\mathcal{A}_{det} = (Z, z_o, Z_f, \delta)$ over X. Its state set Z is equal to the set R^S of all mappings from S into R, which is a finite set by assumption. Furthermore, we put $z_o = S_o$,

$$Z_f = \{z \in Z \mid \sum_{s \in S} z(s) \cdot S_f(s) \geq c\}$$

and the next state $z' = \delta(x,z)$ under the transition function δ is as mapping determined as follows

$$\delta(x,z)(s) = \sum_{s' \in S} z(s') \cdot d(x,s')(s).$$

It is manifest that

$$L(A,c) = \{w \in X^* \mid \delta^*(w,z_0) \in Z_f\}.$$

Thus L is a rational language. Hence $\mathcal{L}_R$ equals $\mathcal{L}_{rat}$.

We call a po-semiring quasi-finite if every finitely generated subsemiring of it is finite. For instance, a po-semiring with idempotent operations is quasi-finite. Thus any distributive lattice with 0 and 1 considered as po-semiring is quasi-finite.

Theorem 3.20. If R is a quasi-finite po-semiring, then $\mathcal{L}_R$ equals $\mathcal{L}_{rat}$.

Proof. Let $A = (S,S_0,S_f,d)$ be an R-fuzzy automaton over X. Denote by D_A the set of all coefficients in S_0, S_f (considered as vectors), and in all transition matrices $d(x)$, $x \in X$. If R_A is the subsemiring generated by D_A, then A can also be regarded as R_A-fuzzy automaton. Since R_A is finite by assumption, $\mathcal{L}_R$ equals $\mathcal{L}_{rat}$ as shown in Theorem 3.19.

Given two po-semirings R and R', a cut-point homomorphism f_c, $c \in R$, is a homomorphism from R into R' satisfying the following condition: $c \leq r$ if and only if $f_c(c) \leq f_c(r)$ for all $r \in R$.

Theorem 3.21. Let A be an R-fuzzy automaton. A language accepted by A with respect to the cut-point $c \in R$ is rational if there exists a cut-point homomorphism f_c such that $f_c(R)$ is finite.

Proof. The assumed property of a cut-point homomorphism yields

$$L(A,c) = \{w \in X^* \mid [A](w) \geq c\} = \{w \in X^* \mid f_c([A](w)) \geq f_c(c)\}.$$

Since a $f_c(R)$-fuzzy automaton A' with

$$[A'](w) = f_c([A](w)) \qquad \text{for all } w \in X^*$$

exists, we have $L(A,c) = L(A',f_c(c))$. Therefore, $L(A,c)$ is rational by Theorem 3.19.

Let R be a po-semiring and let R' be a subset of R. We call the set $N(R',c) = \{r \in R' | c \nleq r\}$ negative cone of R' with respect to the cut-point $c \in R$. A po-semiring R is said to be cone-finite if the unit element 1 of R is the least element of $R \setminus \{0\}$ and, furthermore, the negative cone of every finitely generated subsemiring with respect to any cut-point is finite. For instance, the po-semiring $\mathbb{N}$ of natural numbers or $R = \{r \in \mathbb{Q}_+ | r \geq 1\} \cup \{0\}$ as well as $R = \{r \in \mathbb{R}_+ | r \geq 1\} \cup \{0\}$ are cone-finite.

Theorem 3.22. If R is a cone-finite po-semiring, then $\mathcal{L}_R$ equals $\mathcal{L}_{rat}$.

Proof. Let L be a language accepted by an R-fuzzy automaton $\mathcal{A} = (S, S_0, S_f, d)$ over X with respect to $c \in R$. We construct a finite po-semiring

$$R' = N(R_{\mathcal{A}}, c) \cup \{0, 1, \omega\}$$

by defining

(1) 0 is zero and 1 is unit element

(2) $$r +' r' = \begin{cases} r + r' & \text{if } c \nleq r + r' \\ \omega & \text{if } c \leq r + r' \end{cases}$$

(3) $$r \cdot' r' = \begin{cases} r \cdot r' & \text{if } c \nleq r \cdot r' \\ \omega & \text{if } c \leq r \cdot r' \end{cases}$$

(4) 0 is bottom and ω is top element

(5) $r \leq' r'$ if and only if $r \leq r'$ for all $r, r' \in N(R_{\mathcal{A}}, c)$.

Defining a cut-point homomorphism f_c from R into R' by

$$f_c(r) = \begin{cases} r & \text{if } c \nleq r \\ \omega & \text{if } c \leq r, \end{cases}$$

we conclude, by Theorem 3.21, that $L(\mathcal{A}, c)$ is rational. Consequently, $\mathcal{L}_R$ equals $\mathcal{L}_{rat}$.

An integral slo-monoid R with zero (see Section 1.1) is called pc-finite (or archimedean) if the following condition is fulfilled: $r^n > r'$ for all $n > 0$ implies $r = 1$ for arbitrary $r, r' \in R$. Examples of such structures are given in Section 1.1.

Theorem 3.23. If R is a pc-finite po-semiring, then $\mathcal{L}_R$ equals $\mathcal{L}_{rat}$.

Proof. Let L be a language accepted by an R-fuzzy automaton $\mathcal{A}$ with respect to $c \in R$. In analogy to the proof of Theorem 3.22, we construct a finite po-semiring

$$R' = \{r \in R_{A} | r \nleq c\} \cup \{0\}.$$

Observe that 1 as top element of R belongs to R'. 0 is zero element of R'. Since addition in R coincides with suprema by definition, R' is closed under addition. It only remains to define multiplication

$$r \cdot' r' = \begin{cases} r \cdot r' & \text{if } r \cdot r' \nleq c \\ 0 & \text{if } r \cdot r' \leq c. \end{cases}$$

Obviously, the partial order on R induces a partial order on R'. Defining a cut-point homomorphism f_c from R into R' by

$$f_c(r) = \begin{cases} r & \text{if } r \nleq c \\ 0 & \text{if } r \leq c, \end{cases}$$

we derive, by Theorem 3.21, that L(A,c) is rational. Hence $\mathcal{L}_R$ equals $\mathcal{L}_{rat}$.

The direct product R = R' × R" of two po-semirings R' and R" is that po-semiring R whose operations and partial order are defined component-wise. In order to characterize the family of all R' × R"-fuzzy languages, we use the so-called wedge opertion introduced in [24]. Let $\mathcal{L}'$ and $\mathcal{L}''$ be families of languages, then

$$\mathcal{L}' \sqcap \mathcal{L}'' = \{L | \text{there are } L' \in \mathcal{L}' \text{ and } L'' \in \mathcal{L}'' \text{ such that } L = L' \cap L''\}.$$

Theorem 3.24. Let R' and R" be po-semirings, then

$$\mathcal{L}_{R' \times R''} = \mathcal{L}_{R'} \sqcap \mathcal{L}_{R''}$$

Proof. (1) Let L be an R' × R"-fuzzy language over X accepted by the R' × R"-fuzzy automaton $A = (S,S_o,S_f,d)$ over X with respect to c = (c',c") of R' × R". Now, the following equations are valid

$$\begin{aligned}[A](w) &= S_o \cdot d^{\#}(w) \cdot S_f \\ &= (S_o', S_o) \cdot (d'^{\#}(w), d''^{\#}(w)) \cdot (S_f', S_f) \\ &= (S_o' \cdot d'^{\#}(w) \cdot S_f', S_o \cdot d''^{\#}(w) \cdot S_f).\end{aligned}$$

Since $A' = (S,S_o',S_f',d')$ is an R'-fuzzy automaton over X as well as $A'' = (S,S_o'',S_f'',d'')$ is an R"-fuzzy automaton over X, we deduce for all w of X*:

$$[A](w) \geq c \quad \text{if and only if} \quad [A'](w) \geq c' \quad \text{and} \quad [A''](w) \geq c''.$$

By setting $L' = \{w \in X^* \mid [A'](w) \geq c'\}$ and $L'' = \{w \in X^* \mid [A''](w) \geq c''\}$, it can easily be seen that L belongs to $\mathcal{L}_{R'} \sqcap \mathcal{L}_{R''}$. Thus

$$\mathcal{L}_{R' \times R''} \subseteq \mathcal{L}_{R'} \sqcap \mathcal{L}_{R''}.$$

(2) Let $L' \in \mathcal{L}_{R'}$ be a language over X and $L'' \in \mathcal{L}_{R''}$ be a language over Y. Without loss of generality we assume X = Y. Then there are an R'-fuzzy automaton $A' = (S', S'_0, S'_f, d')$ over X accepting L' with respect to $c' \in R'$ as well as an R''-fuzzy automaton $A'' = (S'', S''_0, S''_f, d'')$ over X accepting L'' with respect to $c'' \in R''$. Observe that the intersection $L' \cap L''$ can be accepted by the following $R' \times R''$-fuzzy automaton $A = (S, S_0, S_f, d)$ over X with respect to $c = (c', c'')$:

$$S_0(s) = \begin{cases} (S'_0(s), 1) & \text{if } s \in S' \\ (1, S_0(s)) & \text{if } s \in S'' \\ (0,0) & \text{otherwise} \end{cases}$$

$$S_f(s) = \begin{cases} (S'_f(s), 1) & \text{if } s \in S' \\ (1, S_f(s)) & \text{if } s \in S'' \\ (0,0) & \text{otherwise} \end{cases}$$

$$d(x)(s_1,s_2) = \begin{cases} (d'(x)(s_1,s_2), 1) & \text{if } s_1,s_2 \in S' \\ (1, d\ (x)(s_1,s_2)) & \text{if } s_1,s_2 \in S'' \\ (0,0) & \text{otherwise.} \end{cases}$$

Therefore, $L = L' \cap L''$ is an $R' \times R''$-fuzzy language. Hence

$$\mathcal{L}_{R' \times R''} \supseteq \mathcal{L}_{R'} \sqcap \mathcal{L}_{R''}$$

which proves the theorem.

Remark. Let $(R_i)_{i \in I}$ be an arbitrary family of po-semirings, then we have (cf. [89]):

$$\mathcal{L}_{\prod_{i \in I} R_i} \subseteq \prod_{i \in I} \mathcal{L}_{R_i},$$

where ΠR_i denotes the direct product of all po-semirings R_i and $\Pi \mathcal{L}_{R_i}$ is the wedge operation extended for arbitrary families of languages. In comparison with coproduct, only inclusion holds true in the infinite case (see Section 3.2). Consider the language $L = \{a^n b^{k \cdot n} \mid n \geq 1,\ k \geq 1\}$ over $X = \{a, b\}$. L can be represented as infinite union of rational languages $L_i = a^i (b^i)^*$. Thus

$$X^* \setminus L = \bigcap\{(X^* \setminus L_i) \mid i \geq 1\}.$$

Since each language $X^* \setminus L_i$ is rational, $X^* \setminus L$ belongs to $\prod_{i\geq 1} \mathcal{L}_i$, where $\mathcal{L}_i = \mathcal{L}_{rat}$ for all $i \geq 1$. But L is not rational *). Therefore, $X^* \setminus L$ is not a $\prod_{i\geq 1} R_i$-fuzzy language, where $R_i = \underline{2}$ for all $i \geq 1$. Notice that this family of $\prod R_i$-fuzzy languages equals $\mathcal{L}_{rat}$. Hence the inclusion stated above is proper.

Theorem 3.25. Let R be the direct product $R = R_1 \times R_2 \times \ldots \times R_n$ of po-semirings $R_1, R_2, \ldots, R_n$. Then $\mathcal{L}_R$ equals $\mathcal{L}_{rat}$ if and only if any R_i-fuzzy language is rational for $i = 1, 2, \ldots, n$.

Considering the multiplicative structure of a given po-semiring, we exhibit an interesting feature of R-fuzzy languages.

Theorem 3.26. The family of all R-fuzzy languages properly includes all rational languages if the multiplicative monoid of R contains a non-trivial subgroup.

Proof. Let R be a po-semiring with the assumed property. Then there must exist an element r of R different from 0 and 1. Without loss of generality, we suppose that $r > 1$ belongs to the subgroup. Consider the following R-fuzzy automaton $A = (\{s_o, s_f\}, s_o, s_f, d)$ over $X = \{x, y\}$ with

$$d(x) = \begin{vmatrix} r & r \\ 0 & 0 \end{vmatrix} \quad \text{and} \quad d(y) = \begin{vmatrix} 0 & 0 \\ 0 & r^{-1} \end{vmatrix}.$$

An easy calculation shows

$$[A](w) = \begin{cases} r^{m-n} & \text{if } w = x^m y^n \text{ for } m,n \geq 1 \\ 0 & \text{otherwise.} \end{cases}$$

Since all powers of r are different, we have

$$L(A, 1) = \{x^m y^n \mid m > n \geq 1\}.$$

It is well-known that this language is not rational. Because of the special choice of transition matrices, addition is not used. Consequently, the assertion of Theorem 3.26 is proved.

The po-semiring $\mathbb{Q}_+$ of all non-negative rational numbers fulfils the assumption of Theorem 3.26. Therefore, $\mathcal{L}_{rat}$ is properly included in the family of all $\mathbb{Q}_+$-fuzzy languages. But this is a known fact. P. Turakainen [81] has investigated stochastic automata where the coefficients of the

*) private communication from R. G. Bucharajev

initial and final vectors and each transition matrix are rational numbers. A language is said to be rational stochastic if it is accepted by such an automaton with respect to a rational cut-point. The family of all rational stochastic languages properly contains $\mathcal{L}_{rat}$ and is properly included in $\mathcal{L}_{stoch}$. Any rational stochastic language is a $\mathbb{Q}_+$-fuzzy language and vice versa.

At the end of this section we focus our attention on the question whether there exists an infinite hierarchy of special R-fuzzy languages. Let $\mathbb{Q}_+^n$ denote the n-fold direct product of $\mathbb{Q}_+$.

Definition 3.7. A $\mathbb{Q}_+^n$-fuzzy language is said to be n-rational for $n \geq 1$. In this context rational languages are called 0-rational. The family of all n-rational languages is denoted by $\mathcal{L}_{n\text{-}rat}$.

At first, some properties of 1-rational languages will be recalled (cf. [19,42,55,60]). $\mathcal{L}_{1\text{-}rat}$ is closed neither under intersection nor under union. But the intersection and the union of a 1-rational language with a rational one is 1-rational.

Theorem 3.27 [37]. For any 1-rational language $L \subseteq X^*$ there exists a pair of nondeterministic automata $\mathfrak{A}$ and $\mathfrak{A}'$ over X (considered as $\mathbb{N}$-fuzzy automata) such that

$$L = \{w \in X^* \mid [\mathfrak{A}](w) \geq [\mathfrak{A}'](w)\}.$$

We denote by $\mathcal{L}_{1\text{-}rat}(=)$ the set of all those languages L for which a pair of $\mathbb{N}$-fuzzy automata $\mathfrak{A}$ and $\mathfrak{A}'$ exists satisfying

$$L = \{w \in X^* \mid [\mathfrak{A}](w) = [\mathfrak{A}'](w)\}.$$

$\mathcal{L}_{1\text{-}rat}(=)$ is a proper subset of $\mathcal{L}_{1\text{-}rat}$.

Let $p = a_0 + a_1u + a_2u^2 + \ldots + a_nu^n$ a polynomial in one variable with coefficients of a commutative po-semiring R. For any R-fuzzy automaton $\mathfrak{A} = (S, S_0, S_f, d)$ over X there exists an R-fuzzy automaton $p\mathfrak{A}$ over X such that

$$[p\mathfrak{A}](w) = p([\mathfrak{A}](w)) \qquad \text{for all } w \in X^*.$$

We define $p\mathfrak{A}$ as follows

$$p\mathfrak{A} = (\bigcup_{i=0}^{n} S^i, \sum_{i=0}^{n} a_i S_0^i, \sum_{i=0}^{n} S_f^i, \sum_{i=0}^{n} d^i)$$

where $S^0 = \{s_0\}$, $S^1 = S$ and $S^{i+1} = S^i \times S$ for $i \geq 1$. The powers S_0^i, S_f^i and d^i are determined by

$$S_o^o(s_o) = S_f^o(s_o) = d^o(x)(s_o,s_o) = 1$$

$$S_o^i(s_1,s_2,\dots,s_i) = S_o(s_1)\cdot S_o(s_2)\cdot\dots\cdot S_o(s_i)$$

$$S_f^i(s_1,s_2,\dots,s_i) = S_f(s_1)\cdot S_f(s_2)\cdot\dots\cdot S_f(s_i)$$

$$d^i(x)((s_1,s_2,\dots,s_i),(s_1',s_2',\dots,s_i')) = d(x)(s_1,s_1')\cdot d(x)(s_2,s_2')\cdot\dots\cdot d(x)(s_i,s_i')$$

for all $s_1,s_2,\dots,s_i,s_1',s_2',\dots,s_i' \in S$ and $i \geq 1$. Now, we derive

$$\begin{aligned}[pA](w) &= (\sum_{i=0}^{n} a_i S_o^i)\cdot(\sum_{i=0}^{n} d^i)^*(w)\cdot(\sum_{i=0}^{n} S_f^i) \\ &= \sum_{i=0}^{n} a_i(S_o^i\cdot d^{i*}(w)\cdot S_f^i) \\ &= \sum_{i=0}^{n} a_i(S_o\cdot d^*(w)\cdot S_f)^i \\ &= p([A](w))\end{aligned}$$

for all $w \in X^*$.

<u>Examples</u>. 1) Let p and q be polynomials in one variable with coefficients in $\mathbb{Q}_+$. Then the languages

$$L_{p\geq q} = \{w \in X^* \mid p(|w|_x) \geq q(|w|_y)\}$$

$$L_{p=q} = \{w \in X^* \mid p(|w|_x) = q(|w|_y)\}$$

over $X = \{x,y\}$ are 1-rational, where $|w|_x$ and $|w|_y$ denote the numbers of symbols x and y in w, respectively. By Theorem 3.27, it is sufficient to show there exist automata A and A' over X so that $[A](w) = |w|_x$ and $[A'](w) = |w|_y$. Consider $A = (\{s_o,s_f\},s_o,s_f,d)$ and $A' = (\{s_o,s_f\},s_o,s_f,d')$ whose transition matrices are defined by

$$d(x) = d'(y) = \begin{vmatrix} 1 & 1 \\ 0 & 1 \end{vmatrix} \qquad d(y) = d'(x) = \begin{vmatrix} 1 & 0 \\ 0 & 1 \end{vmatrix} .$$

Obviously, A and A' have the property in question. In particular, the context-free language $L = \{x^n y^n \mid n \geq 0\}$ is 1-rational because

$$L = L_{u=u} \cap x^*y^*.$$

2) The languages

$$L_{k,\geq} = \{x^m(y^n x^n)^k \mid m \geq n \geq 1\}$$

$$L_{k,=} = \{x^n(y^nx^n)^k | n \geq 1\}$$

over $X = \{x,y\}$ are 1-rational for $k \geq 1$. Only for the case $k = 1$, we exhibit two $\mathbb{N}$-fuzzy automata $\mathcal{A} = (S,s_0,s_f,d)$ and $\mathcal{A}' = (S,s_0,s_f,d')$ over X so that

$$[\mathcal{A}](w) = \begin{cases} (2\cdot3)^m & \text{if } w \in x^my^*x^* \text{ for } m \geq 1 \\ 0 & \text{otherwise} \end{cases}$$

$$[\mathcal{A}'](w) = \begin{cases} 2^n\cdot3^{n'} & \text{if } w \in x^*y^nx^{n'} \text{ for } n,n' \geq 1 \\ 0 & \text{otherwise.} \end{cases}$$

$\mathcal{A}$ as well as $\mathcal{A}'$ have four states, i.e. $S = \{s_0,s,s',s_f\}$ and the transition matrices are defined by

$$d(x) = \begin{vmatrix} 6 & 6 & 0 & 0 \\ 0 & 0 & 0 & 0 \\ 0 & 0 & 1 & 1 \\ 0 & 0 & 0 & 0 \end{vmatrix} \qquad d(y) = \begin{vmatrix} 0 & 0 & 0 & 0 \\ 0 & 1 & 1 & 0 \\ 0 & 0 & 0 & 0 \\ 0 & 0 & 0 & 0 \end{vmatrix}$$

$$d'(x) = \begin{vmatrix} 1 & 1 & 0 & 0 \\ 0 & 0 & 0 & 0 \\ 0 & 0 & 3 & 3 \\ 0 & 0 & 0 & 0 \end{vmatrix} \qquad d'(y) = \begin{vmatrix} 0 & 0 & 0 & 0 \\ 0 & 2 & 2 & 0 \\ 0 & 0 & 0 & 0 \\ 0 & 0 & 0 & 0 \end{vmatrix}$$

In [17] it is shown that every $\mathbb{N}$-fuzzy automaton $\mathcal{A}$ over X can be simulated by a non-deterministic automaton $\mathfrak{A}$ over X such that $[\mathcal{A}](w) = [\mathfrak{A}](w)$ holds for all $w \in X^*$. Thus, by Theorem 3.27, $L_{1,\geq}$ is 1-rational. Since

$$L_{1,=} = \{w \in X^* | [\mathcal{A}](w) = [\mathcal{A}'](w)\} \cap x^*y^*x^*,$$

the language $L_{1,=}$ is also 1-rational. In order to prove that $L_{k,\geq}$ and $L_{k,=}$ are 1-rational for $k > 1$, 2k pair-wise different prime numbers a_1, $a_2,\ldots,a_{2k}$ are used for constructing $\mathbb{N}$-fuzzy automata $\mathcal{A}$ and $\mathcal{A}'$ so that

$$[\mathcal{A}](w) = \begin{cases} (a_1\cdot a_2\cdot\ldots a_{2k})^m & \text{if } w \in x^m(y^*x^*)^k \text{ for } m \geq 1 \\ 0 & \text{otherwise} \end{cases}$$

$$[\mathcal{A}'](w) = \begin{cases} a_1^{n_1}\cdot a_2^{n_2}\ldots a_{2k}^{n_{2k}} & \text{if } w \in x^*y^{n_1}x^{n_2}\ldots x^{n_{2k}} \text{ for } n_i \geq 1 \\ 0 & \text{otherwise} \end{cases}$$

in an analogous way.

3) The languages

$$L_{*,\geq} = \{x^m y (x^l y)^k x^n y \mid m \geq n \geq 1,\ k,l \geq 0\}$$

$$L_{*,=} = \{x^n y (x^l y)^k x^n y \mid n \geq 1,\ k,l \geq 0\}$$

over $X = \{x,y\}$ are 1-rational. Consider the $\mathbb{N}$-fuzzy automata $\mathcal{A}$ and $\mathcal{A}'$ over X given by

$$\mathcal{A} = (\{s_0,s,s',s_f\},s_0,s_f,d) \quad \text{and} \quad \mathcal{A}' = (\{s_0,s,s',s_f\},s_0,s_f,d')$$

where the transition matrices are defined as follows

$$d(x) = \begin{vmatrix} 2 & 0 & 0 & 0 \\ 0 & 1 & 0 & 0 \\ 0 & 0 & 1 & 0 \\ 0 & 0 & 0 & 0 \end{vmatrix} \qquad d'(x) = \begin{vmatrix} 1 & 0 & 0 & 0 \\ 0 & 1 & 0 & 0 \\ 0 & 0 & 2 & 0 \\ 0 & 0 & 0 & 0 \end{vmatrix}$$

$$d(y) = \begin{vmatrix} 0 & 1 & 0 & 0 \\ 0 & 1 & 1 & 0 \\ 0 & 0 & 0 & 1 \\ 0 & 0 & 0 & 0 \end{vmatrix} \qquad d'(y) = \begin{vmatrix} 0 & 1 & 0 & 0 \\ 0 & 1 & 1 & 0 \\ 0 & 0 & 0 & 1 \\ 0 & 0 & 0 & 0 \end{vmatrix}.$$

It can easily be seen that

$$[\mathcal{A}](w) = \begin{cases} 2^m & \text{if } w \in x^m y (x^* y)^* \text{ for } m \geq 1 \\ 0 & \text{otherwise} \end{cases}$$

$$[\mathcal{A}'](w) = \begin{cases} 2^n & \text{if } w \in (x^* y)^* x^n y \text{ for } n \geq 1 \\ 0 & \text{otherwise.} \end{cases}$$

This implies the statement.

4) Let $L_1,L_2,\dots,L_k$ be 1-rational languages over $X = \{x,y\}$. Then the languages

$$L_{\geq}(L_1,L_2,\dots,L_k) = \{x^m y w_1 y x^n y w_2 y \dots y w_k y x^n \mid w_i \in L_i \text{ and } m \geq n\}$$

$$L_{=}(L_1,L_2,\dots,L_k) = \{x^n y w_1 y x^n y w_2 y \dots y w_k y x^n \mid w_i \in L_i\}$$

are 1-rational.

5) Let p,p',p'' be polynomials in one variable with coefficients of $\mathbb{Q}_+$. Then the language

$$L(p,p',p'') = \{w \in X^* \mid p(|w|_x) > p'(|w|_y) > p''(|w|_z)\}$$

over $X = \{x,y,z\}$ is 2-rational. But $L(u,u,u)$ is 1-rational [42].

Theorem 3.28. The families of n-rational languages form an infinite hierarchy

$$\mathcal{L}_{0\text{-rat}} \subset \mathcal{L}_{1\text{-rat}} \subset \mathcal{L}_{2\text{-rat}} \subset \ldots \subset \mathcal{L}_{n\text{-rat}} \subset \ldots$$

Proof. The inclusion of $\mathcal{L}_{n\text{-rat}}$ in $\mathcal{L}_{(n+1)\text{-rat}}$ is trivial for $n \geq 0$. But it is known that $\mathcal{L}_{0\text{-rat}} = \mathcal{L}_{rat}$ is properly included in $\mathcal{L}_{1\text{-rat}}$. Since $\mathcal{L}_{1\text{-rat}}$ is not closed under intersection, it follows that $\mathcal{L}_{1\text{-rat}}$ is a proper subset of $\mathcal{L}_{2\text{-rat}}$. The next steps can be proved by induction over n. In [42] it has been shown that the 2-rational language $L(p,p',p'')$ of Example 5) is not 1-rational if $p = u^k$, $p' = u^{k'}$ and $p'' = u^{k''}$ with $k > k' > k''$ is chosen. In this way we can establish n-rational languages $L(p,p',\ldots,p^{(n)})$ which are not elements of $\mathcal{L}_{(n-1)\text{-rat}}$ for $n \geq 3$.

Theorem 3.29. A language is n-rational if and only if there exist n 1-rational languages $L_1, L_2, \ldots, L_n$ such that $L = L_1 \cap L_2 \cap \ldots \cap L_n$ holds for $n \geq 1$.

Theorem 3.30. For any n-rational language $L \subseteq X^*$ there exist n pairs of non-deterministic automata $\mathfrak{A}_i$ and $\mathfrak{A}_i'$ over X satisfying

$$L = \{w \in X^* \mid [\mathfrak{A}_i](w) \geq [\mathfrak{A}_i'](w) \text{ for } i = 1,2,\ldots,n\}.$$

Remark. In [55] it is noticed that every 1-rational language is context-sensitive. Since the family of all context-sensitive languages is closed under intersection, any n-rational language is context-sensitive by Theorem 3.29.

Open problems:

1) Is the family $\mathcal{L}_{n\text{-rat}}$ closed under complementation for $n \geq 2$?
2) Let L' and L'' be n'-rational and n''-rational languages, respectively. Does there exist a natural number n such that $L' \cup L''$ is n-rational?
3) Is the set $\mathcal{L}_{\omega\text{-rat}} = \bigcup_{n \geq 0} \mathcal{L}_{n\text{-rat}}$ a Boolean algebra?

REFERENCES

[1] Агасандян, Г.А.: Автоматы с переменней структурой.
ДАН СССР I74, 3, 529-530, I967

[2] Arbib, M.A. and Manes, E.G.: A category - theoretic approach to systems in a fuzzy world.
COINS Technical Report 74B-3, Computer and Information Science, Univ. of Massachusetts at Amherst, 1974

[3] Arbib, M.A. and Manes, E.G.: Fuzzy morphism in automata theory.
Lectures Notes in Computer Science Vol 25, 80-86, 1975

[4] Arden, D.N.: Delayed logic and finite state machines.
Theory of Comp. Machine Designe, Univ. of Michigan, Ann Arbor, 1-35, 1960

[5] Autebert, I.M.: Pushdown-automata and families of languages generating cylinders.
Lecture Notes in Computer Science Vol 53, 231-239, 1977

[6] Baer, R.M. and Spanier, E.H.: Referenced automata and metaregular families.
J. Comput. System Sci. 3, 423-446, 1969

[7] Barnes, D.W. and Mack, J.M.: An Algebraic Introduction to Mathematical Logic.
Springer-Verlag, New York, Heidelberg, Berlin 1975

[8] Berstel, J.: Some recent results on recognizable formal power series.
Lecture Notes in Computer Science Vol 56, 39-48

[9] Bellman, R., Kalaba, R. and Zadeh, L.A.: Abstract pattern classification.
J. Math. Anal. Appl. 13, 1-7, 1966

[10] Birkhoff, G.: Lattice Theorie.
American Mathematical Society, Providence 1967

[11] Boasson, L.: Classification of the context-free languages.
Lecture Notes in Computer Science Vol 53, 34-43, 1977

[12] Боднарчук, В.Г.: Метрическое постранство событий I, II.
Кибернетика I, 24-27, II, 22-30, I965

[13] Brunner, J. and Wechler, W.: On behavior of R-fuzzy automata.
Lecture Notes in Computer Science Vol. 45, 210-215, 1976

[14] Cohen, P.M.: Universal Algebra.
Harper and Row, Publ. New York, Evaston and London 1965

[15] Conway, J.E.: Regular Algebra and Finite Machines.
Chapman and Hill, London and Colchester 1971

[16] Ehrig, H., Kiermeier, K.D., Kreowski, H.J. and Kühnel, W.: Universal Theory of Automata. Teubner Verlag, Stuttgart 1974

[17] Eilenberg, S.: Automata, Languages and Machines Vol A. Acad. Press, New York and London 1974

[18] Fliess, M.: Sur certaines familles de séries formelles. These Sc. math., Université Paris VII 1972

[19] Fliess, M.: Propiétés booléennes des languages stochastiques. Math. Systems Theory 7, 353-359, 1974

[20] Fliess, M.: Un calcul symbolique non commutatif pour les asservissements non linéaires et non stationnaires. Lecture Notes in Computer Science Vol 41, 496-509, 1976

[21] Fu, K.S. and Li, T.J.: Formulation of learning automata. Information Sci. 1, 237-256, 1969

[22] Fu, K.S. and Swain, P.H.: On syntactic pattern recognition. Third Intern. Symp. on Comp. and Inform. Sc., 1969

[23] Giles, R.: Lukasiewicz logic and fuzzy sets theory. Internat. J. Man-Machine Studies 8, 313-327, 1976

[24] Ginsburg, S.: Algebraic and Automata-Theoretic Properties of Formal Languages. North-Holland Publ. Company, Amsterdam and Oxford, American Elsevier Publ. Company, New York 1975

[25] Goguen, J.A.: L-fuzzy sets. J. Math. Anal. Appl., 18, 145-174, 1967

[26] Goguen, J.A.: The logic of inexact concepts. Synthese 19, 325-373, 1968-69

[27] Goguen, J.A.: Hierarchical inexact data structures in artificial intelligence problems. Proc. of Fifth Hawii Intern. Conference on Systems Sciences, Honolulu, 345-347, 1972

[28] Goguen, J.A.: Axioms, extensions and applications for fuzzy sets. IBM Research Report RC 4547, Yorktown Heights, N.Y., 1973

[29] Goguen, J.A.: On fuzzy robot planning. In Fuzzy Sets and Their Applications to Cognitive and Decision Processes. (Eds. Zadeh, L.A., Fu, K.S., Tanaka, K. and Shimura, M.), Acad. Press, New York, San Francisco, London, 1975

[30] Gottwald, S.: Untersuchungen zur Mehrwertigen Mengenlehre I, II. Math. Nachr. 72, 298-303, 74, 329-336, 1976

[31] Hasse, M. und Michler, L.: Theorie der Kategorien.
Deutscher Verlag d. Wiss., Berlin 1966

[32] Hirai, H., Asai, K. and Katajima: Fuzzy automaton and its application to learning control systems.
Memo of the Fac. of Eng., Osaka City Univ. 10, 67-73, 1968

[33] Huang, T. and Fu, K.S.: On stochastic context-free languages.
Information Sci. 3, 201-224, 1971

[34] Inagaki, Y., Fukumura, T. and Matuura, H.: Some aspects of linear automata.
Information and Control 20, 439-479, 1972

[35] Kandel, A.: Application of fuzzy logic to the detection of static hazards in combinational switching systems.
Internat. J. Comput. Information Sci. 3, No.2, 129-139, 1974

[36] Kandel, A.: On the properties of fuzzy switching functions.
J. Cybernet. 4, No.1, 119-126, 1974

[37] Karpinski, M.: Note on multiplicity languages.
Preprint of Polish Acad. of Sci. Inst. of Math., Poznań 1975

[38] Kaufmann, A.: Introduction to the Theory of Fuzzy Subsets, Vol I.
Acad. Press, New York, San Francisco, London 1975

[39] Kim, H.H.: Formal grammars characterized by weights.
Ph.D. Thesis, Osaka Univ., Electrical Engineering, Osaka 1976

[40] Klaua, D.: Über einen Ansatz zur mehrwertigen Mengenlehre.
Monatsb. Deutsche Akad. d. Wiss. Berlin 7, 859-867, 1965

[41] Klaua, D.: Stetige Gleichmächtigkeiten kontinuierlichwertiger Mengen.
Monatsb. Deutsche Akad. d. Wiss. Berlin 12, 749-758, 1970

[42] Лапиньш, Я.К.: О нестохастических языках, получаемых как объединение или пересечение стохастических языков.
Автоматика и Вычислительная Техника /АН Лат. ССР/ 4, 6-13, 1974

[43] Lee, S.T. and Zadeh, L.A.: Note on fuzzy languages.
Information Sci. 1, 421-434, 1969

[44] Летичевский, А.А.: Представление контекстно-свободных языков в автоматов с памятью типа push-down.
Кибернетика 2, 80-84, 1965

[45] Manes. E.G.: Algebraic Theories.
Springer-Verlag, New York, Heidelberg, Berlin 1976

[46] Marinos, P.N.: Fuzzy logic and its application to switching systems.
IEEE Trans. Computers C-18, 343-348, 1969

[47] Maurer, H.: Theoretische Grundlagen der Programmiersprachen.
Bibliographisches Institut, Mannheim, Wien und Zürich 1969

[48] Mizumoto, M.: Fuzzy automata and fuzzy grammars.
Ph.D. Thesis, Osaka Univ., Elektrical Engineering, Osaka 1971

[49] Mizumoto, M., Toyoda, J. and Tanaka, K.: Some consideration on fuzzy automata.
J. Comput. System Sci. 3, No.4, 409-422, 1969

[50] Mizumoto, M., Toyoda, J. and Tanaka, K.: Fuzzy languages.
Systems-Computers-Controls 1, 333-340, 1970

[51] Mizumoto, M., Toyoda, J. and Tanaka, K.: N-fold fuzzy grammars.
Information Sci. 5, 25-43, 1973

[52] Mizumoto, M., Toyoda, J. and Tanaka, K.: Variuos kinds of automata with weights.
J. Comput. System Sci. 10, 219-236, 1975

[53] Mizumoto, M. and Tanaka, K.: Fuzzy-fuzzy automata.
Kybernetes 5, 107-112, 1976

[54] Morgan, G. and Pelletier, F.J.: Some notes concerning fuzzy logics.
Preprint 1976

[55] Nasu, M. and Honda, N.: Mappings induced by PGSM-mappings and some recursively unsolvable problems of finite probabilistic automata.
Information and Control 15, No.3, 250-273, 1969

[56] Negoita, C.V.: On the application of the fuzzy sets separation system for automatic classification in information retrieval systems.
Information Sci. 5, 279-286, 1973

[57] Negoita, C.V. and Ralescu, D.A.: Applications of Fuzzy Sets to Systems Analysis.
Birkhäuser Verlag , Basel und Stuttgart 1975

[58] Pavelka, J.: On fuzzy logic I, II, III.
will appear in Z. Math. Logik Grundlagen Math.

[59] Pavelka, J. and Wechler, W.: GÖDEL-BERNAYS models for fuzzy sets.
Manuscript

[60] Paz, A.: Introduction to Probabilistic Automata.
Academic Press, New York and London 1971

[61] Pohl, H.W.: Über kontextfreie stochastische Sprachen.
EIK 12, No.6, 313-323, 1976

[62] Pultr, A.: Closed categories of L-fuzzy sets.
Technische Univ. Dresden, Sekt. Math., WBZ Heft 16/76, 1976

[63] Rasiowa, H.: An Algebraic Approach to Non-Classical Logics. North-Holland Publ. Comp., Amsterdam and London, American Elsevier Publ. Comp., New York 1974

[64] Rescher, N.: Many-Valued Logic. McGraw-Hill, New York 1969

[65] Rosser, J.B. and Turquette, A.R.: Many-Valued Logics. Studies in Logics and Foundations of Mathematics North-Holland Publ. Comp., Amsterdam 1952

[66] Salomaa, A.: On finite automata with a time-variant structure. Information and Control 13, 85-98, 1968

[67] Salomaa, A.: Probabilistic and weighted grammars. Information and Control 15, 529-544, 1969

[68] Salomaa, A.: Formal Languages. Acad. Press, New York, San Francisco and London 1973

[69] Salomaa, A.: Formal Power Series. will appear

[70] Santos, E.S.: Maximin automata. Information and Control 13, 363-377, 1968

[71] Santos, E.S.: Maximin, minimax, and composite sequential machines. J. Math. Anal. Appl. 24, 246-259, 1968

[72] Santos, E.S. and Wee, W.G.: General formulation of sequential machines. Information and Control 12, 5-10, 1968

[73] Schwartz, D.: Mengenlehre über vorgegebenen algebraischen Systemen. Math. Nachr. 53, 365-370, 1972

[74] Schützenberger, P.M.: On the definition of a family of automata. Information and Control 4, 245-270, 1961

[75] Schützenberger, P.M.: On a theorem of R. Jungen. Proc. Amer. Math. Soc. 13, 885-890, 1962

[76] Спивак, М.А.: Введение Абстрактную Теорию Автоматов. Изд. Саратовского Университета, Саратов 1970

[77] Stanat, D.: A homomorphism theorem for weighted context-free grammars. J. Comput. System Sci. 6, 217-232, 1972

[78] Turakainen, P.: On probabilistic automata and their generalizations. Ann. Acad. Sci. Fenn. Ser. AI 429, 1968

[79] Turakainen, P.: On time-variant probabilistic automata with monitors. Ann. Univ. Turku Ser AI 130, 1969

[80] Turakainen, P.: Generalized automata and stochastic languages. Proc. Amer. Math. Soc. 21, 303-309, 1969

[81] Turakainen, P.: On languages representable in rational probabilistic automata. Ann. Univ. Turku Ser. AI 439, 1969

[82] Turakainen, P.: Some closure properties of the family of stochastic languages. Information and Control 14, 319-357, 1971

[83] Wechler, W.: R-fuzzy automata with a time-variant structure. Lecture Notes in Computer Science Vol 28, 73-76, 1974

[84] Wechler, W.: Zur Verallgemeinerung des Theorems von Kleene-Schützenberger auf zeitvariable Automaten. Elektron. Informationsverarbeit. Kybernetik 11, 439-445, 1975

[85] Wechler, W.: Automaten über Inputkategorien. Elektron. Informationsverarbeit. Kybernetik 11, 681-685, 1975

[86] Wechler, W.: R-fuzzy grammars. Lecture Notes in Computer Science Vol 32, 450-456, 1975

[87] Wechler, W.: The concept of fuzziness in the theory of automata. In "Modern Trends in Cybernetics and Systems" (Eds. J. Rose, C. Biliciu). Springer-Verl. Berlin, Heidelberg, New York 1977

[88] Wechler, W.: A hierarchy of n-rational languages. TU-Preprint 07-24-76, Technische Univ. Dresden, 1976

[89] Wechler, W.: Families of R-fuzzy languages. Lecture Notes in Computer Science Vol 56, 117-186, 1977

[90] Вехлер, В. и Агасандян, Г.А.: Автоматы с переменной структурой и метарегулярные ясыки. Техническая Кибернетика I, I46-I48, I974

[91] Wechler, W. and Dimitrov, V.: R-fuzzy automata. In "Information Processing '74", North-Holland Publ. Comp., Amsterdam 1974

[92] Wee, W.G. and Fu, K.S.: A formulation of fuzzy automata and its application as a model of learning systems. IEEE Trans. Systems and Cybernetics SCC-5, 215-223, 1969

[93] Zadeh, L.A.: Fuzzy sets. Information and Control 8, 338-353, 1965

[94] Zadeh, L.A.: Fuzzy languages and their relation to human and machine intelligence. Proc. Intern. Conf. "Man and Computer" Bordeaux 1970, 130-165 S. Karger Verl. Basel, München, New York 1972

[95] Zadeh, L.A.: Fuzzy logic and approximate reasoning. Synthese 30, 407-428, 1975

Appendix: FUZZY CONTROL

by Vladimir Dimitrov

1. Fuzzy control of complex systems

L. A. Zadeh [13] stated the following incompatibility principle: 'As the the complexity of a system increases, our ability to make precise and yet significant statements about its behaviour diminishes until a threshold is reached beyond which precision and significance become a most mutually eclusive characteristics'. At the top of system gradation with respect to complexity the humanistic systems are placed - systems whose 'elements' are human beings able to communicate, to make decisions and to carry out actions in a certain field of activities. Different aspects of humanistic systems are studied in economics, management science etc.

For systems whose description is only possible in a fuzzy way (by using a natural language for instance), a control is put into correspondence in the form of fuzzy instructions to express inprecisely formulated actions and to permit different interpretations by different ways of their executing. Let us call such a control fuzzy.

The incertainty included in a given complex system will be controlled by means of the incertainty included in the fuzzy control instructions. Elementary systems which are deterministically describable can be controlled by a deterministic law. Stochastic systems need a stochastic approach.

As a rule, a humanistic system is controlled by some controlling body which tries to orientate the activities of its individuals achieving some goal. It is supposed that the goals as well as the limitations over the set of actions available for the individuals are presented by the controlling body.

Let S be a set of fuzzy instructions applied to a humanistic system H. Thereby, an instruction is called fuzzy with respect to an individual h of H if h generates a fuzzy set $A: X \to [0,1]$ representing various ways of understanding the meaning of s by h. X is a set of alternatives generated by all individuals of H. The alternatives represent instructions or actions related to the meaning of s. A(x) is the degree of membership of x in A and associated with each x of X its compatibility with the meaning of s. Formally, this situation shall be expressed as follows

$$h \circledast s = A \quad \text{with} \quad A: X \to [0,1]$$

where ⓤ can be read as 'understands'.

The support $|A|$ of a fuzzy set A is defined by $|A| = \{x | A(x) \neq 0\}$. If $A(x) \leq 0.5$ for all $x \in |A|$, then the individual h is neutral with respect to the meaning of s. All $x \in |A|$ for which $A(x) > 0.5$ are called significant. If at least for one $x \in |A|$, $A(x) > 0.5$, the individual h is decisive with respect to s.

Example. Let s = <go slowly>, $h_1, h_2 \in H$, $X = \{1,2,3,4,5\}$ is refered as available speeds (km per hour) at which h_1 and h_2 have to move in order to perform s. Let

$$h_1 @ s = 0.1/5 + 0.5/4 + 0.9/3 + 0.7/2 + 0.5/1$$
$$h_2 @ s = 0.4/4 + 0.6/3 + 0.8/2 + 0.9/1$$

where the fuzzy sets are represented in the form

$$A = \sum_{x \in X} A(x)/x.$$

We can see that h_1 intends to perform the instruction <go slowly> 'faster' than h_2.

The operation of clarification is an important tool in our approach. Let $h @_1 s = A^{(1)}$ (the use of indices is explained below) and let $\tilde{x}$ be an alternative of $|A^{(1)}|$. Assume that h understands $\tilde{x}$ as follows $h @ \tilde{x} = A^{(2)}$. Then the operation of clarification describes creating a new fuzzy set by the rule

$$(h @_2 s)(x) = \begin{cases} A^{(1)}(x) & \text{if } x \neq \tilde{x} \\ \min\{A^{(1)}(\tilde{x}), A^{(2)}(x)\} & \text{otherwise.} \end{cases}$$

The fuzzy set obtained in this way may be interpreted as a more detailed understanding of the initial instruction s by h. If there is another alternative $\tilde{x}' \in |A^{(2)}|$ which is fuzzy with respect to h, i.e. $h @ \tilde{x}' = A^{(3)}$, then applying clarification we construct a new fuzzy set:

$$(h @_3 s)(x) = \begin{cases} A^{(1)}(x) & \text{if } x \neq \tilde{x} \\ \min\{A^{(1)}(\tilde{x}), A^{(2)}(x)\} & \text{if } x \neq \tilde{x},\ x \neq \tilde{x}' \\ \min\{A^{(1)}(\tilde{x}), A^{(2)}(\tilde{x}'), A^{(3)}(x)\} & \text{otherwise} \end{cases}$$

By a successive application of clarification, a so-called clarification tree can be obtained. It describes the process of understanding (clarifying) the meaning of s by h. The root of the tree corresponds to the initial instruction. On the first level of the tree all instructions are located which are in the support of the fuzzy set corresponding to the initial instruction. On the second level all instructions are located which are in the support of the first level instructions etc. The indices in the notations $@_i$ and $A^{(i)}$ denote the level of the clarification tree. The number of the levels can be interpreted as a measure of the complexity of s.

<u>Example</u>. Let s = <buy an interesting and understandable book on cybernetics>:

$$h\,@_1\,s = 0.6/x_1 + 0.7/\tilde{x}_2 + 0.9/\tilde{x}_3$$

where x_1 = <buy 'Cybernetics' by N. Wiener>, $\tilde{x}_2$ = <buy an up to date book on pattern recognition>, and $\tilde{x}_3$ = <buy a book on artificial intelligence not too difficult for understanding>.

$$h\,@\,\tilde{x}_2 = 0.7/x_{21} + 0.6/x_{22}$$

where x_{21} = <buy 'Methodology of Pattern Recognition' by S. Watanabe>, x_{22} = <buy 'Syntactic Pattern Recognition' by K. S. Fu>.

$$h\,@\,\tilde{x}_3 = 0.8/x_{31} + 0.9/x_{32}$$

where $\tilde{x}_{31}$ = <buy 'Artificial Intelligence' by S. Slagle> and $\tilde{x}_{32}$ = <buy 'Artificial Intelligence' by N. Nilsson>. Applying clarification, we get

$$h\,@_2\,s = 0.6/x_1 + 0.7/x_{21} + 0.6/x_{22} + 0.8/x_{31} + 0.9/x_{32}.$$

The instructions $x_1, x_{21}, x_{22}, x_{31}$ and x_{32} are non-fuzzy with respect to h.

The final nodes of a clarification tree are either non-fuzzy instructions (actions) or are not understandable (whose execution is unknown for h). But an instruction which is not understandable in time t may be understood in time $t + \Delta t$. Then it becomes the root of some clarification subtree whose final nodes correspond to the non-fuzzy instructions generated by h.

Next, we are going to intoduce a partial order on a clarification tree. We shall say (instruction s_i) $\leq$ (instruction s_j) if s_i is connected with s_j in the clarification tree and s_j is closer to the root of it.
A fuzzy instruction s of S is called executable by an individual h of H if the corresponding clarification tree only has finite descending chains and at least one of its minimal elements represents a non-fuzzy instruction (action).

The problems of coalition forming and stability can be studied after introducing some measure of similarity in understanding a given instruction s by two individuals h_i and h_k. Such a measure could be defined as follows

$$\delta(h_i,h_k|s) = \max\{\min\{(h_i \circledast s)(x),(h_k \circledast s)(x)|x \in X\}\}$$

or in the following manner

$$\delta(h_i,h_k|s) = \begin{cases} 1 - \frac{1}{n_s} \sum_{x \in X} |(h_i \circledast s)(x) - (h_k \circledast s)(x)| & \text{if } X_s \neq \emptyset \\ 0 & \text{if } X_s = 0, \end{cases}$$

where $X_s = \{x \in X|(h_i \circledast s)(x) > 0.5 \text{ and } (h_k \circledast s)(x) > 0.5\}$ and n_s is the cardinality of X_s.

Fuzzy control is only admissible if the controlling body does not know the way which leads to the stated goal. In this case fuzzy control serves as an instrument for finding this way. Therefore, fuzzy control is 'creative'. Generating different alternatives in response to a given fuzzy instruction, the individuals are able to discover effective ways for achieving the goal.

It turns out that the methods of heuristic search [8,10] can be applied for this purpose (cf. [3,4,5]).

2. Decision making by fuzzy automata

A model of s decision maker (DMM) is considered. The model learns to act in an environment with innate structural and relational incertainty, i.e. no perfect knowledge is available about the environment states and relation between them.

The DMM has a non-empty finite set $X = \{x_1,x_2,\dots,x_m\}$ of actions and a non-empty set Q of states. The state q_t in which the DMM is found at time t is an m-dimensional row vector with coefficients in [0,1]. Each component expresses the degree of preference to the corresponding action (which is prefered by DMM to be chosen at time t).

Let Q_d be the subset of all deterministic row vectors of Q, that are vectors with exact one coefficient equal to 1 and all others equals 0. We call Q_d the subset of decision states and $Q_f = Q \setminus Q_d$ the subset of fuzzy states.

The transition behaviour of DMM is determined by a mapping f from $Q \times I \times Q$ into [0,1], where I is a finite set of inputs. Obviously, f can uniquely extended to a mapping from $Q \times I^* \times Q$ into [0,1].

<u>Definition</u>. A DMM is said to be learnable in time t, $t \in N$, if for all $t' \leq t$ there exists a word $w \in I^*$ with length $|w| = t'$ such that for all fuzzy states $q_k \in Q_f$ there is at least one decision state $q_r \in Q_d$ satisfying $f(q_k, w, q_r) = 1$.

With other words, a DMM is learnable if for any t', $0 \leq t' \leq t$, there is an information flow $w = i_t i_{t+1} \ldots i_{t+t'-1}$ such that for any arbitrary fuzzy state q_k one can find at least one decision state q_r which will be the resulting state of q_k with certainty. Moreover, a learnable DMM must pass through at least one indermediate fuzzy state in order to take a transition from an initial state of decision to another state of decision. This corresponds to the heuristic rule: 'If you want to find a new decision try to forget that one which is known already (let it becomes fuzzy)'. The process of learning may be represented as follows:

fuzzy state (many alternatives are possible).	⟶	decision state (one action is chosen)	⟶	fuzzy state	⟶ ... ⟶	decision state

Let us introduce the following quantitative estimation of the information that changes a given state of a DMM into another:

$$\sum_{i=1}^{m} |q_k(i) - q_l(i)| \qquad (*)$$

where $q_k(i)$ and $q_l(i)$ respectively represent the degrees of preference to the action x_i in the states q_k and q_i.

The minimal information accepted by a DMM for which the sum (*) becomes greater than δ (some fixed value) is called an informon by using Yovits' terminology [12]. Especially, we distinguish negative and positive informons denoted by n-informon and p-informon. An n-informon transforms a given state of decision in some fuzzy state and a p-informon transforms a given fuzzy state into some state of decision.

Let a p-informon be applied to a DMM. The effect is similar to the 'contrast intensification' of fuzzy sets [13], a decrease of fuzziness. Each component of the state vector which is a fuzzy distribution over the actions of DMM may be subjected to a transformation which decreases the values of the components less than 0.5 and increases the values of the components which are greater than 0.5. For example, such a transformation may be given by

$$q(i) \rightarrow \begin{cases} 2 \cdot q(i)^2 & \text{if } 0 \leq q(i) \leq 0.5 \\ 1 - 2 \cdot (1 - q(i))^2 & \text{if } 0.5 < q(i) \leq 1. \end{cases}$$

By repeated application of this transformation, the initial fuzzy state will be transformed in some state of decision.

Let an n-informon be applied to a DMM. The effect of its application is similar to the operation 'fuzzification' of fuzzy sets [13], increasing of fuzziness. The state vector is multiplied by a properly chosen $m \times m$ fuzzy matrix (whose coefficients are elements of $[0,1]$). Each coefficient of this matrix has the role of a 'fuzzifier'.

In which way are the different informons chosen to be applied to DMM? The acceptance of p- and n-informons is controlled by the value structure of a DMM. Every action has some effect in the sense that the action brings gain (reward) or loss (penalty) to the decision maker. A DMM has to know how to choose its actions in order to gain as much as possible. The papers by S. K. Fu et al. [6,7,11] on theory and practice of learning by stochastic and fuzzy automata give a detailed answer to the problem of the selection of actions. Both the gain and the loss received by a given actior are connected with the value structure of the DMM which includes

- fuzzy matrices of the type 'action - output' whose elements express the degree in which a given action could induces the outputs at the time instant t
- fuzzy column vectors whose components characterize the utility of each expected output at the time instant t.

Let an informon $i_t \in I$ be applied to the DMM. If $M(i_t)$ denotes the $m \times n$ matrix of the type 'action - decision' and g_t is the n-dimensional column vector of utility (gain), then $q_t \cdot M(i_t) \cdot g_t$ determines the usefulness of the informon i_t applied on the state q_t.

The question is how to select a sequence of informons so that the summarized utility of DMM is maximal. In practical situations where the number of states and outputs of a DMM is very great the heuristic techniques seem to be of importance for solving this problem [1,2,9]. As a conclusion we should note that the further improvement and extensions of the applicability of DMM are in close connection to the development of 'heuristic' learning.

3. References

[1] Димитров, В.: Застосуванная генетичной теорий для селекций частинних описов у МГВА.
Автоматика 6, 75-80, 1969

[2] Dimitrov, V.: Multilayered stochastic languages for pattern recognition.
1st Intern. Conf. on Pattern Recognition. Washington 1973

[3] Dimitrov, V.: Informal theory of fuzzy control with applications.
Ph. D. Thesis, Bulgarian Acad. Sci., Sofia 1977

[4] Dimitrov, V. and Driankova, L.: Programme system for social choice under fuzzy managing.
Proceedings IFIP Congress '77, Toronto 1977

[5] Dimitrov, V. and Wechler, W.: Optimal fuzzy control of humanistic systems.
Proceedings VI IFAC Congress '75, Boston (USA), 1975

[6] Fu, K.S.: Stochstic Automata as a Model of Learning Systems.
Acad. Press, New York 1970

[7] Fu, K.S. and Li, T.: On stochastic automata and languages.
Information Sci. 1, 403-419, 1969

[8] Harris, L.: A model for adaptive problem solving.
Technical Report TR 72-133, Cornell Univ. Ithaca, 1972

[9] Ivakhnenko, A., Spinu, E. and Dimitrov, V.: Multilayered algorithms of the decision theory.
Proceedings V IFAC Congress '72, Paris 1972

[10] Nilsson, N.: Problem Solving Methods in Artificial Intelligence.
Mc Graw Hill, New York 1971

[11] Wee, W.G. and Fu, K.S.: Simulation of fuzzy automata.
IEEE Trans. Systems and Cybernetics SCC-5,215-223, 1969

[12] Yovits, M. and Whittmore, B.: A generalized conceptual development for the analysis of information flow.
ASIS 24, 3, 1973

[13] Zadeh, L.A.: Outline of a new approach to the analysis of complex systems.
IEEE Trans. Systems, Man and Cybernetics SMC-3, 28-44, 1973

INDEX OF NOTATIONS

The following notations are used at points remote from their explanations which are given on the pages indicated.

SUBJECT INDEX

Kolibri 360 GmbH
Ferdinand-Jühlke-Straße 7
99095 Erfurt, Deutschland
produktsicherheit@kolibri360.de